"Each growing season and subsequent harvest marks a fresh opportunity to unleash Joyce Goldstein's unrelenting passion for preserving peak flavors for another day. My family and I have been fortunate to be on the receiving end of Joyce's jams, chutneys, and preserves, and each time we unscrew one of those lids, it is as if the flavor genie jumps out of the jar. The love and good taste that goes into the cooking and jarring can be tasted in each memorable bite."

—**DANNY MEYER,** author of *Setting the Table*

"I've waited (impatiently) for this glorious book. It's a must for preservers and lovers of flavor. I'll be cooking out of it for the rest of my life."

—**DIANA HENRY,** *London Telegraph* columnist and author of *A Bird in the Hand*

jam
session

jam
session

A Fruit-Preserving Handbook

Joyce Goldstein

Photographs by Ed Anderson

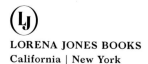

LORENA JONES BOOKS
California | New York

For Barbara

Contents

Fall

Mid-September Through Mid-November

Winter

Late November Through March

HOW I CAME TO PRESERVING

When you've run a successful restaurant and cooking school, one question you are asked quite often is who inspired you to cook. Your mother? Your grandmother? My answer always catches people off guard. There were no great cooks in my family. Most foods were cooked until they were soft and gray. When I was growing up, I was known as a "problem eater." No wonder.

I grew up in Brooklyn, New York, the daughter of Russian immigrants. With both my parents working, we ate out a few times a week. And it was those restaurant meals that awakened my palate. I learned that there was delicious and flavorful food to be had (just not at home). After college and graduate school, where I majored in art history and painting, I had the good fortune to spend an idyllic time living in Italy and traveling around the Mediterranean. I loved exploring the outdoor food markets and talking with the vendors and farmers about their produce and how best to prepare it. In restaurants, I tasted ingredients and dishes that were new to me. It was a great way to discover the signature flavors of the countries, and I was inspired to learn more about these cuisines.

In 1960 when we returned to the States, I looked at our former home, New York City, with new eyes. After the golden light of Rome, New York appeared dark, gray, and cold. I did not want to stay. My former husband had worked for a summer in San Francisco, and he was sure I would love it there because in the

'60s, before the high-rise invasion, it still looked like the Mediterranean.

When we got settled in San Francisco, still inspired by what I learned and tasted during our travels, I started collecting cookbooks, cooking the recipes that interested me, and entertaining friends. From the many compliments I received, I learned that I had a good palate. Soon I was deeply immersed in the world of food and cooking.

In 1967, while browsing in the cookbook section of my neighborhood bookstore in San Francisco, I picked up a small volume called *Fine Preserving* by Catherine Plagemann. Although I had become an avid home cook, I was a city girl from Brooklyn who had never thought of making jams or preserves of any kind. It was not part of my heritage. But now I was living in California, where the produce was abundant and amazing. After leafing through the book and reading the recipes, I thought I would give them a try. Soon I was hooked. I cooked my way through most of that little book, and I've been putting up preserves ever since.

In the California of the 1960s, there were no farmers' markets selling organic produce directly to the public. In 1970, with my growing interest in preserving, I worked at building a relationship with Geraldo dal Porto, the astute produce buyer at Cal-Mart, my neighborhood supermarket. He'd set aside cases of fruits that were cosmetically challenged but ripe and flavorful. I'd buy them at a discount and bring him jars of preserves as a thank-you. Later, while living in Berkeley, I would depend on Bill Fujimoto at Monterey Market, who knew all the local farmers and got their most flavorful fruits and vegetables because his father had taught him to taste before buying, and that looks were not as important as flavor.

In 1977, Governor Jerry Brown passed the Direct Marketing Act, which established certified farmers' markets in California. Success was not instantaneous. It took a lot of politicking and proselytizing by food activists to get communities to set aside market space and sign on to the program. They succeeded in a big way. Today we have farmers' markets all over San Francisco and California, and most of our supermarkets (including warehouse clubs) have designated organic sections.

Ready access to farmers' markets and the opportunity to sample and buy a quantity of seasonal produce has helped bring about a revival of the old-time craft of putting up preserves. Judging from the number of home cooks I see carrying flats of fruit from the farmers' market every week, I know I am not alone in my passion for preserving.

Most commercial condiments and preserves are bland and anonymous, formulated to satisfy a wide audience, including the least adventurous eaters. The flavor of the fruit is usually masked by way too much sugar. The beautiful tension between sweetness and acidity is lost. That is why I make my own.

While I'd like to tell you that making your own preserves is much cheaper than buying them ready-made, I am sorry to say that is just an illusion. Organic fruit is not inexpensive, unless you have your own trees, have friends with trees, or go to U-pick farms. Plus, you have to take your time into consideration, and time is money. But that should not stop you. Make your own preserves because you want better quality and distinctive flavors that reflect your personal palate. My family is spoiled, as they have never had to buy commercial jams or chutneys. I've shipped jam to my grandchildren at college and given cases of preserves as wedding presents to dear friends. When I am invited to dinner, instead of bringing flowers or a bottle of wine, I bring preserves. The hosts are happy to see me. And if they return their empty jars, they get refills.

Having a well-stocked assortment of distinctive homemade preserves and condiments in your pantry will elevate your cooking and make simple meals special. Even a nondescript boneless, skinless chicken breast can come to life with a dollop of excellent conserve or mostarda. A spoonful of lemon chutney or marmalade added to the deglazing liquids in the sauté pan will enliven a chicken or veal piccata. The addition of preserved quince, figs, or lemon enhances a lamb tagine. And simple store-bought vanilla ice cream or pound cake becomes festive with spiced cherry preserves spooned on top.

It takes time to develop a repertoire of reliable recipes that you want to make over and over again. I love to experiment and see what others are doing. In all these years of putting up preserves, I have collected many books on the subject. Most are safe but not sexy. I have noticed that most home preservers don't experiment. Rarely do they revel in preserving's potential to inspire culinary creativity. They fear deviating from their rules and regulations (or making someone ill). Their main focus is on the mechanics of the preserving process and the potential pitfalls of putting up preserves at home. Granted, there is science involved in making preserves, but it is not rocket science. I am very strict when safety is an issue, but I am more permissive when in matters of personal style. Once you have mastered the basic techniques of preserving and the ABCs of safety and process, you can think like a cook and play with your produce. You can be as creative as you like by adding flavor nuances of North Africa, the Middle East, Asia, or the Mediterranean. It's fun to see how far you can travel with an apricot or plum.

When spring arrives, you can find me at the farmers' market, shopping for the first rhubarb, apricots, cherries, and strawberries. It is a brief and unpredictable season, during which apricots or cherries may vary from week to week or vanish from the marketplace unexpectedly.

Summer is a bonanza! Everything is colorful and smells ripe and seductive. It's easy to feel as though you can't put up the fruit fast enough. Where to start? Start with your mouth. Taste everything and taste it again, because beauty does not always deliver maximum flavor. Summer is when peaches and plums arrive, as well as all the other berries. A few figs appear, as well as early tomatoes. The question is whether to put up these early arrivals or to wait until they come on in full force in early fall. So always taste and preserve only the fruit that is truly memorable.

Fall preserving brings mixed emotions. You race to put up the last of the late-summer tomatoes and delicate figs before they vanish for the year. The early-fall pears are good and the apples abundant. Finally, when the quince appear, it is officially fall. But as you stroll the market, out of the corner of your eye you get a glimpse of winter on the horizon. Pomegranates and persimmons are making their first appearance in the stalls that were once filled with plums and peaches. Joy and nostalgia mingle.

Winter brings about a slowing of the preserving year. There is no sense of urgency to grab the best as soon as it appears. After the busy summer and fall, the number of fruits to preserve is limited. They are mostly citrus, hardy, reliable, and abundant. Marmalades have a long shelf life, and thus you may not feel the pressure to produce some every year. In the kitchen, the pace slows down as well. Many of these jams and marmalades come together over the course of a few days, so take your time and enjoy the calmer days of winter preserving.

Whatever time of year, I walk around the farmers' market in a food trance, stopping at stand after stand, sampling the different fruits, and finally selecting those I think will make the best preserves. I want fruit that is just ripe and aromatic, but not overripe and soft. For me, acidity is a key factor in a vibrant preserve with lasting flavor. After I get home and taste the fruit again, I consider my options. Will the apricots be scented with Meyer lemon, ginger, or cardamom? Will they become jam for toast or a spiced condiment to serve with cheese? Will I turn the plums into a chutney or mostarda to serve with roast chicken or a grilled lamb chop? That's when the creative fun begins.

SPICED CHERRIES

QUINCE AND HONEY BUTTER

PLUM TKMALI

RASPBERRY ROSÉ JAM

GREEN TOMATO CHUTNEY

QUINCE MOSTARDA

SPICED FIG

SPICY PEACH WITH SALSA FLAVORS

BLUEBERRY POMEGRANATE JAM

STRAWBERRY BLACK PEPPER POMEGRANATE

MANGO GINGER LIME JAM

CRANBERRY SAUCE

BANANA DATE CHUTNEY

RASPBERRY MEYER LEMON MARMALADE

CHERRY POMEGRANATE MOSTARDA

BLACK RASPBERRY JAM

SPICED WHOLE FIGS

LEBANESE EGGPLANT W WALNUTS

CARROT GINGER JAM

STRAWBERRY PRESERVE

Fruit-Preserv

ITALIAN PLUM
W. ORANGE
BLACK PEPPER

TURKISH PLUM
POMEGRANATE
WALNUT CONSERVE

WOODLAND
CHERRY
PRESERVE

BLACKBERRY
NECTARINE

PLUM
MOSTARDA

QUINCE
CITRUS + HONEY
BUTTER

ASIAN PEAR
CHUTNEY

PERSIAN
CARROT ORANGE
JAM

BLACKBERRY
JELLY

SOUR CHERRY
PRESERVE
W. ROSE + CARDAMOM

BLOOD
ORANGE
MARMALADE

SATSUMA
MANDARIN
MARMALADE

MOROCCAN
SPICED
QUINCE

ng Primer

PRESERVING BASICS

In years past, it was common to call the process of putting up food in jars for long-term storage "canning." Today this is a misnomer because we use vacuum-sealed jars, not cans. "Preserving" is now the more common term. Here are a few other related terms you should know.

Chutney: Fruit that has been cooked with vinegar, sugar, and pungent spices. This mixture is usually chunky and has a good shelf life. It is most often thought of as a condiment for Indian food, but a good chutney can enhance a roast chicken, lamb chop, or cheese.

Condiment: A flavorful sauce or spread that is used as an accompaniment to cooked foods or cheese plates. This term includes chutneys and mostardas as well as other smoother spreads and ketchups.

Conserve: A fruit preserve to which other elements, such as nuts or dried fruits such as raisins, have been added.

Fruit butter: Fruit that has been cooked and then pureed, with sugar added to the puree. The mixture is then cooked slowly for a long time until it thickens and mounds on a spoon rather than attaining the texture of a jam or jelly. As it does not have to gel, which requires a certain amount of sugar, it does not have to be sweet and uses only about one part sugar to three parts puree. Fruit butter can be thickened on the stove top, with lots of stirring to prevent scorching, or can be transferred to a shallow pan and put into a 300°F oven, with occasional stirring until the desired texture is achieved. A bit of honey for flavor can be added at the end of cooking.

Jam: For jam, the fruit is chopped or mashed and cooked down into a relatively smooth spread. There is no desire to keep individual pieces of fruit distinctive. Everything melds together. If the fruit is low in acid, ample lemon juice is added, and if the fruit is low in natural pectin, apple pectin or grated apple may be added. A mixture of ripe and some underripe fruit will increase the pectin level in the jam.

Jelly: Jellies are clear mixtures of sugar and fruit juices. The fruit has to be high in pectin or it will not gel. The most pectin-rich fruits are apples, quince, damson plums, and currants. Other fruits will require the addition of pectin. The fruit is thoroughly cooked to extract maximum flavor, and its juices are drained through a colander lined with dampened cheesecloth or a jelly bag. Then the juices are cooked with sugar, and lemon and pectin are added if the fruit does not have enough natural pectin. I prefer to add Homemade Apple Pectin (page 200) rather than commercial pectin, using about ¾ cup of the pectin to every 4 cups of juice.

To be candid, making jelly is trickier than making jam. Sometimes, mysteriously, a jelly will not set. There are many possible reasons why this might happen: The fruit might not have had enough natural pectin. Too little sugar may have been added. Too much water may have been used in the initial cooking. The jelly could have been undercooked, causing a weak set. Or the jelly may have been overcooked, causing the pectin to break down. In other words, unless you have pectin-rich fruit, can follow the recipe

especially carefully, and have good karma, stick with jam. (Just kidding about the karma.)

Marmalade: A chunky spread made with the pulp, pith, and peel of citrus fruits. It is usually cooked on and off for two days in order to tenderize the peel. Citrus fruits come loaded with their own natural supply of pectin and set up easily.

Mostarda: In Italy, the classic *mostarda di frutta* is served as an accompaniment to *bollito misto*, a platter of assorted boiled meats. This condiment is made with whole or cut-up fruits cooked in a dense sugar syrup that has been spiked with a very potent essential oil called *olio di senape*, or mustard oil. Mostarda is sweet and hot, seductive and delicious.

Olio di senape is not imported to the United States. Food importer Chiara di Geronimo tells me that erucic acid, a component of this mustard oil, is toxic to human skin and organs when used in high doses. For that reason the U.S. Food and Drug Administration does not allow the sale of olio di senape in the United States. The irony is that it is 100 percent natural and the Italians believe it has many health benefits due to its heat-producing properties. It allegedly aids in digestive as well as respiratory ailments. The oil comes in a tiny bottle with an eyedropper and is so powerful that you add it drop by drop (up to three drops per one pint of preserves). If you are in Italy, you can walk into a pharmacy and easily buy a bottle. So what do you do if you are a home preserver and want to make your own mostarda? You either fly to Italy or get creative. I do both.

Because most of us will not have ready access to olio di senape, I have been playing with mostarda-like recipes for a few years. At first I tried using the mustard oil you get in Indian groceries, but it was not right. I have now devised a mostarda formula using powdered mustard, mustard seeds, cayenne, and vinegar to get the bite that plays so wonderfully against the sweet fruit. I have made mostardas with apricots, cherries, and plums. I serve them with poultry, pork, lamb, and veal.

Preserves: This is a generic term that covers all foods that are put up in jars, but I use it specifically to signify preserves in which the fruit is whole or in large pieces, such as whole cherries, whole strawberries, or halved cherry tomatoes. The fruit pieces are distinct and are surrounded by a jellylike syrup. Preserves often have a soft set.

SHOPPING FOR PRODUCE

Most preserving recipes give fruit measurements by the pound (versus flat or box). If you are not interested in putting up a big batch of each jam or chutney, or are short on storage space, shopping by the pound is certainly sensible. In my recipes, I tell you about how many pounds of fruit to buy, but after pitting and cutting, I find that cup measurements are often more accurate for the success of the recipe. With berries, I give the amount in cups and also suggest the number of baskets because that's typically how they are sold, but keep in mind that baskets are not consistent in fill and weight. Strawberries are sold in full pints or smaller baskets, depending upon the farm. Blackberry and raspberry baskets can hold 6 to 8 ounces of fruit. So shop by the basket or flat but cook with the cup measurements I give in the berry recipes.

When you go to the farmers' market and find the most amazing cherries or apricots, you may want to take advantage of the season and buy a flat. Buying fruit by the flat is the most economical way to shop. You can prepare three different recipes with each flat of fruit. If you are not feeling that ambitious, ask a friend or family member to join you in your preserving venture. Often I have enlisted my daughter-in-law, Barbara, as my preserving partner. We divide the labor and the goodies. Our families benefit.

Slightly underripe fruit is more acidic than ripe fruit, so use a mixture of ripe and underripe when selecting your fruit for a recipe. When shopping, try to taste the fruits before you buy and purchase those that have ample acidity, not just sweetness. When you taste the fruit, first you will taste expected notes of sweetness, but there should be a hit of tartness at the end of the taste. Without acidity the jams will lack depth of flavor and nuance.

PREPARATION TIME

When you are preserving by yourself, set aside some open-ended time to work—a quiet morning or an afternoon—because the ritual of preserving is like a meditation, involving repetition and routine. It takes a while to cut up the fruits, prep all of the ingredients, and set up all of the equipment and jars. You taste, you smell, you peel, you chop, you grate, you pit, you weigh, and you measure. You get the jars and lids ready. You don't want to feel pressured to get it done. Enjoy the process, take pleasure in working with your hands and engaging all of your senses and, for a time, relax your overstimulated mind. Preserving is slow food at its best.

Some jams and preserves require an hour or two the day before to start the process and a few hours the next day to finish them. Many condiments, such as mostardas and chutneys, can be prepared in one session. Be sure to read the recipe carefully before you begin, so you'll know how much time to set aside.

TASTE, ADJUST, AND FREESTYLE AS YOU GO

If you taste your preserves only at the end of the cooking process, just before you fill the jars, you may miss the moment to make them better. In cooking and preserving, tasting should be ongoing. It is important to taste the preserves as they simmer on the stove so you can make flavor adjustments as you cook. You might find, upon tasting, that the preserve could be better. It is just missing something. There are a few obvious steps you can take right away. Try a pinch of salt. Or another squeeze of lemon. If those don't bring it together for you, there are other options to bring it into balance. Cultivate the ability to improvise. Let's start with the pantry basics, listed in order of their importance in producing good results.

Sugar: Most of the preserves use granulated white sugar—it is the best sweetener for preserves, with the longest shelf life. You can splurge on organic sugar, but I do not think that is necessary.

If I want to highlight the color of apricots or carrots or mangoes or cherry tomatoes, I use granulated white sugar. Brown sugar adds a deeper note and darker color to preserves and is used in chutneys and condiments.

Some people wonder if they can reduce the amount of sugar in the preserve recipes or use a different kind of sweetener. First let us agree that preserves are not diet food. Yes, they are sweet, but they are eaten in small amounts. They are an enhancement to a meal, not the meal. A spoonful on toast or in yogurt or stirred into a pan sauce will raise your daily calorie count a bit but will not set you on the road to ruin.

Sugar is a crucial ingredient in preserving. It helps with the set. When heated to 220°F (the set point), it bonds with the pectin in the fruit and provides structure and makes the preserve spreadable. Other sweeteners, such as honey and agave syrup, do not hydrate the fruit or retard the growth of spoilers as well as sugar does and will not keep the preserve as bright and color-true to the fruit. Jams made with honey may have a looser texture and darken over time. Without sufficient sugar, the preserves will be runny and prone to developing mold. To assure a good set, sugar should make up 55 to 70 percent of the total weight of the preserve. With fruit that has a high acid content, the precise amount of sugar is less crucial. Preserves made with sugar have a longer shelf life and will last in the refrigerator longer than those made with other sweeteners.

My recipes use white sugar almost exclusively as the sweetener and preservative, but if you like the flavor of honey you may use it in place of some of the sugar. To do so, use ¾ cup of honey to replace 1 cup of sugar. So, for example, if a recipe calls for 5 cups of sugar, use 3 cups of sugar and 1½ cups of honey. To substitute agave syrup for some of the sugar, use ⅔ cup agave syrup in place of 1 cup of sugar. Just keep in mind that these preserves will have a shorter shelf life. (When I add a bit of honey to a fruit butter or preserve, I do it just for the flavor, and I add it toward the end of the cooking process, just before the final plate test.) If you are adding either honey or agave syrup, decrease the amount of liquid in your recipe. Most of the time, especially when the maceration process is used, I do not need to add extra liquid. The exceptions are for chutneys with added vinegar or preserves with fruit juice added; for those I decrease the liquid in the recipe by ½ cup. Alternatively, you can cook the preserve longer to reduce the liquid and achieve the proper texture.

Pectin: Fruits vary in their amount of natural pectin, which is essential for gelling. I do not rely on commercial powdered or liquid pectin for my recipes but instead use my Homemade Apple Pectin (page 200) when more pectin is

Fruits with High Pectin Levels

Apples (tart varieties)
Citrus (lemons, limes, oranges, and tangerines)
Cranberries
Currants
Damson plums
Quince

Fruits with Medium Pectin Levels

Apples (sweet varieties)
Blackberries
Blueberries
Plums
Raspberries
Sour cherries

Fruits with Low Pectin Levels

Apricots
Cherries
Figs
Mangoes
Peaches and nectarines
Pears
Rhubarb
Strawberries

Fruits with High Acid Levels

Cranberries
Currants
Most citrus
Rhubarb

Fruits with Medium Acid Levels

Apples (green)
Blackberries
Blueberries
Japanese plums and damsons
Mangoes (green, unripe)
Plums
Quince
Raspberries
Sour cherries
Strawberries
Sweet oranges

Fruit with Low Acid Levels

Apricots
Figs
Peaches
Pears
Prunes and French plums
Ripe mangoes
Sweet cherries

needed for reaching the gel point. Powdered and liquid pectin are inherently bitter, and if you use them, your preserve will require more sugar to suppress the taste. Too much sugar will mask some of the vibrant flavor of the fruits. There is a relatively new product on the market called Pomona's Pectin that allows you to use less sugar to reach the gel point because it contains low-methoxyl citrus pectin activated by calcium. However, it requires a different preserving technique than is used in most classic preserving recipes, and thus it comes with its own instructions. This calcium-activated pectin produces a soft gel.

By not relying on commercial pectin to reach the gel point, I may have to cook the fruit a bit longer or increase the lemon juice. That is just fine with me, because I think fruit preserves need some acidity to cut the sweetness and to bring out the flavor of the fruit. In most recipes, lemon juice and zest will suffice.

Some recipes tell you to cook sliced or chopped apples with the base fruit and then remove the apples. What a nuisance. If you want to cook apples along with the jam fruit instead of using apple pectin or apple jelly, grate or puree the apples in the food processor so they cook quickly and dissolve in the jam. Or cook the slices in water until tender, then mash them and add the puree to the simmering jam.

Lemon juice: Lemon juice is prized not only for activating pectin but also for intensifying the natural acidity of the fruit and helping maintain its color. I usually indicate the amount of lemon needed for a recipe by the number of lemons (for example, "zest and juice of 2 lemons"). But remember that not all lemons are equally sour, and preference for acidity is personal. I always have freshly squeezed lemon juice in the refrigerator. Meyer lemon juice is lower in acid than regular lemon juice and so should not be counted on to provide the correct acidity level. Fresh lemon juice is fine for most fruit preserves, but for a few recipes, commercial bottled lemon juice is advised because of its predictable acidity level. Bottled lemon juice is recommended when you need to get the fruit you are preserving into the safe PH zone to prevent illness. It has a guaranteed acidity of 4.5 percent, so for safety it is recommended for tomatoes and sometimes for pears, figs, and pumpkin recipes that are low in sugar and low in vinegar or lemon juice. In this book, it is used mainly in tomato sauce (see page 175), for which I use 1 tablespoon of bottled lemon juice or ¼ teaspoon of citric acid crystals for every 2 pounds of low-acid fruit.

Bottled lemon juice tastes quite bitter. You will not detect it in small amounts, but fresh lemon juice, because it is not very bitter, may be increased at will in a recipe, both to create a vibrant taste and to aid you in reaching the set point. There is no need to go overboard and use bottled lemon juice for all preserves.

For recipes that require 4.5 percent acidity to get to a safe PH zone, you can add either bottled lemon juice or citric acid crystals, using ¼ teaspoon per half-pint jar and ½ teaspoon per pint jar.

In the winter, I squeeze extra Meyer lemon (and blood orange) juice and put it in small freezer containers to have on hand to flavor or color spring and summer preserves.

Vinegars: White wine vinegar and apple cider vinegar are used for chutneys and mostardas. Most are at 5 percent acidity, which is needed for long shelf life and recommended for safe preserving. The higher the acidity, the lower the PH.

Salt: Just as in baking and pastry, a pinch of salt will heighten and brighten flavors in a sweet jam.

Flavor enhancers: When fruit, sugar, and lemon are not enough to achieve maximum flavor satisfaction, the following flavor enhancers can balance and brighten a preserve that just misses the mark.

- Black pepper, cayenne, or Maras or Aleppo pepper, or red pepper flakes

- Citrus zests and juice

- Dried fruit, such as raisins, dates, or currants

- Dry mustard powder or mustard seeds

- Fresh chiles, garlic, or onions

- Fresh ginger

- Herbs, such as mint, basil, tarragon, bay leaves, lavender, or lemon verbena

- Pomegranate molasses and balsamic vinegar

- Rose water or orange-flower water and extracts such as vanilla, almond, or Fiori di Sicilia (a mixture of orange-flower and vanilla extracts)

- Rum, brandy, Grand Marnier, amaretto, or kirsch

- Spices, such as ground or whole cinnamon, ground ginger, ground cardamom, Chinese five-spice powder, ground cumin, ground or whole cloves, ground nutmeg, whole star anise, or fennel seeds

Flavored sugars: While rose water and orange-flower water are beautifully aromatic, their flavors will fade over time. Therefore, you might want to create some scented sugars. They permeate the preserves and have longer-lasting power. You can buy rose sugar at some spice shops, or you can create your own. Dried edible rose petals and lavender are available online from purveyors such as Kalustyans and Whole Spice Company.

To make rose sugar, grind ½ cup dried unsprayed and organic rose petals with 1 cup granulated sugar in a food processor.

For lavender sugar, grind 2 to 3 tablespoons unsprayed, organic lavender with 1 cup granulated sugar in a food processor.

For vanilla sugar, cut up a vanilla bean and grind it with 1 cup granulated sugar in a food processor.

PERSONAL STYLE

Some preservers are purists who want just one fruit in a preserve—no additional flavors or textures. Other home preservers like to combine fruits or add textural elements such as nuts, dried fruits, or slivers of lemon peel. I know that after I master a basic jam, I want to riff on it. Playing with flavor options is a creative challenge that I enjoy, and it leads to some interesting and unique preserves. If you don't like taking a flavor chance and want a sure thing, that is just fine. It's okay to stick with the basics.

We all have texture prejudices. Before you make a preserve, taste the fruit and then decide what to make. Pay attention to what the fruit is telling you after a few bites. If the fruit is soft and ripe, a jam is your best bet because its texture will be lost after the initial cooking. If the fruit is quite firm, you might opt for a preserve, conserve, or chutney.

I am not a fan of jellies, but I do make them occasionally. I like to see pieces of fruit, halves of small apricots, or whole berries or cherries in my preserves whenever possible, but I do enjoy a smooth jam or clear jelly from time to time.

Just as we all have different texture preferences, we also have predilections for acidity and spice. I like my flavors to be a bit sharp rather than sweet. At the market, I am always looking for fruit that has an acid backbone. Even then, I am always adding more lemon. If I add ginger, I want to taste it. But you may be one for subtlety. Just keep in mind that the flavor will be the most intense the day you put up the preserve. Over time it will lose some of that intensity. Acid and heat in chutney and other condiments should be overly strong when you jar them because these elements recede after a while. This is why some recipes advise you to let a chutney, pickle, or condiment sit for a month or so before serving, to give the preserve time to settle into flavor balance.

FOOD SAFETY

If you have any fears about food safety or spoilage, please put them aside. I am still standing after eating my preserves all these years. (So, too, are my family and friends.) I am neither a reckless daredevil nor a compulsive worrywart. I am a practical, no-nonsense home cook who has run a restaurant, worked in commercial kitchens, and sold preserves to the public. High-acid foods are safely preserved when heated in a boiling water bath that reaches 212°F, which kills most molds, yeasts, and bacteria. With my preserve recipes, there is no danger of botulism because it cannot survive in the presence of high-acid fruits, ample lemon juice, and vinegar. Low-acid foods need to be preserved in special pressure canners. I do not include those in this book.

PRESERVING EQUIPMENT

First, some basic advice on preserving equipment that will make the job easier and more efficient and enjoyable.

A **preserving pot** needs a heavy bottom to resist scorching and ideally must be both deep and wide. You want a deep pot because many preserves bubble up (and you don't want to stop cooking to clean the stove top), and you want a wide base to enable the faster evaporation of excess liquid. You may want a couple of different sizes—one for small batches of preserves and one for large batches.

Many cooks extol the copper preserving pan and say it is essential if you are serious about preserving. It is an extravagant purchase, and if money is no object, by all means buy one. Copper, however, may react to fruit acids, so it may not be the wisest purchase unless you care for that pan as if it were your child. I do not think a copper preserving pan is essential for success. I find that my **enamel-covered cast-iron pots** do the job very well. (Plus I can use them for soups and stews, too.) While they are generally indestructible, they are not nonstick. When using enamel-covered cast iron, you need to stir your preserves often and pay attention to the liquid levels in the pot. If you have not been attentive while cooking preserves in enamel-covered cast iron—say you stop to answer the phone, momentarily forgetting that you have fruit on the stove—the fruit may scorch and stick. You will come back to find that you have a small caramelized mess on your hands. If this happens, try an initial soaking with hot water for a few hours to dislodge the burnt-on food.

If you caught it early, most of the caked-on gunk will come off. If the charred fruit does not release easily, pour in 2 inches of white vinegar or hydrogen peroxide and 1 tablespoon of baking soda, bring to a boil over medium-high heat, cover, and simmer for 15 minutes. Turn off the heat and let the pot rest for 15 minutes, then clean with a plastic scrubby. You may have to repeat the process. And although you will be muttering under your breath, swearing you will never go through this again, you probably will. (I speak from experience.)

For the boiling water bath you will use to seal the jars, you will need a couple of **stockpots or pasta cooking pots** deep enough to hold your jars and water to cover them by 2 inches. Most pots will hold 4 or 5 jars at a time. If you have **round cake-cooling racks** that fit in the pots, place them in the bottom of each pot; these are optional (for more about this, see page 33). I always keep a full **teakettle** of hot water on the stove to replenish the boiling water over the jars. And I have a **small pan** of hot water to heat the lids.

You will need a couple of **baking sheets** on which to place the jars before filling and after processing in the water bath. The average 11 by 16-inch baking sheet can hold 8 jars; the larger ones, also known as half-sheet pans, are 13 by 18 inches and can hold 12 jars.

Canning jars manufactured by Ball or Kerr are sold at hardware and home stores. They are made of glass that is specially tempered to withstand high heat repeatedly. **Wide-mouth jars** are easier to fill, especially if you are preserving whole fruits, recipes with large pieces of fruit, or batches that are dense, such as fruit butters, that may need to be stirred before sealing. If you can find only the narrow **standard-mouth jars**, your local hardware store may be willing to order the wide-mouth style for you. I prefer wide-mouth jars for ease of filling, but use standard-mouth jars for looser preserves, such as ketchup and tomato sauce, and for jellies and jams that can be easily ladled into the jars.

Jars that have minor chips in the rim will not seal, so inspect your previously used jars and discard those with imperfect rims or use them for other storage. I most often use **half-pint jars**, but if you have a large family, pints will probably be your jar size of choice. I rarely use quarts but have some on hand for large batches of tomato sauce and pickled peaches. The larger the jar, the longer time it will need in the boiling water bath for the heat to penetrate the contents.

You will also need **rings and lids** for closing and sealing the filled jars. Jars and rings may be reused season after season, but you need to use new lids every time.

Hardware and cookware stores now offer a preserving kit that comes with a wide-mouth metal funnel, **clamplike tongs called a jar lifter** (which enables the user to gently deposit the jars in the hot water bath and remove them), and a **lid lifter** (a magnet on a stick). You also can use **long tweezers** (also sterilized) to lift the lids from the hot water and deposit them atop the filled jars.

Invest in a **scale for bulk weight** and a **digital scale** for smaller measurements. It's good to know how much your fruit weighs before you start gathering the other ingredients to complete a recipe. In general, weight measurements are more accurate than volume measurements, but I am not fanatical about this. I often give both weight measurements and cup measurements for most of the preserve recipes, but super-precise measurements are not crucial for success. After all, I have a mouth for tasting, and I know I can make adjustments as I cook.

A **candy thermometer** is nice so you can double-check your gel point if you are not sure how to read the results of your plate test (see page 30).

A reliable **kitchen timer** is a necessity for timing the boiling water bath, gel-point test, and other time-sensitive steps. If you plan to put up multiple batches at a time, invest in two timers.

You need **dry and liquid measuring cups** and **measuring spoons**.

Some **long-handled wooden spoons** are necessary for stirring the preserves while they cook. And also a couple of **large long-handled silicone spatulas** to scrape up any juices and fruit that cling to the bottom of the pot. You'll also need a **slotted spoon** for removing fruit from the cooking liquids.

It probably goes without saying that you need a **cutting board, sharp knives**, a **small paring knife, peelers, melon ball scoop, potato masher**, and a **cherry pitter** (if you want to preserve cherries). In my toolkit, I also have a **wooden chopstick** to remove air bubbles from jars of preserved fruit and dense fruit butters.

You will need a **stainless steel ladle** to deposit the cooked preserves into the jars via a **wide mouth-funnel**. I also have an assortment of **small wooden tasting spoons** to prevent me from burning my mouth on a metal spoon when I am checking the flavor development of a simmering preserve. I treasure mine— bought in Istanbul at the spice bazaar—but you can find small wooden spoons online or in cookware stores.

Pot holders, pot-holder gloves, dish towels, and a **long apron** should be at the ready.

A **colander** or **chinois** is helpful to strain fruit so it doesn't overcook and so the juices can be cooked separately. Instead of getting a jelly bag contraption, set a colander over a bowl and line it with dampened **cheesecloth**, a clean dish towel, or an old (detergent-free) pillowcase to drip-drain cooked fruit for jelly. (No need to buy something you will rarely use, and most of the jelly bag contraptions are rickety at best.) Cheesecloth is also handy for making spice and herb sachets for flavoring fruit while it macerates and preserves while they cook.

A **Microplane grater** is useful when you want to add citrus zest, and a **mandoline** is advised when you want to add thin slices of lemon or ginger to a preserve. Get an OXO or the Japanese Benriner that many chefs swear by, rather than a complicated and expensive mandoline. After a few years of use, when the blades are no longer as sharp as you'd like, you can buy a replacement blade, as they are inexpensive and easy to install.

A **food processor** is best for pureeing ingredients such as citrus fruits, fresh ginger, and onions as well as cooked fruits. You might want to get a mini food processor to grind up small amounts of chiles or garlic, and a standard-size model for citrus, onions, and other bulky ingredients. You can easily buy replacement blades. Be a sport and treat your processor to a new blade every once in a while!

A **food mill** is handy to separate seeds and peel from cooked fruit and tomatoes and for creating purees with a more rustic texture than those prepared in a food processor.

If you plan on making large batches of tomato sauce, you may want to invest in a **Victorio tomato strainer** or a strainer attachment for your KitchenAid mixer.

For making fresh citrus juices, a glass reamer is nice, but given the amount of fresh citrus juice I go through, a **small electric juicer** is way more efficient.

I have a **wire splatter screen**—not essential but nice to have when the quince jam or pumpkin butter starts to bubble up and pop like molten lava. It will help you avoid sugar burns and protect your hair, your clothing, and the stove top. You'll laugh, but **swim goggles** are an extra safety precaution to consider.

I know this seems obvious, but I have had to repeatedly remind line cooks and culinary students to read the recipe through a few times and to make sure they have everything that is needed before they start. Good organization enhances the cooking process.

Finally, clear and clean all your work surfaces, tie on that apron, and get ready to have some fun!

PRESERVING TECHNIQUES AND POINTERS

Now that you've shopped for great fruit and have assembled the required equipment, it's time to address cooking times, recipe yield, jar preparation, and the techniques that will help you prepare delicious preserves that are safe to eat and long lasting. Terms such as "plate test," "processing," and "water bath" will no longer be mysterious, so you can approach preserving with confidence.

GAUGING RECIPE YIELD

Predicting the final yield of preserving recipes requires making educated guesses. Yields will vary from season to season. Every batch of fruit behaves slightly differently. Some fruits shrink more than others. Some fruit may have more water and take longer to thicken. The amount of moisture in the fruit will vary according to the weather during the growing season. Pay close attention to the fruit as it cooks, because sometimes it will soften way before the juices have reached the set point (220°F on a candy thermometer or when it passes the plate test [see page 30]). Rather than cooking whole fruit or pieces so long that they begin to break down, remove a piece to check the texture, and if the fruit is losing its shape before the juices have started to thicken, use a slotted spoon and transfer it to a colander set over a bowl. Continue to cook the juices until they reach the set point. When the syrup is ready, carefully spoon the fruit back into the pot (do not tip it in all at once or you risk burning yourself with the splatter). Give the mixture a stir to distribute the fruit in the syrup and bring all to a boil. Cook for a minute or two longer until it is back to the set point and passes the plate test. For a better distribution of fruit in the jars, let the mixture sit for 5 minutes and then give it one more stir before ladling it into the jars.

A note on recipe batch size: Some recipes, such as the ever-popular strawberry preserves, produce a larger batch. You can decrease the recipe by half if you do not want to make so much.

MACERATING

Whenever possible, I am a firm believer in macerating the fruit before cooking a jam or preserve. To macerate, in your preserving pot or a stainless steel or ceramic bowl, combine the fruit and sugar and let it sit at room temperature or, if your kitchen is very hot, in the refrigerator, overnight, so the fruit gives off its own juices. (You can cover the bowl or pot if you choose. I rarely cover the pot when it is at room temperature but in the refrigerator you might want to cover it with plastic wrap to keep out other odors.) Additional water is rarely needed. (Adding water dilutes the fruit's inherent flavor and increases cooking time.) After maceration, transfer the contents of the bowl to the preserving pot and begin cooking. This technique works well for strawberries, raspberries, peaches, apricots, and even tomatoes.

Some fruits, such as cherries, mangoes, blueberries, plums, currants, figs, and pears, are macerated with sugar at room temperature for an hour or two, cooked very briefly, and then macerated again overnight. And for some preserves, such as citrus marmalades, this process of overnight maceration is done over the course of two days.

SKIMMING

Sometimes when making preserves, a froth or dense film of bubbles will form atop the fruit as it cooks. You can skim off most of it because an excess of this bubbly film will look unsightly in the jars and will give the illusion of fermentation. If you find it difficult to skim all of it away, I suggest you turn off the heat and let the preserve rest for a while, and most of the bubbles will subside. What remains can be stirred into the preserve and will disappear. Some cooks suggest adding a tablespoon or so of cold butter to disperse the bubbles. I prefer to rest it and then give it a stir—that suffices most of the time.

TIMING

It would be gratifying to be able to tell you precisely how long to cook a preserve to reach the set point, but I can't. If I were to say to cook a preserve 5 to 7 minutes longer or 20 to 30 minutes longer for completion, I would be guessing. There are too many variables to make accurate blanket predictions. I do not know the heat levels of your stove, for example. I do not know if you have a heavy-duty pot or a lighter one, nor do I know if your pot is deep or wide. I do not know if you are preserving a small batch of jam in a large pot, which will thicken more quickly, or a large batch in a large pot, which will take longer to reduce and thicken. In other words, any numeric cooking time I give you might be off.

The answer to the question "Are we there yet?" is to use your eyes and common sense. Visual cues will let you know if you have arrived, so pay careful attention to what you see happening in the pot. When you stir the jam, does it still feel runny and loose, or is it becoming thicker

and starting to coat the spoon? Are the bubbles in the pot getting larger? When you lift the spoon or spatula from the pot, does the jam run off quickly or fall more slowly in larger drops, or do the drops run together and form a sheet? A candy thermometer can tell you when you are getting close to the set point but may not be completely accurate. It may say 210°F or 220°F and yet the preserve will still look a bit runnier than you would like. As the preserve cooks, you need to perform the plate test (see next entry) a few times to monitor the progress of the preserve. As you get closer to the set point, keep stirring to prevent scorching. Do not leave the stove to do something else; remain attentive. You are almost there.

Your eyes and mouth will tell you when it is time to stop the cooking and ladle the preserve into jars. When you reach that point, remove the pot from the stove so the preserve does not continue to cook while you fill jars. At that point, the preserve can sit off the heat for a while before going in the jars, giving you time to reboil the water in the stockpot(s) and warm the jars if they have cooled.

THE PLATE TEST

I keep some small plates in the freezer at all times. These are for testing the texture and set of completed preserves. In preserving recipes, this is called the plate test. To do a plate test, drop a spoonful of hot preserves on a frozen plate and turn the plate so it is vertical to the ground for a second or two. If the preserve is finished, the spoonful will not run much and, after a few minutes back in the freezer, will set up semi-firmly if the preserve is ready for jarring. Some say to run your finger through the dollop, and if the jam wrinkles it is set. You can double-check your work with a candy thermometer, inserting it into the preserving pot but being careful that

the probe does not come into contact with the pot itself. When the preserves are about 220°F, you have reached the set point. Some preserves and fruit butters will never achieve a firm set but will instead mound on a spoon or plate. This is called a soft set.

If your preserve is close to setting but not yet there, you can cook it a bit longer (maybe 5 minutes longer, but keep stirring and watching closely because this is when scorching may occur) or add a few more tablespoons of lemon juice. I always have fresh and commercial bottled lemon juice on hand in case the fruit needs it for flavor balance or to facilitate thickening (for more about this, see page 20). Occasionally I use my Homemade Apple Pectin (page 200) as added insurance for fruits that need a thickening boost. About ¾ cup apple pectin per 4 cups of cooked fruit will do the trick.

STERILIZING THE JARS AND LIDS

The jars need to be sterilized before they are filled. You can sterilize them by running them through the dishwasher or by submerging them in boiling water in the water-bath pot for 10 minutes or, after rinsing well, by heating them on a baking pan in a 300°F oven for 25 minutes. It's a nuisance to stop the process and scramble for an extra jar, so sterilize more jars and lids than you think you will need. With that said, if you find you are a jar or two short while in the midst of ladling the preserves into your prepared jars, lower the last-minute additional jars into the boiling water bath for a few minutes, or zap them in the microwave for 2 minutes. Jars need to be mildly hot but not scorching when you fill them. If the jars have cooled down, warm them in a 200°F oven for 10 minutes or place them in the boiling water bath to warm them again. The jars vacuum-seal better when the fruit, jars, and lids are hot.

Simmer the lids for a minute or two in a small pot of hot water, leaving them in the water to keep them hot until you are ready to seal the jars. I alternate stacking the lids front to back (rubber sides away from each other so they don't stick together).

FILLING THE JARS

Have a damp paper towel or clean dishcloth and a thin plastic spatula or wooden chopstick ready. Set the sterilized jars on the work surface near your preserving pot. You need to protect the work surface from the heat of the preserving pot, so put a towel, tray, or trivet under the pot, unless your counters are heat-resistant granite, marble, stone, stainless steel, or ceramic tile. For each jar, placing the wide-mouth funnel in the jar, ladle the hot preserves into the jar, filling it just enough to leave ¼-inch headspace for jams and preserves or 1 inch for whole fruit. Too little headspace can cause food to overflow in the water bath and prevent the jar from sealing. Too much headspace and air inside the jar may prevent a proper vacuum seal from forming. When all of the jars are filled, if there are visible air bubbles or if you want to redistribute the fruit in the preserving juices, run the plastic spatula or wooden chopstick around the inside of the jar. Wipe the rim of each jar well with a damp paper towel or cloth. The rims must be clear of the preserves for a perfect seal. (The main reason a jar does not seal is because the rim was not clean when it was closed.) Set a lid atop the jars and screw on the rings. The jars will be hot, so you won't want to handle them for any longer than you have to. Repeat with any remaining preserves and jars.

PROCESSING THE JARS IN A BOILING WATER BATH

Preserving is often called canning, even though, as I've explained, no cans are involved. Because of the association with the term *canning*, many people confuse the boiling water bath with pressure canning, a technique for preserving low-acid foods that requires a special pressure cooker. I think this is why hearing the phrase "boiling water bath" scares people. Breathe easy. No special pressure canner is needed for the recipes in this book; these recipes are only for high-acid preserves that resist botulism and spoilage. Unless you are making small batches of jam that will be held for no longer than 1 week in the refrigerator, all preserves must be processed in a boiling water bath for safe and successful long-term storage at room temperature. While some jars will seal without this additional processing, the boiling water bath is done to make sure all of the jars seal.

Older preserving cookbooks often did not include instructions for boiling water processing. They simply instructed cooks to ladle the hot preserves from the pot into the hot jars. But this open-kettle method has been deemed unsafe, because some jars may not seal, and those that seal may not hold the seals a long time. Mold can easily develop without the water bath. Some books recommend processing filled jars in the oven instead of in a hot water bath. This technique also has been discredited by the National Center for Home Food Preservation, because it results in incomplete heat circulation and heat penetration. Dry heat is very slow to fully penetrate the contents of the jars, and thus this method cannot ensure the safety of the finished product. The boiling water bath forces more air out of the jars and, by reducing oxygen, helps inhibit mold growth. Hot air isn't nearly as effective as hot liquid. So stick with the boiling water bath.

Some books advise cooks to place round, footed cooling racks or a folded dish towel in the bottom of the pots and set the jars on top to prevent breakage during processing. I confess that I have never done either, and in fifty years of preserving I have had only three jars break (and they may have been old or flawed before filling). But if you have concerns about breakage, and you have a couple of round cake racks that fit your pots, why not use them?

Place a couple of baking sheets on the counter adjacent to your stove or on the work surface where you will be filling the jars. Set one or two stockpots on the stove and fill them with enough water to cover the jars by 1 to 2 inches. Bring the water to a boil over medium-high heat. If at all possible, try to do this as close as possible to the time that you will be putting the preserves into the jars. If the water bath pots have cooled down, you will need to bring them back to a boil when your preserve reaches the set point or passes the plate test (see page 30). If the sterilized jars have cooled down, you will need to warm them, too. I know this may sound like a crazy juggling act—finishing the preserves, keeping the jars hot, and having the boiling water bath ready, all at the same time. Relax. This does not require precise timing. You have some leeway. With practice, you will find your rhythm, create your routine, and get the job done.

The amount of time the jars need to simmer in the hot water bath depends upon the density of the preserves and the size of the jars in which they are preserved. For most preserves, boiling for 8 to 10 minutes will suffice. Denser foods (large pieces of whole fruit, quince, and pumpkin, for example) may require 15 to 20 minutes processing time. For jellies, 5 to 10 minutes of processing will suffice; any longer and you may "break" the gel and end up with a watery preserve. When processing at high altitudes, you'll need to boil the jars a few minutes longer: Add 5 minutes for locations that are up to 3,000 feet above sea level. For higher altitudes, add 10 minutes.

Keep a full kettle of hot water on the stove to replenish the water atop the simmering jars. After the water has boiled, using the jar lifter, gently place the sealed jars in the simmering water and bring the water back to a boil. When the water returns to a boil, set the timer and then decrease the heat to bring the pot to an active simmer. You want to see some bubbling in the pot. "Processing the jars" means that although you are immersing them in a boiling water bath, you are not keeping them at a hard boil. You don't want them to rattle around too much.

Given pot capacity, you may not be able to process all the sealed jars at one time. Do as many as will fit in your pots for the first batch. The remaining sealed jars can wait the extra 10 or even 20 minutes until you can process the next batch.

While processing the jars, I rarely cover the pots, but some sticklers will advise you to do that to prevent evaporation of the water. I prefer to see into my pots and monitor the process, which is why I have that kettle of hot water at the ready in case I need to add more water. I keep the heat at just a bubble so the jars do not rattle around too much. When the timer rings, I turn off the heat and wait 1 to 2 minutes for the jars to settle and then lift them out as carefully as I put them in, placing them on the clean room-temperature baking sheet. Do not put hot jars on a cold surface or they may crack on contact. Some preserving experts recommend placing

the hot jars on a towel-covered surface. I do not do this, because I do not see the need for it; I've never had a jar break this way.

When the jars are settled on the baking sheets, I listen for the cheerful popping sound as they vacuum-seal. It may take an hour or two for all the jars to "ping." Some may have sealed silently in the water bath. And some may not ping until the next morning. When they do, it is music to your ears because that sound lets you know the jar has successfully sealed. Some books advise you against moving the jars for 12 hours so as not to break the seal. I don't always follow that rule and have had no problems. Sometimes I move the tray of jars from the kitchen counter to my big dining room table, where I can more easily label them when they are cold. The jars usually cool completely in less than 12 hours (but who's counting?).

STORING

Before storing the preserves in your pantry, make sure all of the jars have sealed by tapping on the center of the lid—properly sealed jars will have a tinlike sound when tapped, and unsealed jars will ring hollow—and looking to confirm that the lids are depressed in the center. Place the odd jar that does not seal in the refrigerator. Label and date all jars. Stow in a cool, dark place, such as a basement or closet, in a single level, if you have the room. Some preservers warn against stacking jars because doing so may hide jars that didn't seal or cause them to open from pressure but I find this to be a needless worry.

Some preserving books recommend removing the rings on the jars before storing. The rings hold the lids in place during processing, but can be safely removed after the jars are cold. (In fact, the rings may actually loosen after the jars are cold. No need to retighten them.) What is the rationale for removing the rings before storage, once you have ascertained that the jars have successfully sealed and the lids are depressed? The melodramatic reason is that if the lid has separated from the jar and the ring is still on, fermentation could cause the jar to explode. I haven't heard of this happening, but I guess it could. Others say that you might not notice that the seal is broken when you remove the ring and think you loosened it when you twisted off the ring. This is also a little farfetched. If all the jars were successfully sealed when you put them away, you may wonder what could have broken the seal. Answer: Spoilage. If food is spoiled, gases may break the vacuum and loosen the lid. Now is the time to use your eyes and common sense. When you twist off the ring to open a jar, if the seal is broken or the lid is no longer depressed and sounds hollow when you tap it, toss the contents of that jar. If you see mold or fermentation, or the contents of a jar smell bad or look dry and shrunken, do not taste or otherwise evaluate; just toss that jar. If you twist off the ring and the lid comes off the jar without being pried off, the jar is unsealed and spoiled, and you should throw away the contents. Discard any jar whose contents look questionable. Broken seals are a rare occurrence if you have used a boiling water bath to seal the jars.

Truth be told, I stack boxes of jars. I store jars with the rings on. In all the years I have been putting up preserves, I have never had a problem. But if you want to be super cautious, remove the rings before putting the jars away. Wash, dry, and store excess rings in a plastic bag. I suppose you could remove the rings after the jars are cold and, once you have ascertained that the jars have sealed, put the rings back on. But why bother? I think that once you see the jars are sealed and the lids are depressed, you can leave them alone. And unless you have miles of shelving, you may stack cases of jars worry-free. A cardboard flat is a reliable barrier.

SHELF LIFE

While most jams and preserves will keep for about a year, they are at their most vibrant for the first six months. Marmalades, chutneys, and condiments can keep for a few years without fading. If you end up with too much of one preserve, you know to make a smaller batch the next time. The excess that you don't eat can be great host gifts. Or you can repurpose them into sauces, vinaigrettes, and marinades.

A NOTE ABOUT LABELS

I know I could use plain labels from the office supply store, but really, after all the care I take to make my preserves, I want them to look as special as they taste. Some hardware stores sell labels alongside the jars and many styles are available online, but I order labels from Il Papiro or Tassotti in Italy. It's a personal choice. Do not label jars while they are still warm as the labels may not stick.

TROUBLESHOOTING

Even with the utmost care and best of intentions, we sometimes mess up our preserves. Here are a few solutions to some occasional problems.

What to do if the jam is too stiff or too dry: It happens to the best of us. For example, a batch of Meyer lemon marmalade ends up having the texture of a rubber ball. It tastes good but is too stiff to spread. Some jams set up much firmer than they seem when you are spooning them into the jars. Not only citrus. I've had blackberry and plum jams that became bouncy, too. Sometimes the carrots in the carrot preserves or the raisins in a chutney are so thirsty they absorb almost all of the juice and the finished jam is too dry.

I know we all hate to waste food, time, and labor. Do not despair. You can salvage imperfect preserves. Transfer the jam to a clean preserving pot. Discard the lids and thoroughly clean the jars. Get new lids. Heat the jars in the water bath or a low oven (see page 32). If the jam is too firm to stir, break it up with a potato masher. Add water and stir well. The amount of water you add depends upon how stiff the jam is. You want it to be spoonable but not soupy. Bring to a simmer over medium heat. Increase the heat to medium-high and bring to a boil. Do the plate test (see page 30) to gauge runniness. Now that you know this is a pectin bomb, let it be a bit runnier than you might otherwise. Adjust the amount of liquid you need to get it back on track. Simmer and, when you are satisfied, ladle into the sterilized jars, seal, and process in the hot water bath again.

What to do if the jam is too runny: You can try to reboil it, but the fruit will lose some of its freshness and taste a bit "cooked." You might gamble and add more sugar, more lemon, and some additional fresh fruit and try to rescue the jam. Or add some Homemade Apple Pectin (page 200) and reboil. But most of the time, you cannot rescue it without overcooking the fruit, and you might be better off serving it as a sauce.

What to do when you've made too much: Okay, you got carried away and put up too many jars of Blenheim apricot jam. The deal on the fruit was too good to pass up. You've eaten quite a few jars and given away a few. But what remains is a few years old and is starting to darken. It kills you to throw it away.

You can repurpose the jam and turn it into barbecue sauce. Or a marinade for pork or poultry. Or add it to a pan sauce or tagine or stew that can safely go sweeter. You can also thin it and make a sauce for ice cream and panna cotta.

Best preserves for recycling: Berry jams, peach jams, apricot jams, and marmalades.

Berry jams: Thin by stirring in a little water or even a liqueur, such as kirsch, Framboise, or Grand Marnier, to make a sauce for ice cream or panna cotta.

Apricot and berry jams: May be used for cookie fillings or fillings for Sacher torte or linzertorte.

Apricot or peach jams: Add to commercial or homemade barbecue sauce.

Citrus marmalades: Thin with olive oil and lemon juice and turn into marinades or sauces for poultry or pork.

Spring

Strawberries

Strawberries are the most popular berry worldwide, and strawberry jam is probably the most popular jam. I agree with food writer Jane Grigson, who said that strawberries and raspberries are rarely improved by complication. The less done to them the better. No chutneys, mostardas, or offbeat condiments. I worry whenever the strawberry industry has competitions to invent complicated and novel dishes using cooked strawberries, because the contestants' creations rarely show the fruit in its best light.

Ripe strawberries should be eaten or preserved within a day or two. Shop for flavor (the farmers will always let you taste one) and aroma. Serve them at room temperature if you are eating them out of hand.

The average supermarket strawberry is designed for show—the larger the better for display and to dip in chocolate. Most often the large berries are hollow in the center, watery, and lack perfume. Many are grown in pesticide-saturated soil, so my advice is to buy only organic berries. The most popular varieties are Chandler, Albion, and Seascape. As the season progresses from April through the summer, the berries get smaller, so if you are interested in putting up whole-berry preserves, keep this in mind. Your patience will be rewarded.

The main variable with strawberry jam is texture. If the berries are large, you will want to hull them and cut them up into slices or smallish pieces. Some recipes suggest chopping them.

Others call for mashing the berries with a potato masher. I do not see any reason for such abuse. They are so tender that when you cook them, they soften enough to meld into a cohesive jam. Texture is a very personal matter; you may want them to be universally mashed and smooth. I do not mind seeing a soft slice. Strawberry jams will not set up firm but will be a soft set.

If you have access to small berries, show them off and preserve them whole. They are most elegant in this way. And because they are tender, they do not roll off the toast.

Strawberries are a member of the rose family. You may want to try using rose sugar (see page 22) in a batch to see if you like it, substituting it for about a third of the sugar. Keep lemon juice on hand so the preserve is not too cloying and the perfume of the berries comes through.

Simpatico flavorings for strawberries are vanilla, lemon, star anise, real balsamic vinegar, black pepper, pomegranate, mint, basil, and rose.

Strawberries can be paired with rhubarb or currants for a spectacular tart-sweet jam. But few markets carry currants, so you may have to special order them.

Strawberry jam is perfect spread on toast, biscuits, and pancakes; stirred into yogurt; and spooned over ice cream. And, of course, slathered on good old PB&J.

BASIC STRAWBERRY JAM

Because strawberries are not high in pectin, some should be ripe and some underripe. Lemon juice will do the rest of the work.

8 cups (4 pint baskets) strawberries, three-quarters ripe and one-quarter not so ripe

4 cups granulated sugar

Juice of 2 lemons

1 vanilla bean (optional)

Yield: 7 half-pint jars

Place 3 or 4 small plates in the freezer.

Rinse, dry, and hull the strawberries. Cut them into ¼-inch slices.

In a large preserving pot, gently combine the strawberries, sugar, and lemon juice and toss to mix. Set aside to macerate overnight.

The next day, add the vanilla bean, place the pot over medium-high heat, and bring to a boil. Cook for 5 minutes, watching closely because the berries can quickly boil over and you do not want to spend the morning cleaning your stove top. Remove the pot from the heat and let sit, uncovered, for 1 to 2 hours.

Place a baking sheet on the counter near your stove. Heat a kettle of water. Set two stockpots on the stove and fill them with enough water to cover the jars by 1 to 2 inches. Bring the water to a boil over medium-high heat. Sterilize the jars (see page 32) in the water bath.

Bring the strawberry mixture to a boil again over medium-high heat and cook for 3 to 5 minutes, until the berries are tender. At this point, decide how much texture you want in your jam.

If you want to see a few berry slices in your jam, set a colander over a bowl and, using a slotted spoon, transfer the strawberries to the colander and set aside to rest for 1 hour. Add any strawberry juices that have collected in the bowl under the colander to the preserving pot. Taste the liquid and add lemon juice if the strawberry juice is not tart enough. Reduce the strawberry syrup over medium-low heat, stirring frequently, until thickened. Carefully return the berry slices to the jam pot. While stirring, bring to a boil and cook the jam briefly, until it passes the plate test (see page 30), forming a soft set and not running much when you tilt the plate.

If you want to make a smooth jam without any visible slices, after you cook the mixture for the first 3 to 5 minutes, mash the berries with a potato masher. Continue to cook the jam until the berries break down and become a soft puree and the jam passes the plate test, mounding on the plate for a soft set. Remove the pot from the heat. Remove the vanilla bean.

Bring the water bath back to a boil. If the jars have cooled, warm them in the water bath or in a 200°F oven. Simmer the lids in a saucepan of hot water. Place the jars on the baking sheet. Ladle the jam into the jars, leaving ¼-inch headspace. Wipe the rims clean and set the lids on the mouths of the jars. Twist on the rings.

Using a jar lifter, gently lower the jars into the pots. When the water returns to a boil, decrease the heat to an active simmer, and process the jars for 10 minutes. Turn off the heat and leave the jars in the water for 1 to 2 minutes.

Using the jar lifter, transfer the jars from the pots to the baking sheet and let sit for at least 6 hours, until cool enough to handle. Check to be sure the jars have sealed (see page 34). Label and store the sealed jam for 6 months to 2 years. Once open, store in the refrigerator for up to 3 months.

WHOLE STRAWBERRY PRESERVES

When strawberries are small and sweet, they make beautiful preserves. I think it is more elegant to keep the berries whole than to mash them for jam. Cooking the berries in stages causes them to plump up, become translucent, and absorb the syrup.

This can be a two- or three-day process. You can try to speed it up, but if you can be patient (no labor involved, just waiting) and give the strawberries time, you will have a voluptuous preserve. After you have made this recipe a few times, you may want to play with it. For a change of pace, I love to add black pepper and pomegranate molasses for a subtle sweet-tart accent (see page 46). Following Italian tradition, some cooks add a splash of aged artisanal balsamic vinegar (not the cheap supermarket stuff, which is regular vinegar sweetened with caramel), either during maceration or at the end. Occasionally, I add a few tablespoons of chopped fresh mint or basil at the end of cooking. The choice is yours.

16 cups (8 pint baskets) small organic strawberries

6 to 7 cups granulated sugar

5 tablespoons fresh lemon juice, plus more to taste

4 to 6 tablespoons chopped fresh mint or basil (optional)

2 to 4 tablepoons aged balsamic vinegar (optional)

Yield: 14 to 16 half-pint jars

Place 3 or 4 small plates in the freezer.

Rinse, dry, and hull the strawberries.

In a large preserving pot, gently combine the strawberries, 6 cups of the sugar, and the lemon juice and toss to mix. Let sit for at least a few hours or, preferably, overnight to macerate.

Next, place the pot over medium-high heat, and bring to a boil. Remove from the heat and let sit, uncovered, for 1 to 2 hours or overnight.

Taste the strawberry preserves and see if you want to add any of the remaining 1 cup sugar. Bring the strawberry mixture to a boil over medium-high heat, watching closely because the berries can quickly boil over and you do not want to spend the morning cleaning your stove top. Remove the pot from the heat and let sit, uncovered, for 1 to 2 hours. You may now stop the cooking and wait another day or proceed to complete the preserve.

Set a colander over a bowl and, using a slotted spoon, transfer the berries to the colander.

Place two baking sheets on the counter near your stove. Heat a kettle of water. Set two stockpots on the stove and fill them with enough water to cover the jars by 1 to 2 inches. Bring the water to a boil over medium-high heat. Sterilize the jars (see page 32) in the water bath.

Reduce the strawberry syrup over medium-high heat until thickened, skimming and stirring frequently, about 5 minutes. Cook the syrup until it thickens, passes a preliminary plate test (see page 30), and is not runny.

Carefully return the berries to the jam pot, along with any juices that have collected in the bowl under the colander. Increase the heat to high, stir gently, and bring the strawberry mixture to a boil. Cook for 3 minutes. Taste the preserves and add more lemon juice if you think it needs a hit of acid. If you are going to add the mint or basil, do it now. At this point, you can also taste the syrup and add the balsamic vinegar to taste. Continue to cook on high briefly until the preserves pass the final plate test, reaching a soft set that is neither runny nor firm. Remove the pot from the heat and let the mixture rest for 5 minutes.

Bring the water bath back to a boil. If the jars have cooled, warm them in the water bath or in a 200°F oven. Simmer the lids in a saucepan of hot water. Place the jars on the baking sheet.

Stir the preserves to distribute the berries.

Ladle the preserves into the jars, leaving 1-inch headspace. Wipe the rims clean and set the lids on the mouths of the jars. Twist on the rings.

Using a jar lifter, gently lower the jars into the pots. When the water returns to a boil, decrease the heat to an active simmer, and process the jars for 10 minutes. Turn off the heat and leave the jars in the water for 1 to 2 minutes.

Using the jar lifter, transfer the jars from the pots to the baking sheets and let sit for at least 6 hours, until cool enough to handle. Check to be sure the jars have sealed (see page 34). Label and store the sealed preserves for 6 months to 2 years. Once open, store in the refrigerator for up to 3 months.

WHOLE STRAWBERRY PRESERVES WITH BLACK PEPPER AND POMEGRANATE

These preserves are sweet, tart, and surprising. I love the buzz from the black pepper. The pomegranate molasses amplifies the tartness of the lemon and adds depth to the preserves. Start at least a day ahead to allow the berries to macerate.

12 cups (6 pint baskets) small strawberries

7 cups granulated sugar

3 to 4 tablespoons fresh lemon juice

1 to 2 teaspoons freshly ground black pepper

3 to 4 tablespoons pomegranate molasses

Yield: 11 to 12 half-pint jars

Place 3 or 4 small plates in the freezer.

Rinse, dry, and hull the strawberries.

In a large preserving pot, gently combine the strawberries, sugar, and lemon juice and toss to mix. Let sit for a few hours to macerate. Bring to a boil over high heat and boil for 1 minute. Turn off the heat and let sit overnight.

The next day, bring the berry mixture to a boil over medium-high heat and boil for 1 minute. Remove from the heat and let sit, uncovered, for 1 to 2 hours or overnight.

Set a colander over a bowl and, using a slotted spoon, transfer the berries to the colander. Let sit for 30 minutes.

Place two baking sheets on the counter near your stove. Heat a kettle of water. Set two stockpots on the stove and fill them with enough water to cover the jars by 1 to 2 inches. Bring the water to a boil over medium-high heat. Sterilize the jars (see page 32) in the water bath.

Add any juices that are in the bowl to the preserving pot and bring the pot to a boil over medium-high heat. Cook the syrup until it passes the plate test (see page 30), and does not run very much when you tilt the plate.

Carefully return the berries to the preserving pot. Bring to a boil over medium-high heat and cook for 2 to 3 minutes. Add the pepper and pomegranate molasses. Run a final plate test, looking for a soft set that is not too runny. Remove the pot from the heat and let the mixture rest for 5 minutes.

Bring the water bath back to a boil. If the jars have cooled, warm them in the water bath or in a 200°F oven. Simmer the lids in a saucepan of hot water. Place the jars on the baking sheet.

Stir the preserves to distribute the berries.

Ladle the preserves into the jars, leaving 1-inch headspace. Wipe the rims clean and set the lids on the mouths of the jars. Twist on the rings.

Using a jar lifter, gently lower the jars into the pots. When the water returns to a boil, decrease the heat to an active simmer, and process the jars for 10 minutes. Turn off the heat and leave the jars in the water for 1 to 2 minutes.

Using the jar lifter, transfer the jars from the pots to the baking sheet and let sit for at least 6 hours, until cool enough to handle. Check to be sure the jars have sealed (see page 34). Label and store the sealed jam for 6 months to 2 years. Once open, store in the refrigerator for up to 3 months.

Rhubarb

Rhubarb is native to Siberia. This herbaceous perennial is technically a vegetable, but we have come to think of it as a fruit and use it in desserts, so I am including it in this book of fruit preserves. In England it is called the pie plant, but there's more to rhubarb than pie. In parts of the Middle East it is used in place of lemon to add acidity in sauces and soups. Its leaves are poisonous, so we eat just the stalks. For preserving, its intense sourness is countered with sugar.

Rhubarb needs cool weather during the growing season and comes into season in late April or May, with a second harvest that begins in June and runs through July. When shopping for rhubarb, select stalks that are firm, not flabby. You want them to be neither too thin (flavorless) nor too thick (stringy and tough). The stalks' color will vary from pink to red to greenish red, but the color does not affect the flavor. Field-grown rhubarb is redder than rhubarb grown in a hothouse.

Rhubarb and strawberries come into season at about the same time. After the long winter of citrus fruits, we are eager for such new flavors. Strawberries soften rhubarb's sharp angles and add a delicate floral note. They also accentuate the reddish color of the fruit. Rose sugar can add additional perfume. Rhubarb also pairs well with carrots (see Carrot-Rhubarb Jam, page 87), the other spring vegetable we use in desserts.

Over the course of a year, the color of some rhubarb jams will fade a bit or darken. Blending in strawberries and blood orange juice helps retain rhubarb's red color.

Natural flavor pairings for sweet rhubarb preserves are ginger, citrus, vanilla, rose, anise, strawberries, and raspberries.

You can choose to play up rhubarb's inherent bold tartness by using it in a chutney to serve with poultry, lamb, and some fish, such as salmon.

BASIC RHUBARB JAM

You have to be a fan of tart and bitter flavors to love pure rhubarb jam, untempered by sweet and fragrant strawberries. Spread it on toast, pancakes, scones, or biscuits. Or fold it into some strawberries to use as a shortcake filling.

2 pounds rhubarb

3 cups granulated sugar

Juice of 1 lemon or of ½ orange and ½ lemon

Yield: 6 half-pint jars

Place 3 or 4 small plates in the freezer.

Wash, trim (no need to peel it unless it is particularly stringy), and dice the rhubarb. You will have about 8 cups.

In a large preserving pot, gently combine the rhubarb, sugar, and citrus juice and toss to mix. Let sit overnight to macerate. Alternatively, you may skip the overnight maceration and bring the rhubarb mixture to a boil over medium-high heat and cook for 2 minutes. Remove the pot from the heat and let sit for 1 to 2 hours.

Place a baking sheet on the counter near your stove. Heat a kettle of water. Set two stockpots on the stove and fill them with enough water to cover the jars by 1 to 2 inches. Bring the water to a boil over medium-high heat. Sterilize the jars (see page 32) in the water bath.

For a jam with some texture, set a colander over a bowl and, using a slotted spoon, transfer the rhubarb to the colander. If you prefer a smoother texture in your finished jam, do not remove the fruit before proceeding.

If you removed the rhubarb, bring the juices to a boil over medium-high heat and cook until thickened or the mixture registers 220°F on a candy thermometer. If you do a preliminary plate test (see page 30) the juices will not run very much. Carefully add the rhubarb back to the pot, along with any juices that have collected in the bowl under the colander. Bring to a boil over medium-high heat, stirring frequently, and cook about 5 minutes longer, or until it passes the plate test and reaches a soft set.

For the smoother textured jam, cook the fruit with the juices over medium-high heat for 15 to 20 minutes, or until it passes the plate test, achieving a soft set that mounds on the plate and is not runny. Remove the pot from the heat.

Bring the water bath back to a boil. If the jars have cooled, warm them in the water bath or in a 200°F oven. Simmer the lids in a saucepan of hot water. Place the jars on the baking sheet.

Ladle the jam into the jars, leaving ¼-inch headspace. Wipe the rims clean and set the lids on the mouths of the jars. Twist on the rings.

Using a jar lifter, gently lower the jars into the pots. When the water returns to a boil, decrease the heat to an active simmer, and process the jars for 10 minutes. Turn off the heat and leave the jars in the water for 1 to 2 minutes.

Using the jar lifter, transfer the jars from the pots to the baking sheet and let sit for at least 6 hours, until cool enough to handle. Check to be sure the jars have sealed (see page 34). Label and store the sealed jam for 6 months to 2 years. Once open, store in the refrigerator for up to 3 months.

RHUBARB JAM WITH GINGER AND ORANGE

The major variable here is the amount of spiciness of the fresh ginger. Some fresh ginger is mild, and some is quite zippy. Adding a bit more sugar will keep it in check if it is too strong. And vanilla will add balance, too. If the rhubarb has a greenish tinge, and if blood oranges are available, adding their juice will make for a more attractive-looking preserve.

This jam is good on toast, biscuits, scones, and pancakes.

2 pounds rhubarb

Grated zest of 2 oranges

2 cups orange juice or substitute up to 1 cup blood orange juice if you want a redder hue

6 to 8 ounces fresh ginger, peeled, sliced thin, and finely grated in a food processor

4 cups granulated sugar, or more as needed

Fresh lemon juice, as needed

1 to 2 teaspoons vanilla extract (optional)

Yield: 6 half-pint jars

Place 3 or 4 small plates in the freezer.

Wash, trim (no need to peel it unless it is particularly stringy), and dice the rhubarb. You will have about 8 cups.

In a large preserving pot, combine the rhubarb, orange zest and juice, ginger, sugar, and lemon juice and toss to mix. Let sit overnight to macerate.

The next day, place the pot over medium-high heat. Bring to a boil and cook for 10 to 15 minutes. Remove from the heat and let sit, uncovered, for 1 hour.

Place a baking sheet on the counter near your stove. Heat a kettle of water. Set two stockpots on the stove and fill them with enough water to cover the jars by 1 to 2 inches. Bring the water to a boil over medium-high heat. Sterilize the jars (see page 32) in the water bath.

Taste the rhubarb and add sugar and lemon juice to taste if the rhubarb is not tart enough. Return the pot to medium-high heat, bring back to a boil, and cook for about 5 minutes, stirring often to prevent scorching. Taste the jam again and add the vanilla. Cook the jam briefly, until it passes the plate test (see page 30), achieving a soft set that mounds on the plate and is not runny. Remove the pot from the heat.

Bring the water bath back to a boil. If the jars have cooled, warm them in the water bath or in a 200°F oven. Simmer the lids in a saucepan of hot water. Place the jars on the baking sheet.

Ladle the jam into the jars, leaving ¼-inch headspace. Wipe the rims clean and set the lids on the mouths of the jars. Twist on the rings.

Using a jar lifter, gently lower the jars into the pots. When the water returns to a boil, decrease the heat to an active simmer, and process the jars for 10 minutes. Turn off the heat and leave the jars in the water for 1 to 2 minutes.

Using the jar lifter, transfer the jars from the pots to the baking sheet and let sit for at least 6 hours, until cool enough to handle. Check to be sure the jars have sealed (see page 34). Label and store the sealed jam for 6 months to 2 years. Once open, store in the refrigerator for up to 3 months.

RHUBARB, STRAWBERRY, AND ROSE JAM

This is a crowd-pleaser. You can make this with plain sugar, but the rose sugar adds a subtle perfume to the jam. As a change of pace after you've made this a few times, you may use raspberries in place of the strawberries, but it is hard to resist a classic pairing.

Use as a filling for shortcakes, atop rice pudding or panna cotta, or, of course, on toast or biscuits.

2 pounds rhubarb

4 cups (2 pint baskets) strawberries

Juice of 1 lemon

1½ cups granulated sugar

1½ cups rose sugar (see page 22) or granulated sugar

½ cup blood orange juice, for color (optional)

Yield: 9 half-pint jars

Place 3 or 4 small plates in the freezer.

Wash, trim (no need to peel it unless it is particularly stringy), and dice the rhubarb into 1-inch pieces. You will have about 8 cups.

Trim, hull, and quarter the strawberries.

In a large preserving pot, gently combine the rhubarb, strawberries, lemon juice, granulated sugar, and rose sugar or additional granulated sugar, and toss to mix. Let sit overnight to macerate.

The next day, bring the fruit mixture to a boil over medium-high heat. Cook for 5 minutes.

Set a colander over a bowl and, using a slotted spoon, transfer the rhubarb and berries to the colander.

Place two baking sheets on the counter near your stove. Heat a kettle of water. Set two stockpots on the stove and fill them with enough water to cover the jars by 1 to 2 inches. Bring the water to a boil over medium-high heat. Sterilize the jars (see page 32) in the water bath.

Reduce the rhubarb-strawberry syrup until it thickens, passes the plate test (see page 30) and does not run. Carefully return the fruit to the jam pot, along with any juices that have collected in the bowl under the colander, and add the blood orange juice.

Cook the jam briefly until it passes the plate test again, achieving a soft set that mounds on the plate and is not runny. Remove the pot from the heat.

Bring the water bath back to a boil. If the jars have cooled, warm them in the water bath or in a 200°F oven. Simmer the lids in a saucepan of hot water. Place the jars on the baking sheet.

Ladle the jam into the jars, leaving ¼-inch headspace. Wipe the rims clean and set the lids on the mouths of the jars. Twist on the rings.

Using a jar lifter, gently lower the jars into the pots. When the water returns to a boil, decrease the heat to an active simmer, and process the jars for 10 minutes. Turn off the heat and leave the jars in the water for 1 to 2 minutes.

Using the jar lifter, transfer the jars from the pots to the baking sheets and let sit for at least 6 hours, until cool enough to handle. Check to be sure the jars have sealed (see page 34). Label and store the sealed jam for 6 months to 2 years. Once open, store in the refrigerator for up to 3 months.

RHUBARB, BLOOD ORANGE, AND ROSE JAM

This one is a poem. The color is a spectacular deep red. If you store this jam for more than 6 months, the color will fade, but the jam will still taste fine. It just won't be as pretty.

Some blood oranges are quite juicy. Others can be rather dry, especially late in the season, ironically just as the rhubarb is hitting the market. Be prepared and have at least a dozen on hand. In the winter, I squeeze a lot of blood oranges when they are at their peak and freeze the juice in 1- or 2-cup quantities.

2 pounds rhubarb

2 cups blood orange juice

2 tablespoons grated blood orange zest

2 cups rose sugar (see page 22)

Yield: 6 half-pint jars

Place 3 or 4 small plates in the freezer.

Wash, trim (no need to peel it unless it is particularly stringy), and dice the rhubarb into 1-inch pieces. You will have about 8 cups.

In a large preserving pot, gently combine the rhubarb, orange juice and zest, and rose sugar, and toss to mix. Let sit overnight to macerate. Alternatively, you may skip the overnight maceration and bring the rhubarb mixture to a boil over medium-high heat, cooking it for 2 minutes. Remove the pot from the heat and let sit for 1 to 2 hours.

After the resting period, return the pot to medium-high heat, bring to a boil, and cook for 10 minutes, stirring often to prevent scorching, or until most of the rhubarb is soft. Remove the pot from the heat and let sit for 1 to 2 hours more. The jam may thicken as it sits.

Place a baking sheet on the counter near your stove. Heat a kettle of water. Set two stockpots on the stove and fill them with enough water to cover the jars by 1 to 2 inches. Bring the water to a boil over medium-high heat. Sterilize the jars (see page 32) in the water bath.

Bring the jam to a boil and cook until it passes the final plate test (see page 30). The jam should mound on the plate and not run. Remove the pot from the heat.

Bring the water bath back to a boil. If the jars have cooled, warm them in the water bath or in a 200°F oven. Simmer the lids in a saucepan of hot water. Place the jars on the baking sheet.

Ladle the jam into the jars, leaving ¼-inch headspace. Wipe the rims clean and set the lids on the mouths of the jars. Twist on the rings.

Using a jar lifter, gently lower the jars into the pots. When the water returns to a boil, decrease the heat to an active simmer, and process the jars for 10 minutes. Turn off the heat and leave the jars in the water for 1 to 2 minutes.

Using the jar lifter, transfer the jars from the pots to the baking sheet and let sit for at least 6 hours, until cool enough to handle. Check to be sure the jars have sealed (see page 34). Label and store the sealed jam for 6 months to 2 years. Once open, store in the refrigerator for up to 3 months.

Apricots

Over the years, supermarket apricots have become a sad travesty of what the fruit used to be. Because apricots are tender and easily bruised, many old trees have been torn out and newer hardier varieties planted in their stead. Now we get pretty golden orbs, firm on the outside, cottony in texture on the inside, and devoid of much flavor and aroma. By aiming for long shelf life, the growers have taken the life out of the fruit. Fortunately, the organic apricots at my farmers' market sing with sweetness, acidity, and perfume. I always look forward to the arrival of the early Apaches, which then give way to Pattersons, Robadas, Golden Sweets, Tiltons, and Royal Blenheims.

The apricot originated in China, and its cultivation spread to Iran, Turkey, and the rest of the Middle East, where it is still grown in abundance. Spanish explorers carried them from the Mediterranean to the New World and planted them in the California missions. The famous Blenheim, however, came to us from England. It was discovered in the garden of the Duke of Marlborough in Blenheim Palace in the 1830s. Blenheims (sometimes labeled Royal Blenheims) are prestigious and not widely available, so more organic farmers want to cultivate them. The Blenheims at my market vary in appearance and quality. Most are small, pale, even greenish, and a few don't have much flavor. But when they are good, they are certainly worth your time. The best are fragrant and floral in taste, just not as blush red on the outside as the Tilton and other varieties.

When shopping for apricots, buy organic fruit that is fragrant and plump. You want the apricot to give just a bit when you touch it. Avoid green, underripe fruit, as it will not get any better or riper at home. Avoid soft apricots, as they can develop mold or dark spots and you will have wasted your money. Firm, ripe apricots can be stored for a day or two at room temperature, arranged in a single layer on a baking sheet or platter. Ripe apricots may be stored in the refrigerator for a day or two, but they will lose some of their perfume.

Some cooks crack the pits and extract the kernel inside, because the kernels can be used to impart a bitter almond flavor to the jam. If you are able to extricate them from the shell—no small feat—put a few apricot kernels in a tea strainer, add it to the preserve as it cooks, and then discard the kernels.

Natural flavor-pairing affinities for apricot are almond, vanilla, Fiori di Sicilia, lemon, ginger, cardamom, and herbs such as lavender or lemon verbena.

BASIC APRICOT JAM

Of all the jams that I preserve, this is the one I make in large batches because it is a family favorite. My family loves it plain or with other flavor enhancements (see the variations). This is a two-day project. Macerate the apricots overnight and then make the jam the next day.

It is good on toast, spooned into yogurt, as a cookie or cake filling, or thinned and used as a glaze for almond or sponge cake.

5 pounds whole apricots, pitted and halved (8 cups)

4 cups granulated sugar

Juice of 2 lemons

Yield: 9 or 10 half-pint jars

Place 3 or 4 small plates in the freezer.

Cut any large apricot halves into quarters.

In a large preserving pot, gently combine the apricots with the sugar and toss to mix. Add the juice of 1 lemon and gently stir to mix. Let sit overnight to macerate.

The next day, bring the fruit mixture to a boil over medium-high heat. Cook for 2 minutes. Remove from the heat and let sit, uncovered, for 1 hour.

If you want the fruit to retain some of its shape in the finished jam, set a colander over a bowl and, using a slotted spoon, transfer the apricots to the colander.

Place two baking sheets on the counter near your stove. Heat a kettle of water. Set two stockpots on the stove and fill them with enough water to cover the jars by 1 to 2 inches. Bring the water to a boil over medium-high heat. Sterilize the jars (see page 32) in the water bath.

Reduce the apricot syrup, stirring frequently, until thickened. Carefully return the apricots to the jam pot, along with any juices that have collected in the bowl under the colander. Add the remaining lemon juice to taste.

Cook the jam briefly until it passes the plate test (see page 30), achieving a soft set that mounds on the plate and does not run very much. Remove the pot from the heat.

Bring the water bath back to a boil. If the jars have cooled, warm them in the water bath or in a 200°F oven. Simmer the lids in a saucepan of hot water. Place the jars on the baking sheet.

Ladle the jam into the jars, leaving ¼-inch headspace. Wipe the rims clean and set the lids on the mouths of the jars. Twist on the rings.

Using a jar lifter, gently lower the jars into the pots. When the water returns to a boil, decrease the heat to an active simmer, and process the jars for 10 minutes. Turn off the heat and leave the jars in the water for 1 to 2 minutes.

Using the jar lifter, transfer the jars from the pots to the baking sheets and let sit for at least 6 hours, until cool enough to handle. Check to be sure the jars have sealed (see page 34). Label and store the sealed jam for 6 months to 2 years. Once open, store in the refrigerator for up to 3 months.

VARIATIONS

— Add 1 tablespoon dried lavender in a sachet, or substitute 1 cup lavender sugar (see page 22) for 1 cup of the granulated sugar.

— Add vanilla extract or substitute 1 cup vanilla sugar (see page 22) for 1 cup of the granulated sugar.

— Add 2 teaspoons ground cardamom.

— Add 1 to 2 teaspoons almond extract or amaretto liqueur.

— Add lemon verbena leaves.

APRICOT-GINGER JAM

The ginger can be added in either of two ways: pureed in the food processor so it permeates the jam, or in strips so you get little hits of ginger as you eat the jam. To make the strips, peel the ginger, slice it thinly on a mandoline, and then stack the slices and cut into fine strips.

This is a two-day project. Macerate the apricots with sugar overnight, and then make the jam the next day.

This jam is good on toast or used as cookie filling, and is wonderful spooned atop ice cream. Thinned with a little soy sauce, it makes a fine glaze for pork roast or baked ham.

5 pounds apricots, pitted and halved (8 cups)

4 cups granulated sugar

3 tablespoons fresh lemon juice, or more as needed

5 to 6 ounces fresh ginger, peeled and pureed (¼ cup) or finely julienned (½ cup)

Yield: 10 half-pint jars

Place 3 or 4 small plates in the freezer.

Cut any large apricot halves into quarters.

In a large preserving pot, gently combine the apricots with the sugar and toss to mix. Add the lemon juice and ginger and gently stir to mix in. Let sit overnight to macerate.

The next day, bring the apricot mixture to a boil over medium-high heat. Cook for 2 minutes. Remove from the heat and let sit, uncovered, for 1 hour.

If you want the fruit to retain some of its shape in the finished jam, set a colander over a bowl and, using a slotted spoon, transfer the apricots to the colander.

Place two baking sheets on the counter near your stove. Heat a kettle of water. Set two stockpots on the stove and fill them with enough water to cover the jars by 1 to 2 inches. Bring the water to a boil over medium-high heat. Sterilize the jars (see page 32) in the water bath.

Reduce the apricot syrup, stirring frequently, until thickened. Carefully return the apricots to the jam pot, along with any juices that have collected in the bowl under the colander. Cook the jam briefly until it passes the plate test (see page 30), achieving a soft set that is not too running. Remove the pot from the heat.

Bring the water bath back to a boil. If the jars have cooled, warm them in the water bath or in a 200°F oven. Simmer the lids in a saucepan of hot water. Place the jars on the baking sheets.

Ladle the jam into the jars, leaving ¼-inch headspace. Wipe the rims clean and set the lids on the mouths of the jars. Twist on the rings.

Using a jar lifter, gently lower the jars into the pots. When the water returns to a boil, decrease the heat to an active simmer, and process the jars for 10 minutes. Turn off the heat and leave the jars in the water for 1 to 2 minutes.

Using the jar lifter, transfer the jars from the pots to the baking sheets and let sit for at least 6 hours, until cool enough to handle. Check to be sure the jars have sealed (see page 34). Label and store the sealed jam for 6 months to 2 years. Once open, store in the refrigerator for up to 3 months.

APRICOT—MEYER LEMON PRESERVES

For this recipe, it is important to blanch the lemon slices to remove their bitterness; don't skip this step.

This jam is good on toast or muffins with butter, ricotta, or mascarpone, or spooned atop panna cotta or rice pudding.

5 pounds apricots, pitted and halved (8 cups)	6 cups granulated sugar
	½ cup water
3 small Meyer lemons or 2 small Eureka or Lisbon lemons	1 large sprig (about 12 leaves) lemon verbena (optional)

Yield: 10 half-pint jars

Place 3 or 4 small plates in the freezer.

Cut any large apricot halves into quarters.

Cut the lemons into very thin slices on a mandoline. If the lemons are small, cut the slices in half. If they are large, cut the slices into quarters. You want ½ to ¾ cup of lemon slices.

Bring a saucepan of water to a boil over medium-high heat. Add the lemon slices and boil for 2 minutes. Remove the slices with a wire skimmer and rinse with cold water. For Meyer lemons, taste the slices and, if they are still bitter, repeat the process one more time. For regular Eureka or Lisbon lemons, blanch the slices two more times, blanching them three times in all.

In a large, heavy-bottomed pot, gently combine the apricots, lemon slices, sugar, and water and toss to mix. Let sit overnight to macerate.

The next day, add the lemon verbena and bring the pot to a boil over medium-high heat. Cook for 2 minutes. Remove from the heat and let sit, uncovered, for 1 hour.

If you want the fruit to retain some of its shape in the finished preserve, set a colander over a bowl and, using a slotted spoon, transfer the apricots to the colander.

Place two baking sheets on the counter near your stove. Heat a kettle of water. Set two stockpots on the stove and fill them with enough water to cover the jars by 1 to 2 inches. Bring the water to a boil over medium-high heat. Sterilize the jars (see page 32) in the water bath.

Reduce the apricot syrup, stirring frequently, until thickened. Carefully return the apricots to the pot, along with any juices that have collected in the bowl under the colander.

Cook the preserve briefly until it passes the plate test (see page 30), achieving a soft set that mounds on the plate and is not runny. Remove the pot from the heat.

Bring the water bath back to a boil. If the jars have cooled, warm them in the water bath or in a 200°F oven. Simmer the lids in a saucepan of hot water. Place the jars on the baking sheet.

Ladle the jam into the jars, leaving ¼-inch headspace. Wipe the rims clean and set the lids on the mouths of the jars. Twist on the rings.

Using a jar lifter, gently lower the jars into the pots. When the water returns to a boil, decrease the heat to an active simmer, and process the jars for 10 minutes. Turn off the heat and leave the jars in the water for 1 to 2 minutes.

Using the jar lifter, transfer the jars from the pots to the baking sheets and let sit for at least 6 hours, until cool enough to handle. Check to be sure the jars have sealed (see page 34). Label and store the sealed jam for 6 months to 2 years. Once open, store in the refrigerator for up to 3 months.

APRICOT CHUTNEY

In the Middle East and North Africa, apricots are often paired with lamb, so I like to serve this chutney with lamb curry and lamb roasts. It's also excellent with pork, chicken, and turkey and works well as a condiment for a salumi or charcuterie plate.

5 pounds apricots, pitted and halved (8 cups)

1 lime, cut into small pieces

3 cloves garlic

2 large yellow onions, diced

4 ounces fresh ginger, peeled and sliced

3 cups apple cider vinegar, plus more as needed

3½ cups firmly packed brown sugar or 3 cups granulated sugar, if you want a brighter color

1 teaspoon ground allspice

1 teaspoon ground cloves

1 teaspoon ground ginger

1 tablespoon ground cinnamon

1 teaspoon ground cayenne

2 teaspoons salt

2 cups raisins

Yield: 7 pint jars

Place 3 or 4 small plates in the freezer.

Cut any large apricot halves into quarters.

Combine the lime, garlic, onions, and ginger in a food processor or blender. Add a splash of the vinegar and pulse until pureed.

In a preserving pot over medium-high heat, combine the apricots and onion mixture. Add the sugar, the rest of the 3 cups of vinegar, the allspice, cloves, ginger, cinnamon, cayenne, and salt and stir to combine well.

Place a baking sheet on the counter near your stove. Heat a kettle of water. Set two stockpots on the stove and fill them with enough water to cover the jars by 1 to 2 inches. Bring the water to a boil over medium-high heat. Sterilize the jars (see page 32) in the water bath.

Bring the apricot mixture to a boil over medium-high heat and cook, stirring frequently, then decrease the heat to low and simmer, stirring occasionally to prevent sticking.

After the mixture has simmered for 30 minutes, add the raisins and stir continuously because the raisins have a tendency to sink to the bottom of the pot and scorch. If the raisins become fully plumped, they will likely have absorbed much of the liquid, so you will need to add enough vinegar or water to rehydrate the mixture. Taste and add salt or cayenne if you like. Do the plate test (see page 30). The chutney should be chunky and syrupy, not dry. Remove the pot from the heat.

Bring the water bath back to a boil. If the jars have cooled, warm them in the water bath or in a 200°F oven. Simmer the lids in a saucepan of hot water. Place the jars on the baking sheet.

Ladle the chutney into the jars, leaving ¼-inch headspace. Wipe the rims clean and set the lids on the mouths of the jars. Twist on the rings.

Using a jar lifter, gently lower the jars into the pots. When the water returns to a boil, decrease the heat to an active simmer, and process the jars for 10 minutes. Turn off the heat and leave the jars in the water for 1 to 2 minutes.

Using the jar lifter, transfer the jars from the pots to the baking sheet and let sit for at least 6 hours, until cool enough to handle. Check to be sure the jars have sealed (see page 34). Label and store the sealed jam for 6 months to 2 years. Once open, store in the refrigerator for up to 3 months.

APRICOT MUSTARD

Back when I had my San Francisco restaurant, Square One, we made a mustard with dried apricots. (It was really good with our house-made sausages.) One morning not long ago, while pondering what to do with a flat of beautiful apricots, I remembered that mustard and thought I'd try using fresh apricots and changing the procedure a little. That experiment led to this potent spread, a smooth, spreadable mustard that's flavored with cooked, pureed apricots. This is a two-day project. Macerate the apricots with sugar overnight and then make the mustard the next day. The recipe can easily be halved if you prefer to make less.

This is an ideal spread for a ham or chicken sandwich, and it's good on grilled cheese, too. You can also use it as a glaze for baked ham or roast pork.

5 pounds apricots, pitted and halved (8 cups)

½ cup freshly squeezed orange juice or water

2 cups granulated sugar

2 cups Colman's mustard powder

3 cups apple cider vinegar

2 teaspoons ground cinnamon

2 teaspoons ground ginger

1 tablespoon salt, or more as needed

1 teaspoon ground cayenne

¼ cup yellow mustard seeds

Fresh lemon juice, as needed

Yield: 12 to 14 half-pint jars

Place 3 or 4 small plates in the freezer.

Cut any large apricot halves into quarters.

In a large preserving pot, gently combine the apricots with the orange juice and sugar and toss to mix. Let sit overnight to macerate.

The next day, bring the mixture to a boil over medium-high heat. Cook the apricots until they are very soft. Remove from the heat and let them cool until just warm.

Transfer the apricot mixture to a food processor and process until pureed. Return the puree to the preserving pot.

In a mixing bowl, whisk together the mustard powder, vinegar, cinnamon, and ginger. Add the mustard mixture to the apricot puree. Stir in the salt, cayenne, and mustard seeds.

Place two baking sheets on the counter near your stove. Heat a kettle of water. Set two stockpots on the stove and fill them with enough water to cover the jars by 1 to 2 inches. Bring the water to a boil over medium-high heat. Sterilize the jars (see page 32) in the water bath.

Simmer the mustard mixture over medium-high heat, stirring until thick. Taste the mustard and add a squeeze or two of lemon juice and/or a generous pinch of salt. It should be spicy. Stir well, taste again, and cook briefly until the mustard passes the plate test (see page 30) and mounds on the plate. Remove the pot from the heat.

Bring the water bath back to a boil. If the jars have cooled, warm them in the water bath or in a 200°F oven. Simmer the lids in a saucepan of hot water. Place the jars on the baking sheets.

Ladle the mustard into the jars, leaving ¼-inch headspace. Wipe the rims clean and set the lids on the mouths of the jars. Twist on the rings.

Using a jar lifter, gently lower the jars into the pots. When the water returns to a boil, decrease the heat to an active simmer, and process the jars for 10 minutes. Turn off the heat and leave the jars in the water for 1 to 2 minutes.

Using the jar lifter, transfer the jars from the pots to the baking sheets and let sit for at least 6 hours, until cool enough to handle. Check to be sure the jars have sealed (see page 34). Label and store the sealed jam for 6 months to 2 years. Once open, store in the refrigerator for up to 3 months.

APRICOTS IN FRAGRANT SYRUP

Why bother with preserving your own when you can buy canned fruit in plain sugar syrup? Because you can create a syrup that is distinctive and shows off the fruit to its best advantage.

Apricots are delicate and cook very, very quickly. Most recipes call for cooking the fruit way too long. To keep their shape, apricot halves should cook for 3 to 5 minutes and whole apricots for 8 to 10 minutes. You can put the cardamom seeds in a cheesecloth sachet or tea strainer if you do not want them floating around in the syrup, but I like to see them and don't mind biting into them.

Serve the apricots with ice cream, or as a garnish for panna cotta or rice pudding.

2 pounds small, firm apricots	¼ cup thin julienne strips of fresh young ginger
2 cups granulated sugar	
2 cups water	1 teaspoon cardamom seeds, in a cheesecloth sachet or tea strainer or loose
1 vanilla bean, cut into thirds	
3 strips lemon zest	1 to 2 tablespoons fresh lemon juice (optional)

Yield: 1 wide-mouth quart jar for whole apricots or 3 half-pint jars for apricot halves

Remove any stems still attached to the apricots. If you prefer to preserve apricot halves, pit and halve the apricots.

Place a baking sheet on the counter near your stove. Heat a kettle of water. Set a stockpot on the stove and fill it with enough water to cover the jar(s) by 1 to 2 inches. Bring the water to a boil over medium-high heat. Sterilize the jar(s) (see page 32) in the water bath. Simmer the lid(s) in a saucepan of hot water. Leave in the water to keep warm.

In a large preserving pot, combine the sugar, water, vanilla bean, lemon zest, ginger, and cardamom. Bring the syrup to a boil over medium-high heat. Carefully taste the syrup and add lemon juice if desired. Simmer the syrup until it starts to thicken, about 5 minutes longer. Decrease the heat to low. Add the apricots and simmer gently for 3 to 5 minutes for apricot halves or 8 to 10 minutes for whole apricots.

Place the jar(s) on the baking sheet. With a slotted spoon, transfer the fruit to the hot, sterilized jar(s).

Return the syrup to a boil over medium-high heat and reduce until it is thick. Carefully ladle the syrup over the fruit in the jar(s), leaving 1-inch headspace. Run a chopstick around the inside of the jar(s) to remove any air bubbles. Wipe the rim(s) clean and set the lid(s) on the mouth(s) of the jar(s). Twist on the ring(s).

Bring the water bath back to a boil.

Using a jar lifter, gently lower the jar(s) into the pot. When the water returns to a boil, decrease the heat to an active simmer, and process the jar(s) for 10 minutes. Turn off the heat and leave the jar(s) in the water for 1 to 2 minutes.

Using the jar lifter, transfer the jar(s) from the pot to the baking sheet and let sit for at least 6 hours, until cool enough to handle. Check to be sure the jars have sealed (see page 34). Label and store the sealed preserves for 6 months to 2 years. Once open, store in the refrigerator for up to 3 months.

VARIATIONS

— Substitute strips of orange peel
   for the lemon peel.

— Add a few tablespoons of orange-
   flower water.

— Stir in 1 to 2 teaspoons amaretto
   liqueur just before ladling the
   syrup into the jar(s).

Cherries

Cherries are among the most prized fruits of spring. I cross my fingers that they arrive as expected and stay at the market for a while, because an early rain can damage the crop and cut their availability short. In the West we grow mainly sweet cherries. With luck their season is about six weeks, so jump at the chance to preserve them. Select those that are shiny and have greener stems. The earliest red cherries, Brooks, give way to the crunchy Sweetheart, Black Tartarian, and Burlat varieties, and then come the deep red and sweet Bings. The pretty Rainier and Queen Anne cherries lack sufficient flavor intensity for jams and are best eaten out of hand, although you can pickle them.

Sour cherries are cultivated mainly east of the Rockies and are abundant in Michigan. Every once in a while, local sour cherries appear at the markets in San Francisco, and they are snapped up in a flash. One year their arrival was even announced in my market's newsletter. I was at the Lagier Ranch stand at 7:30 on the appointed morning to get as much of their first and only crop as I could carry home. I felt lucky, greedy, and guilty for grabbing so many on the one day they were available. If you know someone who has a sour cherry tree, hope that their crop is so abundant that they will have to give you some.

Pectin level is a major concern in making cherry preserves. Cherries are low in natural pectin and may need the addition of apple pectin to set. Whenever I prepare to make cherry preserves, I bring up a jar of apple pectin from the jam cellar for insurance, just in case it is needed. Sometimes, with enough citrus or tart berries added, the preserve sets to my satisfaction. But I want to be prepared just in case they don't.

Another challenge with cherries is the time it takes to pit them. That's the meditation! Try to slow down and enjoy it. After I pit the cherries, I usually try to leave them whole to display my handwork.

Natural flavor pairings for cherries are cardamom, lemon, orange, bay leaves, vanilla, star anise, cinnamon, almond, amaretto, kirsch, and brandy.

Cherry preserves can be used as cake filling, as a lattice tart filling, and as a spread for toast and pancakes. They pair beautifully with almond butter on a sandwich. You may also use them as a topping for cheesecake, custard, ice cream, almond panna cotta, and rice pudding. Deglazing a pan with wine and cherry preserves produces a lovely sauce for sautéed duck breasts or pork chops.

Some notes on yield:

- 12 pounds (1 flat) of cherries makes 18 to 20 half-pint jars (call a friend!).

- 6 pounds will give you about 10 half-pint jars.

- 3 pounds yield 5 to 6 half-pint jars.

BASIC CHERRY JAM

If you want a smoother preserve (and do not want your cherries to roll off your breakfast toast), you may halve the cherries or coarsely chop them after pitting. If you plan on serving cherry preserves as a sauce for panna cotta or cake or rice pudding, then whole pitted cherries make a flashier presentation.

6 pounds sweet cherries

9 cups granulated sugar

Juice of 2 lemons, plus more as needed

1 whole vanilla bean or vanilla extract (optional)

1 cinnamon stick (optional)

Up to 1 cup Homemade Apple Pectin (page 200)

¼ cup kirsch or 1 teaspoon almond extract (optional)

Yield: 9 to 10 half-pint jars

Place 3 or 4 small plates in the freezer.

Stem and pit the cherries. You will have about 16 cups.

In a large preserving pot, gently combine the cherries, sugar, and lemon juice. Bring to a boil over medium-high heat and boil for 1 to 2 minutes. Add the vanilla bean and cinnamon; if using vanilla extract instead of a vanilla bean, don't add it yet. Turn off the heat and let sit overnight to macerate.

The next day, place two baking sheets on the counter near your stove. Heat a kettle of water. Set two stockpots on the stove and fill them with enough water to cover the jars by 1 to 2 inches. Bring the water to a boil over medium-high heat. Sterilize the jars (see page 32) in the water bath.

If the cherries seem very soft, set a colander over a bowl and, using a slotted spoon, transfer them to the colander. If the cherries are firm, keep them in the syrup during cooking.

Bring the mixture to a boil over medium-high heat and reduce until it has thickened.

If you removed the cherries, carefully return them to the preserving pot now, along with any juices that have collected in the bowl under the colander.

Bring the fruit and syrup to a boil over medium-high heat. Do a preliminary plate test (see page 30) to see how thick the jam is and then add the apple pectin (using the full cup if you like a thicker jam) and cook for about 5 minutes over high heat. If using the vanilla extract, add it, or add the kirsch or almond extract, during the final minute of cooking. Taste and add another squeeze of lemon juice if you think the preserve needs a kick of acidity. Discard the vanilla bean and cinnamon stick. Repeat the plate test and, when you are satisfied with the set, remove the pot from the heat.

Bring the water bath back to a boil. If the jars have cooled, warm them in the water bath or in a 200°F oven. Simmer the lids in a saucepan of hot water. Place the jars on the baking sheet.

Ladle the jam into the jars, leaving ¼-inch headspace. Wipe the rims clean and set the lids on the mouths of the jars. Twist on the rings.

Using a jar lifter, gently lower the jars into the pots. When the water returns to a boil, decrease the heat to an active simmer, and process the jars for 10 minutes. Turn off the heat and leave the jars in the water for 1 to 2 minutes.

Using the jar lifter, transfer the jars from the pots to the baking sheet and let sit for at least 6 hours, until cool enough to handle. Check to be sure the jars have sealed (see page 34). Label and store the sealed jam for 6 months to 2 years. Once open, store in the refrigerator for up to 3 months.

SWEETHEART CHERRY JAM WITH STAR ANISE

Cherries and anise are an elegant flavor combination. If you use whole star anise, remove them after cooking. If you use ground anise, start with a teaspoon, taste, and then add a bit more if you like.

3 pounds sweet cherries

3 whole star anise pods, or 1 teaspoon ground anise

3 tablespoons fresh lemon juice, plus more as needed

4 cups granulated sugar

Up to 1 cup Homemade Apple Pectin (page 200)

Yield: 6 to 7 half-pint jars

Place 3 or 4 small plates in the freezer.

Stem and pit the cherries. You will have about 8 cups.

In a large preserving pot, gently combine the cherries, star anise, lemon juice, and sugar. Let it sit overnight to macerate.

The next day, bring the cherry mixture to a boil over medium-high heat. Turn off the heat and let sit for 1 hour.

Place a baking sheet on the counter near your stove. Heat a kettle of water. Set a stockpot on the stove and fill it with enough water to cover the jars by 1 to 2 inches. Bring the water to a boil over medium-high heat. Sterilize the jars (see page 32) in the water bath.

Return the cherry mixture to a boil over medium-high heat, then decrease the heat and simmer until thickened, skimming and stirring frequently. Taste and add more lemon juice if needed. Do the plate test (see page 30), and if the jam is too runny, add the apple pectin (using the full cup if you like a thicker jam) and cook for 5 minutes longer, until it passes the plate test, achieving a soft set that mounds on the plate and is not runny. Remove the pot from the heat.

Bring the water bath back to a boil. If the jars have cooled, warm them in the water bath or in a 200°F oven. Simmer the lids in a saucepan of hot water. Place the jars on the baking sheet.

Ladle the jam into the jars, leaving ¼-inch headspace. Wipe the rims clean and set the lids on the mouths of the jars. Twist on the rings.

Using a jar lifter, gently lower the jars into the pots. When the water returns to a boil, decrease the heat to an active simmer, and process the jars. for 10 minutes Turn off the heat and leave the jars in the water for 1 to 2 minutes.

Using the jar lifter, transfer the jars from the pot to the baking sheet and let sit for at least 6 hours, until cool enough to handle. Check to be sure the jars have sealed (see page 34). Label and store the sealed jam for 6 months to 2 years. Once open, store in the refrigerator for up to 3 months.

CHERRY-BERRY JAM

This jam came about because I overbought at the market and had fruit left over—a happy accident that is worth doing on purpose.

2½ pounds Bing cherries

2 cups (1 pint basket) strawberries

2 cups granulated sugar

2 cups rose sugar (see page 22)

¼ cup lemon juice, plus more as needed

2 cups (3 six-ounce baskets) raspberries

Up to 1 cup Homemade Apple Pectin (page 200)

Yield: 8 half-pint jars

Place 3 or 4 small plates in the freezer.

Stem, pit, and halve or coarsely chop the cherries. You will have about 6 cups.

Hull and slice the strawberries.

In a large preserving pot, gently combine the cherries, strawberries, granulated sugar, rose sugar, and lemon juice. Bring to a boil over medium-high heat and cook for 1 to 2 minutes. Turn off the heat and let sit overnight to macerate.

The next day, bring the cherry mixture to a boil over medium-high heat and cook for 5 minutes. Turn off the heat and let sit for 2 to 3 hours.

Place a baking sheet on the counter near your stove. Heat a kettle of water. Set two stockpots on the stove and fill them with enough water to cover the jars by 1 to 2 inches. Bring the water to a boil over medium-high heat. Sterilize the jars (see page 32) in the water bath.

Bring the cherry mixture back to a boil over medium-high heat, add the raspberries, and cook for 5 more minutes. Taste the jam and add another squeeze of lemon juice if needed. Do the plate test (see page 30). If the jam has not thickened enough, stir in the apple pectin (using the full cup if you like a thicker jam) and cook for 5 minutes, stirring frequently, until it thickens and passes the plate test, achieving a soft set that is neither runny nor stiff. Remove the pot from the heat.

Bring the water bath back to a boil. If the jars have cooled, warm them in the water bath or in a 200°F oven. Simmer the lids in a saucepan of hot water. Place the jars on the baking sheet.

Ladle the jam into the jars, leaving ¼-inch headspace. Wipe the rims clean and set the lids on the mouths of the jars. Twist on the rings.

Using a jar lifter, gently lower the jars into the pots. When the water returns to a boil, decrease the heat to an active simmer, and process the jars for 10 minutes. Turn off the heat and leave the jars in the water for 1 to 2 minutes.

Using the jar lifter, transfer the jars from the pots to the baking sheet and let sit for at least 6 hours, until cool enough to handle. Check to be sure the jars have sealed (see page 34). Label and store the sealed jam for 6 months to 2 years. Once open, store in the refrigerator for up to 3 months.

WOODLAND CHERRY PRESERVES

While browsing in the cookbook bin at my local bookstore, I discovered a copy of *Sweet Magic*, Michel Richard's dessert book. In it, I learned that some French chefs like to add a bay leaf or two to cherry compotes. Intrigued, I thought I'd give it a try for a cherry preserve. The flavor is subtle and mysterious. Sort of woodsy. If you can find sour cherries, they are a great match for the bay leaves, but regular cherries will work, too.

3 pounds cherries

3 small fresh bay leaves

5 cups granulated sugar

3 tablespoons fresh lemon juice

Up to 1 cup Homemade Apple Pectin (page 200)

Yield: 6 to 7 half-pint jars

Place 3 or 4 small plates in the freezer.

Stem and pit the cherries. You will have about 8 cups.

In a large preserving pot, gently combine the cherries, bay leaves, sugar, and lemon juice. Bring to a boil over medium-high heat and cook for 1 to 2 minutes. Turn off the heat and let sit overnight to macerate.

The next day, place a baking sheet on the counter near your stove. Heat a kettle of water. Set two stockpots on the stove and fill them with enough water to cover the jars by 1 to 2 inches. Bring the water to a boil over medium-high heat. Sterilize the jars (see page 32) in the water bath.

Bring the cherry mixture to a boil again over medium-high heat and cook for 5 minutes.

If the cherries seem very soft, set a colander over a bowl and, using a slotted spoon, transfer them to the colander.

If the cherries are firm, bring the fruit and syrup to a boil over medium-high heat, add the apple pectin (using the full cup if you like a thicker jam), and cook for 5 minutes.

If you removed the cherries, carefully return them to the jam pot now, along with any juices that have collected in the bowl under the colander.

Bring the cherry mixture back to a boil, and cook over high heat for 5 minutes, skimming and stirring frequently, until it passes the plate test (see page 30), achieving a soft set that is neither runny nor stiff. Remove the pot from the heat and discard the bay leaves.

Bring the water bath back to a boil. If the jars have cooled, warm them in the water bath or in a 200°F oven. Simmer the lids in a saucepan of hot water. Place the jars on the baking sheet.

Ladle the preserves into the jars, leaving ¼-inch headspace. Wipe the rims clean and set the lids on the mouths of the jars. Twist on the rings.

Using a jar lifter, gently lower the jars into the pots. When the water returns to a boil, decrease the heat to an active simmer, and process the jars for 10 minutes. Turn off the heat and leave the jars in the water for 1 to 2 minutes.

Using the jar lifter, transfer the jars from the pots to the baking sheet and let sit for at least 4 hours, until cool enough to handle. Check to be sure the jars have sealed (see page 34). Label and store the sealed preserves for 6 months to 2 years. Once open, store in the refrigerator for up to 3 months.

CHERRY-ORANGE MARMALADE

No additional apple pectin is needed for this recipe because the oranges add sufficient pectin for it to set.

3 pounds sweet cherries

2 organic oranges

4 to 5 cups granulated sugar

3 to 4 tablespoons fresh lemon juice

4 small fresh bay leaves (optional)

Yield: 7 half-pint jars

Place 3 or 4 small plates in the freezer.

Stem and pit the cherries. You will have about 8 cups.

Cut the unpeeled oranges into quarters, remove any seeds, and place the quarters in the bowl of a food processor. Pulse until pulverized.

In a large preserving pot, gently combine the cherries, oranges, sugar, lemon juice, and bay leaves.

Bring to a boil over medium-high heat and cook for 1 to 2 minutes. Turn off the heat and let sit overnight to macerate.

The next day, bring the cherry mixture to a boil again over medium-high heat and cook for 5 minutes. Turn off the heat and let sit for 2 to 3 hours.

Place a baking sheet on the counter near your stove. Heat a kettle of water. Set two stockpots on the stove and fill them with enough water to cover the jars by 1 to 2 inches. Bring the water to a boil over medium-high heat. Sterilize the jars (see page 32) in the water bath.

Bring the cherry mixture to a boil over medium-high heat, and cook, skimming and stirring frequently, until it passes the plate test (see page 30), achieving a soft set that is neither runny nor stiff.

Remove and discard the bay leaves. Remove the pot from the heat.

Bring the water bath back to a boil. If the jars have cooled, warm them in the water bath or in a 200°F oven. Simmer the lids in a saucepan of hot water. Place the jars on the baking sheet.

Ladle the marmalade into the jars, leaving ¼-inch headspace. Wipe the rims clean and set the lids on the mouths of the jars. Twist on the rings.

Using a jar lifter, gently lower the jars into the pots. When the water returns to a boil, decrease the heat to an active simmer, and process the jars for 10 minutes. Turn off the heat and leave the jars in the water for 1 to 2 minutes.

Using the jar lifter, transfer the jars from the pots to the baking sheet and let sit for at least 6 hours, until cool enough to handle. Check to be sure the jars have sealed (see page 34). Label and store the sealed marmalade for 6 months to 2 years. Once open, store in the refrigerator for up to 3 months.

BING CHERRY AND MEYER LEMON PRESERVES

The lemon in this recipe should provide sufficient pectin for the preserves to set. However, it's a good idea to have Homemade Apple Pectin (page 200) at the ready and add during the last 5 to 7 minutes of cooking if you are not having luck achieving the set point.

Spoon the preserves over cheesecake for a delicious dessert.

3 pounds Bing cherries

2 Meyer lemons, sliced paper-thin on a mandoline, slices cut into quarters, and seeds removed

4 cups granulated sugar

3 to 4 tablespoons fresh lemon juice, plus more as needed

½ teaspoon freshly ground black pepper (optional)

Yield: 6 half-pint jars

Place 3 or 4 small plates in the freezer.

Stem and pit the cherries. You will have about 8 cups.

Bring a saucepan of water to a boil over medium-high heat. Drop in the lemon slices and blanch for 1 minute. Remove with a wire skimmer, rinse with cold water, and then repeat.

In a large preserving pot, gently combine the blanched lemon, cherries, sugar, and lemon juice. Bring to a boil over medium-high heat and cook for 1 to 2 minutes. Turn off the heat and let sit overnight to macerate.

The next day, place a baking sheet on the counter near your stove. Heat a kettle of water. Set two stockpots on the stove and fill them with enough water to cover the jars by 1 to 2 inches.

Bring the water to a boil over medium-high heat. Sterilize the jars (see page 32) in the water bath.

Bring the cherry mixture to a boil over medium-high heat. Taste and add a squeeze more of lemon juice, if needed. Stir in the pepper. Cook, skimming and stirring frequently, until it thickens and passes the plate test (see page 30), achieving a soft set that is neither runny nor stiff. Remove the pot from the heat.

Bring the water bath back to a boil. If the jars have cooled, warm them in the water bath or in a 200°F oven. Simmer the lids in a saucepan of hot water. Place the jars on the baking sheet.

Ladle the preserves into the jars, leaving ¼-inch headspace. Wipe the rims clean and set the lids on the mouths of the jars. Twist on the rings.

Using a jar lifter, gently lower the jars into the pots. When the water returns to a boil, decrease the heat to an active simmer, and process the jars for 10 minutes. Turn off the heat and leave the jars in the water for 1 to 2 minutes.

Using the jar lifter, transfer the jars from the pots to the baking sheet and let sit for at least 6 hours, until cool enough to handle. Check to be sure the jars have sealed (see page 34). Label and store the sealed preserves for 6 months to 2 years. Once open, store in the refrigerator for up to 3 months.

CHERRY PRESERVES
WITH CARDAMOM

Sour cherries are prized in the Middle East. The Turks and Iranians make fabulous preserves with this wonderfully tart and aromatic fruit. If you can find sour cherries, great. If not, sweet cherries will also be delicious. For a variation, use 1 or 2 cups of rose sugar (see page 22) in place of the granulated sugar.

This preserve is lovely spooned over vanilla or honey ice cream or panna cotta, as well as almond cake.

3 pounds sour or sweet cherries

4 cups granulated sugar

Juice of 1 or 2 lemons

1 teaspoon ground cardamom, or as needed

Up to 1 cup Homemade Apple Pectin (page 200)

Yield: 7 to 8 half-pint jars

Place 3 or 4 small plates in the freezer.

Stem and pit the cherries. You will have about 8 cups.

In a large preserving pot, gently combine the cherries, sugar, lemon juice, and cardamom. Bring to a boil over medium-high heat and cook for 1 to 2 minutes. Turn off the heat and let sit overnight to macerate.

The next day, place a baking sheet on the counter near your stove. Heat a kettle of water. Set two stockpots on the stove and fill them with enough water to cover the jars by 1 to 2 inches. Bring the water to a boil over medium-high heat. Sterilize the jars (see page 32) in the water bath.

Bring the cherry mixture to a boil again over medium-high heat and cook for 5 minutes.

Set a colander over a bowl and, using a slotted spoon, transfer the cherries to the colander.

Bring the syrup to a boil over medium-high heat and cook until thickened.

Carefully return the cherries to the preserving pot, along with any juices that have collected in the bowl under the colander. Bring the preserves to a boil over high heat, add the apple pectin (using the full cup if you like a thicker preserve), and cook, stirring frequently, until it passes the plate test (see page 30), achieving a soft set that mounds on the plate and is not runny. Remove the pot from the heat.

Bring the water bath back to a boil. If the jars have cooled, warm them in the water bath or in a 200°F oven. Simmer the lids in a saucepan of hot water. Place the jars on the baking sheet.

Ladle the preserves into the jars, leaving ¼-inch headspace. Wipe the rims clean and set the lids on the mouths of the jars. Twist on the rings.

Using a jar lifter, gently lower the jars into the pots. When the water returns to a boil, decrease the heat to an active simmer, and process the jars for 10 minutes. Turn off the heat and leave the jars in the water for 1 to 2 minutes.

Using the jar lifter, transfer the jars from the pots to the baking sheet and let sit for at least 6 hours, until cool enough to handle. Check to be sure the jars have sealed (see page 34). Label and store the sealed preserves for 6 months to 2 years. Once open, store in the refrigerator for up to 3 months.

CHERRY MOSTARDA

For this sweet and spicy condiment you start by making the syrup and then adding the fruit later. Usually the cherries hold their shape, but if they start to soften too much or become mushy, transfer them to a colander, complete cooking the syrup, and add them back at the end. If you do not have Meyer lemons, you may use two small Eureka lemons instead.

This is excellent served with poultry, pork, ham, cheeses, and charcuterie.

3½ pounds sweet cherries

2 Meyer lemons, sliced paper-thin on a mandoline, slices cut into quarters, and seeds removed

4 cups granulated sugar

2 cups red wine vinegar or apple cider vinegar

½ cup fresh lemon juice

½ cup water

2 tablespoons mustard seeds (optional)

1 tablespoon Chinese five-spice powder

4 teaspoons freshly ground black pepper, plus more as needed

1 teaspoon ground cayenne

⅓ cup Colman's dry mustard powder

2 teaspoons salt

¼ cup pomegranate molasses

8 ounces fresh ginger, peeled, sliced, and cut into slivers

Up to 1 cup Homemade Apple Pectin (page 200)

Yield: About 15 half-pint or 7 pint jars

Place 3 or 4 small plates in the freezer.

Stem and pit the cherries. You will have about 10 cups.

Bring a saucepan of water to a boil over medium-high heat. Drop in the lemon slices and blanch for 30 seconds. Remove with a wire skimmer, rinse with cold water, and then repeat.

In a large preserving pot, gently combine the blanched lemon, sugar, vinegar, lemon juice, water, mustard seeds, five-spice powder, black pepper, cayenne, dry mustard powder, salt, pomegranate molasses, and ginger.

Bring to a boil over medium-high heat, and cook for 1 to 2 minutes. Turn off the heat and let sit for 1 hour.

Place two baking sheets on the counter near your stove. Heat a kettle of water. Set two stockpots on the stove and fill them with enough water to cover the jars by 1 to 2 inches. Bring the water to a boil over medium-high heat. Sterilize the jars (see page 32) in the water bath.

Bring the spiced syrup to a boil over medium-high heat and cook for 5 minutes. As it starts to thicken, add the cherries and return to a boil, cooking for 10 to 15 minutes and no longer.

Do a preliminary plate test (see page 30) to see how the mostarda is thickening. If the mixture is not thickening, add the apple pectin (using the full cup if you like a thicker preserve) and cook for 5 minutes. If the mixture is thickening, you can skip adding the apple pectin.

Bring the cherry mostarda back to a boil and cook over high heat, skimming and stirring frequently, until it passes the plate test, achieving a soft set that mounds on the plate and is not runny. Remove the pot from the heat.

Bring the water bath back to a boil. If the jars have cooled, warm them in the water bath or in a 200°F oven. Simmer the lids in a saucepan of hot water. Place the jars on the baking sheet.

Ladle the mostarda into the jars, leaving ¼-inch headspace. Wipe the rims clean and set the lids on the mouths of the jars. Twist on the rings.

Using a jar lifter, gently lower the jars into the pots. When the water returns to a boil, decrease the heat to an active simmer, and process the jars for 10 minutes. Turn off the heat and leave the jars in the water for 1 to 2 minutes.

Using the jar lifter, transfer the jars from the pots to the baking sheet and let sit for at least 6 hours, until cool enough to handle. Check to be sure the jars have sealed (see page 34). Label and store the sealed mostarda for 6 months to 2 years. Once open, store in the refrigerator for up to 3 months.

TURKISH CHERRY–ROSE PRESERVES

I know sour cherries are the Turkish choice for this preserve, but if you cannot find these tart, tiny ones, use whatever cherries you have on hand. You might want to increase the lemon a bit to mimic the tartness of the sour cherry.

I love this preserve spooned over ice cream or almond cake.

3 pounds sour cherries or Bing cherries

3 tablespoons lemon juice, plus more as needed

3 cups granulated sugar

2 cups rose sugar (see page 22)

Up to 1 cup Homemade Apple Pectin (page 200)

Yield: 8 to 9 half-pint jars

Place 3 or 4 small plates in the freezer.

Stem and pit the cherries. You will have about 8 cups.

In a large preserving pot, gently combine the cherries, lemon juice, granulated sugar, and rose sugar. Bring to a boil over medium-high heat and cook for 1 to 2 minutes. Turn off the heat and let sit overnight to macerate.

The next day, place two baking sheets on the counter near your stove. Heat a kettle of water. Set two stockpots on the stove and fill them with enough water to cover the jars by 1 to 2 inches. Bring the water to a boil over medium-high heat. Sterilize the jars (see page 32) in the water bath.

Bring the cherry mixture to a boil again over medium-high heat and cook for 5 minutes.

Set a colander over a bowl and, using a slotted spoon, transfer the cherries to the colander.

Bring the syrup to a boil over medium-high heat, add the apple pectin (using the full cup if you like a thicker jam), and cook for 5 minutes.

Carefully return the cherries to the pot, along with any juices that have collected in the bowl under the colander.

Bring the cherry mixture back to a boil, and cook over high heat for 5 minutes, skimming and stirring frequently, until it passes the plate test (see page 30), achieving a soft set that is neither runny nor stiff. Remove the pot from the heat.

Bring the water bath back to a boil. If the jars have cooled, warm them in the water bath or in a 200°F oven. Simmer the lids in a saucepan of hot water. Place the jars on the baking sheet.

Ladle the preserves into the jars, leaving ¼-inch headspace. Wipe the rims clean and set the lids on the mouths of the jars. Twist on the rings.

Using a jar lifter, gently lower the jars into the pots. When the water returns to a boil, decrease the heat to an active simmer, and process the jars for 10 minutes. Turn off the heat and leave the jars in the water for 1 to 2 minutes.

Using the jar lifter, transfer the jars from the pots to the baking sheets and let sit for at least 4 hours, until cool enough to handle. Check to be sure the jars have sealed (see page 34). Label and store the sealed preserves for 6 months to 2 years. Once open, store in the refrigerator for up to 3 months.

BRANDIED CHERRIES

Next New Year's Eve, drop a few of these into your glass of bubbly! They are great over ice cream as well. You do not have to process these in the water bath unless you prefer to store them at room temperature instead of in the refrigerator. Simply add the brandy, close the jars, and store in the refrigerator for 4 to 6 weeks before using. Some cooks like to add a cinnamon stick or cloves while cooking the syrup.

1½ pounds sweet cherries

¾ cup granulated sugar

¾ cup water

4 cardamom pods (optional)

1 cinnamon stick (optional)

½ cup brandy, or more as needed

Yield: 2 pint jars

Stem and pit the cherries. You will have about 4 cups.

Place a baking sheet on the counter near your stove. Heat a kettle of water. Set a stockpot on the stove and fill it with enough water to cover the jars by 1 to 2 inches. Bring the water to a boil over medium-high heat. Sterilize the jars (see page 32) in the water bath; leave in the water to keep warm.

In a saucepan, combine the sugar, water, cardamom, cinnamon and brandy and bring to a boil over medium-high heat, stirring until the sugar is dissolved. Decrease the heat to medium and cook until the syrup has thickened, 8 to 10 minutes. Remove the pan from the heat.

Simmer the lids in a saucepan of hot water. Place the jars on the baking sheet.

Using a large slotted spoon, transfer the cherries to the jars. Pour the brandy syrup over the fruit and top off with additional brandy to cover, leaving ½-inch headspace. Stir with a chopstick to mix the brandy with the syrup. Wipe the rims clean and set the lids on the mouths of the jars. Twist on the rings.

You now have two options: Transfer the jars to the refrigerator and store for up to 1 month before opening so the brandy flavor has time to develop, or process the jars in the water bath for storage at room temperature.

To process the jars, bring the water bath back to a boil.

Using a jar lifter, gently lower the jars into the pot. When the water returns to a boil, decrease the heat to an active simmer, and process the jars for 10 minutes. Turn off the heat and leave the jars in the water for 1 to 2 minutes.

Using the jar lifter, transfer the jars from the pot to the baking sheet and let sit for at least 6 hours, until cool enough to handle. Check to be sure the jars have sealed (see page 34). Label and store the sealed cherries for up to 2 years. Once open, store in the refrigerator for up to 1 year.

SPICED WHOLE CHERRIES

This recipe is an oldie but a goodie. It was inspired by Catherine Plagemann's version, and fifty years later, it is still one of the first preserves I make every year. Sometimes I like to add a bit of black pepper to the syrup.

These cherries are good as a topping for custard, rice pudding, and sautéed duck breasts. They also pair well with cream cheese and salumi.

2 pounds sweet cherries

4 cups granulated sugar

1 cup apple cider vinegar

½ teaspoon ground cinnamon

¼ teaspoon ground cloves

¼ teaspoon ground allspice

Freshly ground black pepper (optional)

Yield: 5 half-pint jars

Place 3 or 4 small plates in the freezer.

Stem and pit the cherries. You will have 5 to 6 cups.

In a large preserving pot, gently combine the sugar, vinegar, cinnamon, cloves, allspice, and black pepper. Bring to a boil over medium-high heat and cook for 1 to 2 minutes; then add the cherries, turn off the heat, and let sit for 1 hour.

Place a baking sheet on the counter near your stove. Heat a kettle of water. Set a stockpot on the stove and fill it with enough water to cover the jars by 1 to 2 inches. Bring the water to a boil over medium-high heat. Sterilize the jars (see page 32) in the water bath.

Bring the cherry mixture to a boil over medium-high heat, and cook, skimming and stirring frequently, until the preserve has thickened and passes the plate test (see page 30), achieving a soft and syrupy set. Remove the pot from the heat.

Bring the water bath back to a boil. If the jars have cooled, warm them in the water bath or in a 200°F oven. Simmer the lids in a saucepan of hot water. Place the jars on the baking sheet.

Ladle the cherries and syrup into the jars, leaving 1-inch headspace. Wipe the rims clean and set the lids on the mouths of the jars. Twist on the rings.

Using a jar lifter, gently lower the jars into the pot. When the water returns to a boil, decrease the heat to an active simmer, and process the jars for 10 minutes. Turn off the heat and leave the jars in the water for 1 to 2 minutes.

Using the jar lifter, transfer the jars from the pot to the baking sheet and let sit for at least 6 hours, until cool enough to handle. Check to be sure the jars have sealed (see page 34). Label and store the sealed cherries for 6 months to 2 years. Once open, store in the refrigerator for up to 3 months.

Carrots

Like rhubarb, carrots are a vegetable. But if we can love carrot cake, surely we can embrace carrot jam. While you can buy carrots all year long, late spring, summer, and early fall are when the sweetest carrots appear in the market. They come in many colors and sizes. Red, purple, white, and the familiar orange. There are the long and thin Danvers and Nantes and the round and chubby Chantenays and Thumbelinas. Do not be fooled by the bags of so-called baby carrots you find in the supermarket. As we know from experience in cooking and in life, looks are not everything. They are just large starchy ones that have been abraded and trimmed to look like the real baby carrots sold at farmers' markets. For these preserves, choosing really flavorful carrots is key. Carrots pair well with citrus, and fortunately lemons and oranges are always available. You can use regular oranges or blood oranges if you want a deeper color in your carrot jam.

Grating carrots in the food processor is the way to go. Some cooks slice the carrots, cook them, and mash them, but I think the shreds look elegant, and they become tender quickly during cooking. However, if you prefer a smooth, uniform texture, you can cook and mash sliced carrots and use the puree as if you were making Roasted Pumpkin Butter (page 248).

The carrot jams are rather dense and intense and don't have much excess liquid. So when you spread them on toast or an English muffin, they need a creamy contrast. They really shine if you pair them with crème fraiche, mascarpone, ricotta, cream cheese, or labne.

Natural flavor-pairing affinities for carrot preserves are orange and lemon, cardamom, cinnamon, ginger, anise, orange-flower water, and rose water.

While most fruit preserves last for a few months in the refrigerator after opening, and even a few weeks at room temperature, carrot (and pumpkin) preserves do not have a long shelf life after they've been opened. Refrigerate them after opening and eat within 2 weeks.

BASIC CARROT JAM

This jam is good on toast, pancakes, biscuits, and English muffins, and even makes a great sauce for a shortcake dessert.

1 pound carrots

2 cups water, or more as needed

1 cup orange juice

2½ to 3 cups granulated sugar

Grated zest of 2 lemons

4 to 6 tablespoons fresh lemon juice

Yield: 4 half-pint jars

Peel, trim, and grate the carrots, using a food processor. You will have about 4 cups.

In a large preserving pot, gently combine the carrots, water, and orange juice. Bring to a boil over medium-high heat, then decrease the heat to low and simmer for 10 minutes. Turn off the heat and let it sit, uncovered, for 1 hour for the carrots to soften and drink up some of the liquid.

Place a baking sheet on the counter near your stove. Heat a kettle of water. Set a stockpot on the stove and fill it with enough water to cover the jars by 1 to 2 inches. Bring the water to a boil over medium-high heat. Sterilize the jars (see page 32) in the water bath.

Add 2½ cups of the sugar, the zest, and 4 tablespoons of the lemon juice to the carrots. Return to a boil over medium-high heat, then decrease the heat to low and simmer until the jam has thickened and the carrots are tender and have taken on a glassy appearance. The juices will be quite syrupy. Taste and add more lemon juice for brightness if you think it needs it, some or all of the remaining ½ cup of sugar to adjust the sweetness, and up to ½ cup more

water if you think it is too dry. Cook for a few minutes to incorporate the sugar and water. Do a plate test (see page 30). It should mound on the plate and be syrupy, not dry. Remove the pot from the heat.

Bring the water bath back to a boil. If the jars have cooled, warm them in the water bath or in a 200°F oven. Simmer the lids in a saucepan of hot water. Place the jars on the baking sheet.

Ladle the jam into the jars, leaving ¼-inch headspace. Wipe the rims clean and set the lids on the mouths of the jars. Twist on the rings.

Using a jar lifter, gently lower the jars into the pot. When the water returns to a boil, decrease the heat to an active simmer, and process the jars for 15 minutes. Turn off the heat and leave the jars in the water for 1 to 2 minutes.

Using the jar lifter, transfer the jars from the pot to the baking sheet and let sit for at least 6 hours, until cool enough to handle. Check to be sure the jars have sealed (see page 34). Label and store the sealed jam for 6 months to 2 years. Once open, store in the refrigerator for up to 2 weeks.

CARROT-GINGER JAM

In my book *Cucina Ebraica: Flavors of the Italian Jewish Kitchen,* there's a recipe for a delicious and surprising double-crust carrot-ginger tart, which is what inspired this recipe. I decided a version of the filling would be a good preserve. At first this jam will look soupy, but the carrots gradually drink up the liquid. Pay attention and watch the juiciness quotient. If the mixture seems dry, add a bit more water or juice. The lemon juice is the key flavor enhancer, as it heightens the ginger's zing. Fresh ginger varies in intensity. If it is mild, you might want to add a bit of heat—such as a pinch of hot pepper—at the end of cooking.

Use the jam as a filling for a tart or spread it on toast with cream cheese.

Scant 2 pounds carrots	4 cups granulated sugar
1 orange	6 to 8 tablespoons fresh lemon juice
1 lemon	
6 ounces fresh ginger	Pinch of ground ginger (optional)
2 cups water	Pinch of ground cayenne or Aleppo or Maras pepper (optional)
1 cup orange juice	

Yield: 7 half-pint jars

Place 3 or 4 small plates in the freezer.

Peel, trim, and grate the carrots, using a food processor. Remove from the food processor bowl and set aside. You will have about 6 cups.

Halve and seed the orange and lemon. Cut the citrus into chunks, add to the food processor bowl, and pulse until pureed. Remove from the food processor bowl and set aside.

Peel and slice the ginger. Add to the food processor bowl and pulse until pureed. You will have about 1 cup.

In a large preserving pot, gently combine the carrots, orange and lemon, ginger, water, and orange juice. Bring to a boil over medium-high heat, then decrease the heat to low and simmer for 10 minutes. Turn off the heat and let it sit, uncovered, for 1 hour.

Add the sugar and 3 to 4 tablespoons of the lemon juice and bring to a boil over medium-high heat. Turn off the heat and let sit, uncovered, for 30 minutes.

Place a baking sheet on the counter near your stove. Heat a kettle of water. Set two stockpots on the stove and fill them with enough water to cover the jars by 1 to 2 inches. Bring the water to a boil over medium-high heat. Sterilize the jars (see page 32) in the water bath.

Taste the jam and stir in the remaining 3 to 4 tablespoons of lemon juice as needed. If the ginger is too mild, add a pinch of ground ginger or hot pepper. Bring to a boil over medium-high heat; then decrease the heat to low and simmer the jam for a few minutes longer, until it thickens

CONTINUED

and passes the plate test (see page 30), achieving a soft set and mounding on the plate. It should be syrupy, not dry. Remove the pot from the heat.

Bring the water bath back to a boil. If the jars have cooled, warm them in the water bath or in a 200°F oven. Simmer the lids in a saucepan of hot water. Place the jars on the baking sheet.

Ladle the jam into the jars, leaving ¼-inch headspace. Wipe the rims clean and set the lids on the mouths of the jars. Twist on the rings.

Using a jar lifter, gently lower the jars into the pots. When the water returns to a boil, decrease the heat to an active simmer, and process the jars for 15 minutes. Turn off the heat and leave the jars in the water for 1 to 2 minutes.

Using the jar lifter, transfer the jars from the pots to the baking sheet and let sit for at least 6 hours, until cool enough to handle. Check to be sure the jars have sealed (see page 34). Label and store the sealed jam for 6 months to 2 years. Once open, store in the refrigerator for up to 2 weeks.

CARROT-RHUBARB JAM

They say that plants that grow together go together. Rhubarb and carrots appear at the farmers' market at about the same time, so why not pair them for a bright-colored jam? The addition of cardamom or Fiori di Sicilia gives this jam a Middle Eastern aura.

Use as a spread on toast, folded into yogurt, or spooned over rice pudding.

Generous 1 pound carrots	4 cups granulated sugar
About 1 pound rhubarb	¼ to 1 teaspoon ground cardamom (optional)
Grated zest and juice of 2 oranges	1 tablespoon Fiori di Sicilia (optional)
Grated zest and juice of 2 lemons, plus more juice as needed	

Yield: 5 half-pint jars

Place 3 or 4 small plates in the freezer.

Peel, trim, and grate the carrots, using a food processor. You will have about 4 cups.

Wash, trim (no need to peel it unless it is particularly stringy), and dice the rhubarb. You will have about 4 cups.

In a large preserving pot, gently combine the rhubarb, carrots, orange zest and juice, lemon zest and juice, and sugar and toss to mix. Let sit overnight to macerate.

The next day, bring to a boil over medium-high heat. Cook for 15 minutes. Remove from the heat and let sit, uncovered, for 1 hour. Add the cardamom. Taste and adjust the flavor, adding more lemon juice as needed.

Place a baking sheet on the counter near your stove. Heat a kettle of water. Set a stockpot on the stove and fill it with enough water to cover the jars by 1 to 2 inches. Bring the water to a boil over medium-high heat. Sterilize the jars (see page 32) in the water bath.

Cook the jam, stirring to prevent scorching, until it has thickened and passes the plate test (see page 30), mounding on the plate. Add the Fiori di Sicilia to taste. Remove the pot from the heat.

Bring the water bath back to a boil. If the jars have cooled, warm them in the water bath or in a 200°F oven. Simmer the lids in a saucepan of hot water. Place the jars on the baking sheet.

Ladle the jam into the jars, leaving ¼-inch headspace. Wipe the rims clean and set the lids on the mouths of the jars. Twist on the rings.

Using a jar lifter, gently lower the jars into the pot. When the water returns to a boil, decrease the heat to an active simmer, and process the jars for 10 minutes. Turn off the heat and leave the jars in the water for 1 to 2 minutes.

Using the jar lifter, transfer the jars from the pot to the baking sheet and let sit for at least 6 hours, until cool enough to handle. Check to be sure the jars have sealed (see page 34). Label and store the sealed jam for 6 months to 2 years. Once open, store in the refrigerator for up to 1 month.

PERSIAN CARROT JAM

It is probably not a coincidence that carrot jam is so popular in Iran. The wild ancestor of the carrot originated in ancient Persia. Carrot jam is on every breakfast buffet table in Iran, to be paired with clotted cream or mild soft cheese atop flatbread. I found most Persian jams to be very sweet, so my goal was to create a jam that had a better balance between carrots and citrus, with mild spices. For more punch, you could add grated fresh ginger. Not very Persian, but lively.

Generous 2 pounds full-flavored carrots

2 oranges

3 cups water or 2 cups water plus 1 cup orange juice, plus more as needed

4 to 5 cups granulated sugar

1 to 2 tablespoons grated fresh ginger, or dried ground ginger to taste (optional)

¼ cup fresh lemon juice, plus more as needed

2 teaspoons ground cardamom

Splash of orange flower water (optional)

Yield: 6 half-pint jars

Place 3 or 4 small plates in the freezer.

Peel, trim, and grate the carrots, using a food processor. You will have about 7 cups.

Grate the zest of the oranges into a small bowl. Pare away the white pith from the fruit, separate the segments over the bowl so the juices are collected, remove the seeds, and chop the fruit. Combine the zest and fruit.

Place a baking sheet on the counter near your stove. Heat a kettle of water. Set two stockpots on the stove and fill them with enough water to cover the jars by 1 to 2 inches. Bring the water to a boil over medium-high heat. Sterilize the jars (see page 32) in the water bath.

In a large preserving pot, gently combine the carrots and water or combined water and orange juice. Bring to a boil over medium-high heat, then decrease the heat to low and simmer for 10 minutes. Turn off the heat and let it sit, uncovered, for 10 to 15 minutes.

Add the orange zest and fruit, 4 cups of the sugar, and the ginger to the carrots and cook over medium heat for about 20 minutes, or until thickened. Stir in the lemon juice and cardamom. Taste and add more lemon juice for brightness if you think it needs it and some or all of the remaining 1 cup of sugar to adjust the sweetness.

Simmer the jam a few minutes longer and then drop a spoonful onto one of the cold plates. After 1 minute, tilt the plate or run your finger through the jam to test the texture. It should be thick, the carrots translucent, and the juices somewhat reduced but still syrupy.

If the juices have been mostly absorbed, add just enough water or orange juice to thin the jam until it is syrupy. Simmer for a few minutes and then add the orange flower water. Remove the pot from the heat.

Bring the water bath back to a boil. If the jars have cooled, warm them in the water bath or in a 200°F oven. Simmer the lids in a saucepan of hot water. Place the jars on the baking sheet.

Ladle the jam into the jars, leaving ¼-inch headspace. Wipe the rims clean and set the lids on the mouths of the jars. Twist on the rings.

Using a jar lifter, gently lower the jars into the pots. When the water returns to a boil, decrease the heat to an active simmer, and process the jars for 15 minutes. Turn off the heat and leave the jars in the water for 1 to 2 minutes.

Using the jar lifter, transfer the jars from the pots to the baking sheet and let sit for at least 6 hours, until cool enough to handle. Check to be sure the jars have sealed (see page 34). Label and store the sealed jam for 6 months to 2 years. Once open, store in the refrigerator for up to 2 weeks.

Mangoes

In India there are more than five hundred varieties of mango. Our mango learning curve in the United States is much less steep, as we are limited to just a few varieties cultivated in Mexico, the Caribbean, South America, and Florida.

The most prevalent varieties are Haden, Tommy Atkins, Kent, and Ataulfos. Mangoes come into season in the spring and last into summer. When ripe, their aroma is tantalizing, with a hint of resin, and their taste is sweet and tart. Kidney-shaped Ataulfos are sweet and mild. Some of the oval green varieties, even those with a slight red blush, can be more astringent and medicinal. Their flesh is yellow, smooth, and a bit slippery when sliced. Getting the flesh off the flat central pit is the challenge, and then the cook is in luck, because what clings to the pit is the cook's treat. Wear a bib or eat it over the sink.

Ripe mangoes are ideal for jam and softer-textured conserves. The firmer ones are best for chutney, as they will hold their shape. Mangoes pair well with spices, such as cardamom and ginger, but the classic pairing is with lime. They bring out the best in each other.

Natural flavor-pairing affinities for mangoes are lime, lemon, orange, cardamom, cinnamon, ginger, chiles, vanilla, hot peppers, and coconut.

GOLDEN MANGO AND LEMON CHUTNEY

This is a pretty, glowing, gold chutney. It is good with seafood because it is bright and tart and has a nice lemony kick. Do not substitute brown sugar for the granulated sugar if you want to keep the golden hue of the fruit in the finished chutney. Choose yellow mangoes that are on the firmer side.

7 firm yellow Ataulfo or Champagne mangoes

1 cup golden raisins

Orange juice, lemon juice, or hot water, to just cover raisins

2 cups granulated sugar, plus more as needed

4 cloves garlic

2 small yellow onions, cut into large dice

2 organic lemons, seeded and coarsely chopped

4 ounces fresh ginger, peeled and sliced

4 fresh red chiles, stemmed and chopped

2 cups apple cider vinegar

1 tablespoon salt, plus more as needed

1 teaspoon ground cardamom

1 teaspoon cardamom seeds

2 teaspoons yellow mustard seeds

1 teaspoon ground ginger

Fresh lemon juice, as needed

Yield: 10 half-pint jars

Place 3 or 4 small plates in the freezer.

Hold one of the mangoes vertically and slice the flesh away from the pit on both sides. Peel the halves and cut the flesh into large dice. Repeat with the remaining 6 mangoes. You will have 7 cups.

Place the raisins in a small bowl with the orange or lemon juice or water to cover. Set aside to plump.

In a large preserving pot, gently combine the mangoes and sugar.

Combine the garlic, onions, lemons, fresh ginger, and chiles in the bowl of a food processor and pulse until pulverized. Add ¾ cup of the vinegar and pulse again. Add this mixture to the mangoes.

Add the salt, ground cardamom, cardamom seeds, mustard seeds, ground ginger, and the remaining 1¼ cups vinegar.

Place two baking sheets on the counter near your stove. Heat a kettle of water. Set two stockpots on the stove and fill them with enough water to cover the jars by 1 to 2 inches. Bring the water to a boil over medium-high heat. Sterilize the jars (see page 32) in the water bath.

Bring the mango mixture to a boil over medium-high heat, then decrease the heat and simmer for 15 to 20 minutes. Add the raisins, stirring often (to prevent the raisins from sinking and scorching), and simmer until the chutney has thickened. The raisins will absorb some of the liquid, so if there is not enough juice and syrup to cover the fruit, add lemon juice to cover and thin the mixture.

CONTINUED

Taste and adjust the sweet-tart ratio, adding more sugar, lemon juice, and salt as needed. Do a plate test (see page 30). The chutney should mound on the plate but still be syrupy. If the chutney is not ready, cook a few more minutes and then repeat the plate test until it passes. Remove the pot from the heat.

Bring the water bath back to a boil. If the jars have cooled, warm them in the water bath or in a 200°F oven. Simmer the lids in a saucepan of hot water. Place the jars on the baking sheets.

Ladle the chutney into the jars, leaving ¼-inch headspace. Wipe the rims clean and set the lids on the mouths of the jars. Twist on the rings.

Using a jar lifter, gently lower the jars into the pots. When the water returns to a boil, decrease the heat to an active simmer, and process the jars for 10 minutes. Turn off the heat and leave the jars in the water for 1 to 2 minutes.

Using the jar lifter, transfer the jars from the pots to the baking sheet and let sit for at least 6 hours, until cool enough to handle. Check to be sure the jars have sealed (see page 34). Label and store the sealed chutney for 6 months to 2 years. Once open, store in the refrigerator for up to 3 months.

MANGO-LIME JAM

Look for soft, ripe mangoes for this jam. The Ataulfo or Champagne varieties are best.

The flavor variable is the amount of ginger you add. It can be a subtle hint or a bit more assertive.

For texture, the question is to mash or not to mash. While you want pieces of mango for chutney, you want a jam to be more spreadable. Ergo, mash the fruit a bit.

This jam is good on toast and French toast, as well as on ham and cheese sandwiches, and is wonderful when warmed and spooned over coconut ice cream or coconut panna cotta.

3 or 4 mangoes

Grated zest and juice of 4 limes

2 tablespoons grated fresh ginger, or up to ¼ cup if you like

2½ cups granulated sugar

Pinch of salt

¼ teaspoon ground cinnamon (optional)

Fresh lemon juice, as needed

Yield: 4 half-pint jars

Place 3 or 4 small plates in the freezer.

Hold one of the mangoes vertically and slice the flesh away from the pit on both sides. Peel the halves and cut the flesh into ¼-inch dice. Repeat with the remaining 2 or 3 mangoes. You will have about 4 cups.

In a large preserving pot, gently combine the mangoes, zest and juice of 2 of the limes, and the ginger. Stir in the sugar. Bring to a boil over medium-high heat and cook for 1 minute. Turn off the heat and let sit for 1 hour. Repeat this process until the mango is soft, two or three more times. When the mangoes are tender, mash them to a coarse puree with a potato masher. Or let them cool and then puree in a food processor.

Bring the mango puree to a boil over medium-high heat. Add the zest and juice of the remaining 2 limes and the salt and cinnamon. Taste and increase the tartness by adding lemon juice. Turn off the heat and let sit, uncovered, for 1 hour or until cool.

Place a baking sheet on the counter near your stove. Heat a kettle of water. Set a stockpot on the stove and fill it with enough water to cover the jars by 1 to 2 inches. Bring the water to a boil over medium-high heat. Sterilize the jars (see page 32) in the water bath.

Bring the mango jam to a boil over medium-high heat, then turn off the heat. Do the plate test (see page 30), checking to see if the jam has achieved a soft set and mounds on the plate. If the jam is not ready, cook a few more minutes and then repeat the plate test until it passes. Remove the pot from the heat.

CONTINUED

Bring the water bath back to a boil. If the jars have cooled, warm them in the water bath or in a 200°F oven. Simmer the lids in a saucepan of hot water. Place the jars on the baking sheet.

Ladle the jam into the jars, leaving ¼-inch headspace. Wipe the rims clean and set the lids on the mouths of the jars. Twist on the rings.

Using a jar lifter, gently lower the jars into the pot. When the water returns to a boil, decrease the heat to an active simmer, and process the jars for 10 minutes. Turn off the heat and leave the jars in the water for 1 to 2 minutes.

Using the jar lifter, transfer the jars from the pot to the baking sheet and let sit for at least 6 hours, until cool enough to handle. Check to be sure the jars have sealed (see page 34). Label and store the sealed jam for 6 months to 2 years. Once open, store in the refrigerator for up to 3 months.

GREEN MANGO CHUTNEY

This classic mango chutney is good with curries, especially seafood.

3 large, not-too-ripe Kent or Tommy Atkins mangoes or other green mangoes

½ cup golden raisins

Orange juice or water, to just cover raisins, plus more as needed

1½ cups granulated sugar or firmly packed brown sugar, plus more as needed

1 cup chopped yellow onion

2 or 3 large cloves garlic

1 serrano chile, stemmed, chopped

1 fresh red chile, stemmed, chopped

2 small limes, cut into small pieces, plus lime juice as needed

2 to 3 ounces fresh ginger, peeled and sliced

1½ cups apple cider vinegar

1 teaspoon ground cinnamon

1 teaspoon ground cloves

1 tablespoon salt

Yield: 3 pint and 1 half-pint or 7 half-pint jars

Place 3 or 4 small plates in the freezer.

Hold one of the mangoes vertically and slice the flesh away from the pit on both sides. Peel the halves and cut the flesh into large dice. Repeat with the remaining 2 mangoes. You will have 5 to 6 cups.

Place the raisins in a small bowl with the orange juice or water to cover. Set aside to plump.

In a large preserving pot, gently combine the mangoes and sugar.

Combine the onion, garlic, chiles, limes, and ginger in the bowl of a food processor and pulse until pulverized. Add ¾ cup of the vinegar and pulse again. Add this mixture to the mangoes.

Add the cinnamon, cloves, salt, and the remaining ¾ cup vinegar.

Place a baking sheet on the counter near your stove. Heat a kettle of water. Set two stockpots on the stove and fill them with enough water to cover the jars by 1 to 2 inches. Bring the water to a boil over medium-high heat. Sterilize the jars (see page 32) in the water bath.

Bring the mango mixture to a boil over medium-high heat; then decrease the heat and simmer for 15 minutes. Add the raisins and simmer, stirring often (to prevent the raisins from sinking and scorching), until the chutney has thickened. The raisins will absorb some of the liquid, so if there is not enough juice and syrup to cover the fruit, add orange juice or water to cover and thin the mixture.

Taste and adjust the sweet-tart ratio, adding more sugar or lime juice as needed. Do the plate test (see page 30). The chutney should mound on the plate and be syrupy. If the chutney is not ready, cook a few more minutes and repeat the plate test until it passes. Remove the pot from the heat.

Bring the water bath back to a boil. If the jars have cooled, warm them in the water bath or in a 200°F oven. Simmer the lids in a saucepan of hot water. Place the jars on the baking sheet.

Ladle the chutney into the jars, leaving ¼-inch headspace. Wipe the rims clean and set the lids on the mouths of the jars. Twist on the rings.

Using a jar lifter, gently lower the jars into the pots. When the water returns to a boil, decrease the heat to an active simmer, and process the jars for 10 minutes. Turn off the heat and leave the jars in the water for 1 to 2 minutes.

Using the jar lifter, transfer the jars from the pots to the baking sheet and let sit for at least 6 hours, until cool enough to handle. Check to be sure the jars have sealed (see page 34). Label and store the sealed chutney for 6 months to 2 years. Once open, store in the refrigerator for up to 3 months.

Summer

Peaches and Nectarines

For many of us, peaches are the quintessential summer fruit. Fragrant, juicy, and beautiful, they are best for eating out of hand (maybe over the sink) but are also good for preserving.

Peaches originated in China and made their way to the Mediterranean via Persia. Thus their Latin name is *Prunus persica*. European settlers brought them to America, and today they are widely cultivated in many parts of the country.

Peaches and nectarines are technically the same fruit with only one single gene of difference—the one that gives peaches their fuzz. When ripe, peaches are easily peeled by dipping them in boiling water for a minute or two and then in ice water. Nectarines rarely need peeling, as their skin is so thin and fuzz free.

Peaches have a softer texture than nectarines and are more fragile and bruise easily. Nectarines are hardier. But taste the flesh blindfolded and you'd have a difficult time distinguishing between a fully ripe nectarine and a ripe peach. For everyday eating, store them at room temperature until they are fully ripe. They will resist mold if you keep them well spaced on a sheet pan or platter so they do not touch. If you have bought too many, store them in the refrigerator to slow spoilage (but they will lose their perfume). You should not store them for longer than 1 week. For preserving, buy them when they are firm-ripe and aromatic.

Both fruits come in clingstone and freestone varieties. The early-season fruits are mostly clingstones and need to be cut from the pit in chunks. Freestones open with a twist and easily release from their pits when you cut them at their natural seams. Both come in white- and yellow-fleshed varieties. The white-fleshed ones are very sweet but rather one-dimensional in flavor and low in acid. They are best for eating but do not make a dynamic preserve. The yellow-fleshed fruits are deeper in flavor and have greater acidity. Every preserve you can make with peaches you can also make with nectarines.

White nectarine varieties to look for include Arctic Glow, Arctic Rose, Snow Queen, Heavenly White, and Arctic Blaze.

For yellow nectarines, try Flavortop, Fantasia, Flamekist, Le Grand, Zee Glo, August Red, or Ruby Gold.

White peach varieties are Babcock, Snow King, Arctic Supreme, and White Lady.

For yellow peaches, look for Sun Crest, O Henry, Flavor Crest, Cal Red, Rio Oso, Elegant Lady, Summer Lady, June Pride, Summerset, Crimson Lady, and Indian Blood.

Flavor affinities for peaches and nectarines are vanilla, citrus, ginger, cardamom, almond, berries, lavender, lemon verbena, and mint.

PEACH PUREE JAM

This is a very old-fashion jam. It is very smooth, a little dark, and a bit cooked in flavor, but that is the way prior generations liked it (and maybe how you remember it). Today we tend to cook our fruit for shorter amounts of time and do not puree peaches very often, preferring a chunkier texture. This one's for those of you who are sentimental.

2 pounds peaches

1 cup water

2½ to 3 cups granulated sugar

About 2 tablespoons fresh lemon juice, as needed

1 teaspoon vanilla extract (optional)

Yield: 4 half-pint jars

Place 3 or 4 small plates in the freezer.

Bring a stockpot of water to a boil. Prepare a bowl of ice water. Peel the peaches by dipping them in the boiling water for a minute or two and then dunking them in the ice water. The peels should slip off. If not, use a peeler with a serrated swivel blade to remove the peels. Halve the peaches, remove the pits, and chop the flesh. You will have 6 to 7 cups. Crack the pits with a hammer if you can.

Put the pieces of peach and their pits in a stockpot, along with the 1 cup water. (You can omit the pits, but keeping them in adds a subtle almond flavor to the jam.) Simmer until the fruit is soft. Drain and discard the pits. Press the peaches through a food mill or place in the bowl of a food processor and pulse to puree. You will have about 3 cups of puree.

Place a baking sheet on the counter near your stove. Heat a kettle of water. Set a stockpot on the stove and fill it with enough water to cover the jars by 1 to 2 inches. Bring the water to a boil over medium-high heat. Sterilize the jars (see page 32) in the water bath.

In a large preserving pot over medium-low heat, combine the puree, 2½ cups of the sugar, and the lemon juice and stir until the sugar dissolves. Taste and add the lemon juice, remaining ½ cup sugar as needed, and the vanilla extract.

Increase the heat to medium-high and cook, stirring frequently, until the mixture thickens and passes the plate test (see page 30), achieving a soft set that is neither runny nor stiff. Remove the pot from the heat.

Bring the water bath back to a boil. If the jars have cooled, warm them in the water bath or in a 200°F oven. Simmer the lids in a saucepan of hot water. Place the jars on the baking sheet.

Ladle the jam into the jars, leaving ¼-inch headspace. Wipe the rims clean and set the lids on the mouths of the jars. Twist on the rings.

Using a jar lifter, gently lower the jars into the pot. When the water returns to a boil, decrease the heat to an active simmer, and process the jars for 10 minutes. Turn off the heat and leave the jars in the water for 1 to 2 minutes.

Using the jar lifter, transfer the jars from the pot to the baking sheet and let sit for at least 6 hours, until cool enough to handle. Check to be sure the jars have sealed (see page 34). Label and store the sealed jam for 6 months to 1 year. Once open, store in the refrigerator for up to 3 months.

PEACH-LIME SALSA-JAM

I am constantly disappointed in super-market jalapeños. They seem to be bred for looks and size, taste like bell peppers, and no longer have much heat. Now when I make guacamole or salsa, I use serrano chiles, as they still have some zip. With the addition of the chiles and lime, this jam becomes sort of a peach salsa. I might not give it to young kids for pancakes or put it on breakfast toast, but it sure would be great with cream cheese, spread on a chicken or ham sandwich, or dolloped onto a pork chop or duck breast. In other words, this jam has character.

2 pounds peaches	Walnut-size knob of fresh ginger, peeled and sliced thin
3 cups granulated sugar	
2 tablespoons fresh lemon juice	Pinch of salt
2 serrano chiles	Grated zest and juice of 2 limes

Yield: 5 half-pint jars

Place 3 or 4 small plates in the freezer.

Bring a stockpot of water to a boil. Prepare a bowl of ice water. Peel the peaches by dipping them in the boiling water for a minute or two, and then dunking them in the ice water. The peels should slip off. If not, use a peeler with a serrated swivel blade to remove the peels. Halve the peaches, remove the pits, and dice the flesh. You should have 6 to 7 cups.

In a large preserving pot, gently combine the peaches, sugar, and lemon juice and toss to mix. Let sit for a few hours or overnight to macerate.

In a small food processor, pulverize the peppers with the ginger and salt. Add to the peach mixture. Stir in the lime zest and juice.

Place a baking sheet on the counter near your stove. Heat a kettle of water. Set a stockpot on the stove and fill it with enough water to cover the jars by 1 to 2 inches. Bring the water to a boil over medium-high heat. Sterilize the jars (see page 32) in the water bath.

Bring the peach mixture to a boil over medium-high heat, stirring frequently, until the jam has thickened and passes the plate test (see page 30), achieving a soft set that mounds on the plate and is not runny. Remove the pot from the heat.

Bring the water bath back to a boil. If the jars have cooled, warm them in the water bath or in a 200°F oven. Simmer the lids in a saucepan of hot water. Place the jars on the baking sheet.

Ladle the jam into the jars, leaving ¼-inch headspace. Wipe the rims clean and set the lids on the mouths of the jars. Twist on the rings.

Using a jar lifter, gently lower the jars into the pot. When the water returns to a boil, decrease the heat to an active simmer, and process the jars for 10 minutes. Turn off the heat and leave the jars in the water for 1 to 2 minutes.

Using the jar lifter, transfer the jars from the pot to the baking sheet and let sit for at least 6 hours, until cool enough to handle. Check to be sure the jars have sealed (see page 34). Label and store the sealed jam for 6 months to 2 years. Once open, store in the refrigerator for up to 3 months.

PEACH MELBA JAM

Peach Melba combines vanilla ice cream with poached peach halves and raspberry sauce. I never tire of this classic dessert, as it is a perfect balance of creaminess, sweetness, tartness, and perfume. The last time I served Peach Melba, I decided to try combining peaches and raspberries in a jam, because they work together so well in that dessert.

Peaches take longer to cook than the berries, so you start them first and add the raspberries at the end of cooking. The berries will break down a bit, but it doesn't matter. If you are a purist, you can instead make a basic peach jam (see page 103) and a basic raspberry jam (see page 130) in two separate pots and combine them when both have set.

Add Peach Melba Jam to yogurt, spoon it over vanilla ice cream or panna cotta, or spread on toast.

2 pounds peaches

4 cups granulated sugar, plus more as needed

2 tablespoons fresh lemon juice, plus more as needed

3 cups (4 half-pint baskets) raspberries, plus more as needed

1 teaspoon vanilla or almond extract (optional)

Yield: 6 half-pint jars

Place 3 or 4 small plates in the freezer.

Bring a stockpot of water to a boil. Prepare a bowl of ice water. Peel the peaches by dipping them in the boiling water for a minute or two and then dunking them in the ice water. The peels should slip off. If not, use a peeler with a serrated swivel blade to remove the peels. Halve the peaches, remove and discard the pits, and dice the flesh. You will have 6 to 7 cups.

In a large preserving pot, gently combine the peaches, sugar, and lemon juice. Cover the pot and let it sit overnight to macerate.

The next day, place a baking sheet on the counter near your stove. Heat a kettle of water. Set two stockpots on the stove and fill with enough water to cover the jars by 1 to 2 inches. Bring the water to a boil over medium-high heat. Sterilize the jars (see page 32) in the water bath.

Bring the peach mixture to a boil over high heat and cook, stirring frequently, until the jam starts to thicken.

Add the raspberries and return to a boil, then decrease the heat to medium and cook until the jam passes the plate test (see page 30), achieving a soft set that mounds on the plate and is not runny.

Taste and adjust the flavor balance, adding a squeeze more of lemon juice or a few table-spoons of sugar if the raspberries are very tart. Return to a boil and cook for 1 to 2 minutes. Taste and add the vanilla or almond extract. Remove the pot from the heat.

Bring the water bath back to a boil. If the jars have cooled, warm them in the water bath or in a 200°F oven. Simmer the lids in a saucepan of hot water. Place the jars on the baking sheet.

Ladle the jam into the jars, leaving ¼-inch headspace. Wipe the rims clean and set the lids on the mouths of the jars. Twist on the rings.

Using a jar lifter, gently lower the jars into the pots. When the water returns to a boil, decrease the heat to an active simmer, and process the jars for 10 minutes,. Turn off the heat and leave the jars in the water for 1 to 2 minutes.

Using the jar lifter, transfer the jars from the pots to the baking sheet and let sit for at least 6 hours, until cool enough to handle. Check to be sure the jars have sealed (see page 34). Label and store the sealed jam for 6 months to 2 years. Once open, store in the refrigerator for up to 3 months.

PEACH-GINGER JAM

Given peaches' Chinese origin, I think of peaches and ginger as a classic flavor combination. At my Asian supermarket there are two kinds of ginger: the young, pink, thin-skinned Hawaiian ginger that is delicate in flavor and available for only a month or two, and the hardier regular ginger, which has a bit more bite and is available year-round. So it is up to you to decide how intensely gingery you want this jam to be. As another variable, instead of grating the ginger you may use ½ cup of julienned ginger. I find the texture contrast appealing.

Serve as a topping for ice cream or rice pudding, or as a condiment for pork and duck.

2 pounds peaches	2½ to 3 cups granulated sugar
3 tablespoons fresh lemon juice, plus more as needed	4 to 5 ounces ginger, grated (¼ cup) or julienned (½ cup)

Yield: 6 to 8 half-pint jars

Place 3 or 4 small plates in the freezer.

Bring a stockpot of water to a boil. Prepare a bowl of ice water. Peel the peaches by dipping them in the boiling water for a minute or two, and then dunking them in the ice water. The peels should slip off. If not, use a peeler with a serrated swivel blade to remove the peels. Halve the peaches, remove the pits, and dice the flesh. You should have 6 to 7 cups. Sprinkle with the lemon juice to hold the color.

In a large preserving pot, gently combine the peaches, 2½ cups sugar, and the ginger; toss to mix. Let sit for at least a few hours or overnight to macerate.

Place a baking sheet on the counter near your stove. Heat a kettle of water. Set two stockpots on the stove and fill them with enough water to cover the jars by 1 to 2 inches. Bring the water to a boil over medium-high heat. Sterilize the jars (see page 32) in the water bath.

Bring the peach mixture to a boil over medium-high heat; then decrease the heat and simmer, stirring frequently, until it thickens. Taste and add another squeeze of lemon and the remaining ½ cup sugar if needed. Simmer a few minutes longer. Do the plate test (see page 30). The jam is ready when it achieves a soft set that mounds on the plate and is not runny. Remove the pot from the heat.

Bring the water bath back to a boil. If the jars have cooled, warm them in the water bath or in a 200°F oven. Simmer the lids in a saucepan of hot water. Place the jars on the baking sheet.

Ladle the jam into the jars, leaving ¼-inch headspace. Wipe the rims clean and set the lids on the mouths of the jars. Twist on the rings.

Using a jar lifter, gently lower the jars into the pots. When the water returns to a boil, decrease the heat to an active simmer, and process the jars for 10 minutes. Turn off the heat and leave the jars in the water for 1 to 2 minutes.

Using the jar lifter, transfer the jars from the pots to the baking sheet and let sit for at least 6 hours, until cool enough to handle. Check to be sure the jars have sealed (see page 34). Label and store the sealed jam for 6 months to 2 years. Once open, store in the refrigerator for up to 3 months.

VARIATION

— For Peach and Cardamom Jam, veer toward the Middle East and substitute 2 to 3 teaspoons of ground cardamom for the ginger.

SICILIAN PEACH AND LEMON PRESERVES

In Sicily, peaches are called *persiche* because they supposedly came to Italy from Persia. Some would call this preserve a *marmellata* because of the sliced lemons. Blanching the lemon slices tames their bitterness and softens them a bit so they cook in the same time as the peaches.

At the end of cooking when you do the final tasting, you may decide to stir in some vanilla extract, but I think that Fiori di Sicilia or orange-flower water would be more in keeping with the peaches' origin.

To use, spread on toast, stir into yogurt, or spoon over pound cake or almond cake.

4 pounds peaches

6 cups granulated sugar

1 large Eureka or Meyer lemon, halved, sliced paper-thin on a mandoline, slices cut into quarters, and seeds removed

1 to 2 tablespoons fresh lemon juice (optional)

1 to 2 tablespoons Fiori di Sicilia, orange-flower water, or a mixture of vanilla extract and orange-flower water, to taste (optional)

Yield: 10 half-pint jars

Place 3 or 4 small plates in the freezer.

Bring a stockpot of water to a boil. Prepare a bowl of ice water. Peel the peaches by dipping them in the boiling water for a minute or two and then dunking them in the ice water. The peels should slip off. If not, use a peeler with a serrated swivel blade to remove the peels. Halve the peaches, remove the pits, and dice the flesh. You should have about 12 cups.

In a large preserving pot, gently combine the peaches and sugar and toss to mix. Let sit for a few hours or overnight to macerate.

Bring a saucepan of water to a boil over medium-high heat. Drop in the lemon slices and blanch for 1 minute. Remove with a wire skimmer, rinse with cold water, and repeat twice. (Meyer lemons may need only one blanching to soften and lose their bitterness.) Add the blanched lemon slices to the peach mixture and stir to combine.

Place two baking sheets on the counter near your stove. Heat a kettle of water. Set two stockpots on the stove and fill them with enough water to cover the jars by 1 to 2 inches. Bring the water to a boil over medium-high heat. Sterilize the jars (see page 32) in the water bath.

Bring the peach mixture to a boil over medium-high heat, decrease the heat to low, and simmer until thick, stirring frequently. Taste and add lemon juice, as needed. Cook until the preserve passes the plate test (see page 30), achieving a soft set that mounds on the plate and is not runny. Stir in the Fiori di Sicilia extract, flower water, or combination of flower water and vanilla extract. Taste again. Remove the pot from the heat.

Bring the water bath back to a boil. If the jars have cooled, warm them in the water bath or in a 200°F oven. Simmer the lids in a saucepan of hot water. Place the jars on the baking sheet.

Ladle the preserves into the jars, leaving ¼-inch headspace. Wipe the rims clean and set the lids on the mouths of the jars. Twist on the rings.

Using a jar lifter, gently lower the jars into the pots. When the water returns to a boil, decrease the heat to an active simmer, and process the jars for 10 minutes. Turn off the heat and leave the jars in the water for 1 to 2 minutes.

Using the jar lifter, transfer the jars from the pots to the baking sheet and let sit for at least 6 hours, until cool enough to handle. Check to be sure the jars have sealed (see page 34). Label and store the sealed preserves for 6 months to 2 years. Once open, store in the refrigerator for up to 3 months.

PEACH OR NECTARINE CHUTNEY

One or two serrano chiles or jalapeños can be used instead of or in addition to the cayenne. True Aleppo pepper may become a thing of the past. Maras pepper is grown just across the border in Turkey, and the two are interchangeable.

Use this as you would any chutney: with curries, on ham and cheese sandwiches, and as a condiment for roasted poultry or pork.

5 pounds ripe but not soft freestone peaches

6 ounces fresh ginger, peeled, trimmed, and sliced (about 1 cup)

4 large cloves garlic, sliced

1 yellow onion, coarsely chopped

1 lime or 2 lemons, very thinly sliced

3 cups apple cider vinegar, plus more as needed

2 teaspoons ground cayenne, plus more to taste

1½ tablespoons ras el hanout or garam masala (optional)

1 to 2 teaspoons freshly ground black pepper

1½ teaspoons Maras or Aleppo pepper

1 tablespoon ground cinnamon

1 teaspoon Chinese five-spice powder

1 teaspoon ground cumin

2 tablespoons salt

2 tablespoons brown mustard seeds (optional)

¼ cup fresh lemon juice, or 1 stalk lemongrass, white part finely minced

3½ cups granulated or firmly packed brown sugar

1½ cups raisins

Yield: 8 pint jars

Place 3 or 4 small plates in the freezer.

Bring a stockpot of water to a boil. Prepare a bowl of ice water. Peel the peaches by dipping them in the boiling water for a minute or two and then dunking them in the ice water. The peels should slip off. If not, use a peeler with a serrated swivel blade to remove the peels. Halve the peaches, remove the pits, and dice the flesh into 1½-inch pieces. You should have 15 cups.

In the bowl of a food processor, combine the ginger, garlic, onion, lime or lemons, and 1 cup of the vinegar and pulse to puree. You will have about 2 cups of puree.

In a large preserving pot, gently combine the peaches, ginger-garlic puree, cayenne, ras el hanout, black pepper, Maras or Aleppo pepper, cinnamon, five-spice powder, cumin, salt, and mustard seeds, stirring to mix well. Stir in the lemon juice or lemon grass, sugar, and the remaining 2 cups vinegar. Bring to a boil over medium-high heat, then decrease the heat and simmer until thickened but still juicy, 20 to 30 minutes.

Place a baking sheet on the counter near your stove. Heat a kettle of water. Set two stockpots on the stove and fill them with enough water to cover the jars by 1 to 2 inches. Bring the water to a boil over medium-high heat. Sterilize the jars (see page 32) in the water bath.

Add the raisins to the chutney and simmer, stirring frequently (to prevent the raisins from sinking and scorching), until thickened. The raisins will drink up some of the liquid, so do not overreduce the chutney. If the chutney seems dry, add more vinegar or water until the mixture is syrupy. Do a plate test (see page 30). Remove the pot from the heat.

Bring the water bath back to a boil. If the jars have cooled, warm them in the water bath or in a 200°F oven. Simmer the lids in a saucepan of hot water. Place the jars on the baking sheet.

Ladle the chutney into the jars, leaving ¼-inch headspace. Wipe the rims clean and set the lids on the mouths of the jars. Twist on the rings.

Using a jar lifter, gently lower the jars into the pots. When the water returns to a boil, decrease the heat to an active simmer, and process the jars for 10 minutes. Turn off the heat and leave the jars in the water for 1 to 2 minutes.

Using the jar lifter, transfer the jars from the pots to the baking sheet and let sit for at least 6 hours, until cool enough to handle. Check to be sure the jars have sealed (see page 34). Label and store the sealed chutney for 6 months to 2 years. Once open, store in the refrigerator for up to 3 months.

PICKLED PEACHES

When I had my restaurant, Square One, we started a Fourth of July tradition of serving pickled peaches with our fried chicken. Now my family insists that we have these peaches in the pantry, because we eat fried chicken more than once a year.

12 firm-ripe peaches

1½ cups apple cider vinegar

1½ cups water

3 cups granulated sugar

3 or 4 cinnamon sticks

10 to 12 whole cloves

3 or 4 strips lemon zest

1 teaspoon black peppercorns, slightly bruised (optional)

Yield: 3 or 4 quart jars

Bring a stockpot of water to a boil. Prepare a bowl of ice water. Peel the peaches by dipping them in the boiling water for a minute or two and then dunking them in the ice water. The peels should slip off. If not, use a peeler with a serrated swivel blade to remove the peels. Ideally, you can leave the peaches whole and still fit them in your wide-mouth quart jars. But if they are too large to fit through the mouth of a jar, cut them in half.

Place a baking sheet on the counter near your stove. Heat a kettle of water. Set two stockpots on the stove and fill them with enough water to cover the jars by 1 to 2 inches. Bring the water to a boil over medium-high heat. Sterilize the jars (see page 32) in the water bath; leave in the water to keep warm.

Combine the vinegar, 1½ cups water, sugar, cinnamon, cloves, lemon zest, and peppercorns in a medium nonaluminum saucepan. Bring the mixture to a boil over medium-high heat, stirring until the sugar dissolves. Decrease the heat to low and simmer the syrup for 10 minutes.

Simmer the lids in a saucepan of hot water. Place the jars on the baking sheet.

Poach 3 or 4 peaches at a time in the syrup for 2 minutes. Then, using a slotted spoon, transfer the peaches to the jars. Spoon the hot syrup over peaches, leaving 1-inch headspace. Distribute the cinnamon sticks, cloves, and lemon peels among the jars. Wipe the rims clean and set the lids on the mouths of the jars. Twist on the rings.

Using a jar lifter, gently lower the jars into the pots. When the water returns to a boil, set the timer for 20 minutes, decrease the heat to an active simmer, and process the jars. Turn off the heat and leave the jars in the water for 1 to 2 minutes.

Using the jar lifter, transfer the jars from the pots to the baking sheet and let sit for at least 6 hours, until cool enough to handle. Check to be sure the jars have sealed (see page 34). Label and store the sealed peaches for 6 months to 1 year. Once open, store in the refrigerator for up to 3 months.

VARIATION

— For White Wine Vinegar Syrup: Make a syrup of 4 cups white wine vinegar and 4 cups granulated sugar. Add 2 teaspoons whole cloves, 1 cinnamon stick, 1 teaspoon pickling spice, and slivers of fresh ginger.

Red Currants

During the last five years or so, currants seem to have vanished from my local supermarkets. Now they are a "specialty item" and need to be ordered ahead of time. If it's the same in your area, you might as well ask for a flat or two if you are special-ordering them. One flat of currants is 4½ pounds (twelve 6-ounce boxes).

Because of their high pectin content, currant preserves are great to have on hand to add to other fruits that may have lower pectin or that fall a bit flat in the flavor. Currants pair really well with raspberries and strawberries, and if you add some currant puree to the berries, you won't have to cook them as long to reach the gel point, thus keeping their flavor more vibrant. You can turn the currant puree into a delicious jam by cooking it with sugar and a bit of lemon juice.

RED CURRANT JAM

Currant jam is great served with cream cheese, roast pork, turkey, or anything that needs a big hit of tartness.

4½ pounds currants, stemmed

2 cups water

3 to 4 cups granulated sugar

Juice of 1 lemon

Yield: 6 half-pint jars

Place 3 or 4 small plates in the freezer.

In a large preserving pot, gently combine the currants and water. Bring the pot to a boil over medium-high heat; then decrease the heat and simmer for 5 minutes. Turn off the heat and let sit for 20 minutes.

Run the currant mixture through a food mill or process in a food processor. You should have about 4 cups of currant puree.

Transfer the puree to the pot and bring to a boil over medium-high heat. Cover the pot, decrease the heat, and simmer for 5 minutes. Turn off the heat and let sit for 30 minutes. At this point, the currant puree can be refrigerated for a few days until you are ready to use it to add to one of the berry jams.

Place a baking sheet on the counter near your stove. Heat a kettle of water. Set two stockpots on the stove and fill them with enough water to cover the jars by 1 to 2 inches. Bring the water to a boil over medium-high heat. Sterilize the jars (see page 32) in the water bath.

In a large preserving pot, combine the currant puree, 3 cups of the sugar (4 cups for a sweeter jam), and the lemon juice.

Bring to a boil over medium-high heat and cook, stirring frequently and skimming as necessary, until the jam passes the plate test (see page 30), achieving a rather firm set. Remove the pot from the heat.

Bring the water bath back to a boil. If the jars have cooled, warm them in the water bath or in a 200°F oven. Simmer the lids in a saucepan of hot water. Place the jars on the baking sheet.

Ladle the jam into the jars, leaving ¼-inch headspace. Wipe the rims clean and set the lids on the mouths of the jars. Twist on the rings.

Using a jar lifter, gently lower the jars into the pots. When the water returns to a boil, decrease the heat to an active simmer, and process the jars for 10 minutes. Turn off the heat and leave the jars in the water for 1 to 2 minutes.

Using the jar lifter, transfer the jars from the pots to the baking sheet and let sit for at least 6 hours, until cool enough to handle. Check to be sure the jars have sealed (see page 34). Label and store the sealed jam for 6 months to 2 years. Once open, store in the refrigerator for up to 3 months.

RED CURRANT— STRAWBERRY PRESERVES WITH BLACK PEPPER

This preserve is sweet, tart, and a bit spicy. My grandchildren think this is the best jam ever!

12 cups (6 pint baskets) petite strawberries, stemmed

7 cups granulated sugar

Juice of 2 lemons

3 cups currant puree (see Red Currant Jam, facing page)

½ to 1 teaspoon freshly ground black pepper (optional)

Yield: 12 half-pint jars

Place 3 or 4 small plates in the freezer.

In a large preserving pot, combine the berries, sugar, and lemon juice and set aside to macerate for a few hours. Bring to a boil over medium-high heat, then remove from the heat. Let sit overnight.

The next day, bring the berry mixture to a boil and cook for a few minutes. Remove from the heat and let sit for 1 hour so the berries can plump up a bit.

Set a colander over a bowl and, using a slotted spoon, transfer the strawberries to the colander.

Place two baking sheets on the counter near your stove. Heat a kettle of water. Set two stockpots on the stove and fill them with enough water to cover the jars by 1 to 2 inches. Bring the water to a boil over medium-high heat. Sterilize the jars (see page 32) in the water bath.

Reduce the strawberry syrup until thickened, skimming and stirring frequently.

Add the currant puree to the strawberry syrup and bring to a boil over medium-high heat. Cook until thickened, skimming and stirring frequently. Carefully return the strawberries to the pot, along with any juices that have collected in the bowl under the colander. Add black pepper to taste. Boil until the jam thickens and passes the plate test (see page 30). Let rest for 5 minutes. Stir once to distribute the berries. Remove the pot from the heat.

Bring the water bath back to a boil. If the jars have cooled, warm them in the water bath or in a 200°F oven. Simmer the lids in a saucepan of hot water. Place the jars on the baking sheets.

Ladle the preserves into the jars, leaving ¼-inch headspace. Wipe the rims clean and set the lids on the mouths of the jars. Twist on the rings.

Using a jar lifter, gently lower the jars into the pots. When the water returns to a boil, decrease the heat to an active simmer, and process the jars for 10 minutes. Turn off the heat and leave the jars in the water for 1 to 2 minutes.

Using the jar lifter, transfer the jars from the pots to the baking sheets and let sit for at least 6 hours, until cool enough to handle. Check to be sure the jars have sealed (see page 34). Label and store the sealed preserves for 6 months to 2 years. Once open, store in the refrigerator for up to 3 months.

RED CURRANT— RASPBERRY PRESERVES

Establishing the balance of flavor between the sweet-tart raspberries and the tart currants is a personal decision. You may want the raspberries to dominate, in which case you'll use less than the full amount of currant puree I call for (and prefer).

4 cups (6 six-ounce baskets) raspberries

4 to 5 cups granulated sugar

Juice of 1 lemon

2 cups currant puree (see Red Currant Jam, page 118), or less or more as preferred

Yield: 12 half-pint jars

Place 3 or 4 small plates in the freezer.

In a large preserving pot, gently combine the raspberries, 4 cups of the sugar, and the lemon juice. Let sit overnight to macerate.

The next day, place two baking sheets on the counter near your stove. Heat a kettle of water. Set two stockpots on the stove and fill them with enough water to cover the jars by 1 to 2 inches. Bring the water to a boil over medium-high heat. Sterilize the jars (see page 32) in the water bath.

Place the raspberry mixture over medium-high heat and bring to a boil. Cook for about 5 minutes, then add the currant puree. Return the mixture to a boil and cook, skimming and stirring frequently to prevent seeds from settling on the bottom of the pot and sticking. As you cook, taste and adjust the amount of currant puree and sugar, adding more to taste. Cook until the mixture thickens and passes the plate test (see page 30), achieving a soft set that mounds on the plate and is not runny. Remove the pot from the heat.

Bring the water bath back to a boil. If the jars have cooled, warm them in the water bath or in a 200°F oven. Simmer the lids in a saucepan of hot water. Place the jars on the baking sheets.

Ladle the preserves into the jars, leaving ¼-inch headspace. Wipe the rims clean and set the lids on the mouths of the jars. Twist on the rings.

Using a jar lifter, gently lower the jars into the pots. When the water returns to a boil, decrease the heat to an active simmer, and process the jars for 10 minutes. Turn off the heat and leave the jars in the water for 1 to 2 minutes.

Using the jar lifter, transfer the jars from the pots to the baking sheets and let sit for at least 6 hours, until cool enough to handle. Check to be sure the jars have sealed (see page 34). Label and store the sealed preserves for 6 months to 2 years. Once open, store in the refrigerator for up to 3 months.

RED CURRANT JELLY

Currant jelly used to be a staple in every pantry. It was kept on hand to glaze berry and plum tarts and to make the now-obscure Cumberland sauce to serve with roast meats. It was served with cream cheese for elegant tea sandwiches. Because of its high pectin content, I keep it on hand to thicken recalcitrant berry, plum, or cherry jams and appreciate the tart zing it adds to the blend—it's sort of a colorful and tart version of apple pectin.

4½ pounds currants, stemmed	4 to 5 cups granulated sugar
2 to 3 cups water	Juice of 1 lemon

Yield: 5 or 6 half-pint jars

Place 3 or 4 small plates in the freezer.

In a large preserving pot, combine the currants and water. Bring to a boil over medium-high heat, decrease the heat to low, and simmer for 10 to 15 minutes, mashing the currants as they cook.

Transfer the currants and their juices to a dampened cheesecloth-lined colander or a jelly bag set over a bowl. Let drain for several hours or overnight.

Measure the currant juice. Transfer it to the preserving pot. Measure out the same amount of sugar and add to juice. Taste and add a squeeze of lemon juice if needed.

Place a baking sheet on the counter near your stove. Heat a kettle of water. Set two stockpots on the stove and fill them with enough water to cover the jars by 1 to 2 inches. Bring the water to a boil over medium-high heat. Sterilize the jars (see page 32) in the water bath.

Bring the currants and sugar to a boil over medium-high heat. Once the mixture boils, do not stir. Skim if necessary and cook until it passes the plate test (see page 30), achieving a relatively firm set. Remove the pot from the heat.

Bring the water bath back to a boil. If the jars have cooled, warm them in the water bath or in a 200°F oven. Simmer the lids in a saucepan of hot water. Place the jars on the baking sheet.

Ladle the jelly into the jars, leaving ¼-inch headspace. Wipe the rims clean and set the lids on the mouths of the jars. Twist on the rings.

Using a jar lifter, gently lower the jars into the pots. When the water returns to a boil, decrease the heat to an active simmer, and process the jars for 5 minutes. Turn off the heat and leave the jars in the water for 1 to 2 minutes.

Using the jar lifter, transfer the jars from the pots to the baking sheet and let sit for at least 6 hours, until cool enough to handle. Check to be sure the jars have sealed (see page 34). Label and store the sealed jelly for 6 months to 2 years. Once open, store in the refrigerator for up to 3 months.

Raspberries, Boysenberries, Blackberries, Black Raspberries, and Blueberries

Although strawberries are the harbinger of spring, the berry bonanza comes in summer in the form of raspberries, boysenberries, blackberries, blueberries, olallieberries, loganberries, tayberries, and, for the fortunate few who can find them, black raspberries. The major variables are size, texture, amount of seeds, and the sweet-tart ratio. They can be combined with currants and apples for a bit of extra pectin. Raspberries are my favorite berry because of their perfume.

Blackberries seem to be the most versatile and durable. Unlike strawberries, which can be made into a whole berry preserve, most of these berries are for jam and pie fillings. They lose their contours when cooked. Berry jams are, of course, great on toast, scones, muffins, and biscuits. They may be spooned into yogurt or over ice cream or panna cotta. Berry jams also make great cookie and cake fillings, such as for linzertorte.

To seed or not to seed? That is up to you. I like to put blackberries through the food mill, as I find their seeds get a bit tough over time. And blackberries make a really good jelly.

Simpatico flavor pairings for berries are vanilla, cinnamon, star anise, basil, mint, lemon verbena, citrus, pomegranate, black pepper, rose, and violet.

RASPBERRY-PLUM JAM

This deliciousness is what happened when I got carried away at the market and ended up with leftover fruit from two different recipes. It was another happy accident that led me to now make this jam on purpose.

2 pounds red-fleshed plums

4 cups (6 six-ounce baskets) raspberries

4 cups granulated sugar

2 tablespoons fresh lemon juice

1 teaspoon ground star anise

½ cup water or pomegranate, apple, or prune juice (optional)

⅓ cup chopped mint leaves

Yield: 6 to 7 half-pint jars

Place 3 or 4 small plates in the freezer.

Halve and pit the plums, then cut into pieces. You will have about 4 cups.

In a large, preserving pot, gently combine the plums and raspberries with the sugar, lemon juice, and star anise and toss to mix. Set aside to macerate overnight. (If you don't have time to macerate the fruit overnight, after adding the star anise, add the water or fruit juice and stir gently to distribute. Place the pot over medium-high heat and boil the mixture for 5 minutes. Remove from the heat and let rest, uncovered, for 1 hour.)

Stir in the mint.

The next day, bring the fruit and water or fruit juice to a boil over medium-high heat. Cook for 5 minutes. Remove from the heat and let sit, uncovered, for 1 hour.

Place a baking sheet on the counter near your stove. Heat a kettle of water. Set two stockpots on the stove and fill them with enough water to cover the jars by 1 to 2 inches. Bring the water to a boil over medium-high heat. Sterilize the jars (see page 32) in the water bath.

Cook the jam over medium heat, stirring frequently, until the mixture thickens and passes the plate test (see page 30), achieving a soft set. Remove the pot from the heat.

Bring the water bath back to a boil. If the jars have cooled, warm them in the water bath or in a 200°F oven. Simmer the lids in a saucepan of hot water. Place the jars on the baking sheet.

Ladle the jam into the jars, leaving ¼-inch headspace. Wipe the rims clean and set the lids on the mouths of the jars. Twist on the rings.

Using a jar lifter, gently lower the jars into the pots. When the water returns to a boil, decrease the heat to an active simmer, and process the jars for 10 minutes. Turn off the heat and leave the jars in the water for 1 to 2 minutes.

Using the jar lifter, transfer the jars from the pots to the baking sheet and let sit for at least 6 hours, until cool enough to handle. Check to be sure the jars have sealed (see page 34). Label and store the sealed jam for 6 months to 2 years. Once open, store in the refrigerator for up to 3 months.

RASPBERRY-ROSE JAM

Raspberries and strawberries are in the rose family, so I like to accent the fruit with rose petals (in the form of rose sugar). You can omit them, but they make for a very aromatic and romantic jam. Edible dried rose petals can be found in Middle Eastern groceries or online. They are also sold by spice companies, such as Whole Spice Company in Napa Valley, California, and Kalustyans in New York, which also carry powdered roses and rose sugar. I don't strain out the raspberry seeds, as they are tiny and, unlike blackberry seeds, do not toughen with time. One flat of raspberries is 12 baskets, each about 6 ounces, totaling 4½ to 5 pounds. This recipe can be halved.

8 cups (12 six-ounce baskets) organic raspberries

2 cups rose sugar (see page 22)

5 to 6 cups granulated sugar

Juice of 2 large lemons

¼ cup rose water (optional)

Yield: 16 half-pint jars

Place 3 or 4 small plates in the freezer.

Pick over the raspberries and discard any leaves. To preserve the berries' fragrance, do not wash them.

In a large preserving pot, gently combine the raspberries, rose sugar, granulated sugar (adding more or less to taste, depending on the sweetness of the berries), and the lemon juice. Let sit for 3 hours or up to overnight. The fruit will have given off some juices.

Place the pot over medium-high heat and bring to a boil. Cook for 5 minutes, stirring gently. Remove from the heat and set aside, uncovered, for 30 minutes.

Place two baking sheets on the counter near your stove. Heat a kettle of water. Set two stockpots on the stove and fill them with enough water to cover the jars by 1 to 2 inches. Bring the water to a boil over medium-high heat. Sterilize the jars (see page 32) in the water bath.

Return the raspberries to medium-high heat and boil, stirring gently, until the jam passes the plate test (see page 30), achieving a soft set. Stir in the rose water. Remove the pot from the heat.

Bring the water bath back to a boil. If the jars have cooled, warm them in the water bath or in a 200°F oven. Simmer the lids in a saucepan of hot water. Place the jars on the baking sheets.

Ladle the jam into the jars, leaving ¼-inch headspace. Wipe the rims clean and set the lids on the mouths of the jars. Twist on the rings.

Using a jar lifter, gently lower the jars into the pots. When the water returns to a boil, decrease the heat to an active simmer, and process the jars for 10 minutes. Turn off the heat and leave the jars in the water for 1 to 2 minutes.

Using the jar lifter, transfer the jars from the pots to the baking sheets and let sit for at least 6 hours, until cool enough to handle. Check to be sure the jars have sealed (see page 34). Label and store the sealed jam for 6 months to 2 years. Once open, store in the refrigerator for up to 3 months.

BASIC BLACKBERRY JAM

Supposedly, blackberries are short on natural pectin, so adding apples is recommended to compensate. But adding too much apple will produce a jam that has a rubbery texture. Much less apple (barely any, actually) is required than is typically called for. If you have Homemade Apple Pectin (page 200) on hand, use that instead. If using fresh apple, you may even want to cook the apple first in a bit of water until it is soft, and then add it to the berry puree as needed.

1 to 2 tart apples, peeled, cored, and chopped (optional)

8 cups (10 baskets) blackberries

1 cup water

4 cups granulated sugar

Juice of 2 lemons, or more as needed

½ teaspoon ground cinnamon (optional)

½ teaspoon freshly ground black pepper (optional)

Yield: 7 to 8 half-pint jars

Place 3 or 4 small plates in the freezer.

Bring a small saucepan of water to a boil. Add the apple and cook until soft. Drain well. Mash to a puree.

In a large preserving pot, combine the blackberries and 1 cup water. Crush the berries a bit with a potato masher. Let sit overnight to macerate. (If you do not have time to macerate the berries, just proceed with the instructions.)

Next, place the preserving pot over medium-high heat and bring to a boil. Cook for 5 minutes.

Process the berries through a food mill to extract the seeds, reserving all of the fruit pulp and juice.

Transfer the berry pulp and juices to the preserving pot. Stir in the sugar and apple.

Place over medium heat and bring to a gentle boil. Cook, stirring frequently, until the mixture thickens.

Place a baking sheet on the counter near your stove. Heat a kettle of water. Set two stockpots on the stove and fill them with enough water to cover the jars by 1 to 2 inches. Bring the water to a boil over medium-high heat. Sterilize the jars (see page 32) in the water bath.

Taste the berry mixture and add the lemon juice, as needed. Stir in the cinnamon and black pepper. Cook until the jam passes the plate test (see page 30), achieving a soft, slightly runny set. This jam firms up well as it cools, so do not cook until it reaches a firm set. Remove the pot from the heat.

Bring the water bath back to a boil. If the jars have cooled, warm them in the water bath or in a 200°F oven. Simmer the lids in a saucepan of hot water. Place the jars on the baking sheet.

Ladle the jam into the jars, leaving ¼-inch headspace. Wipe the rims clean and set the lids on the mouths of the jars. Twist on the rings.

Using a jar lifter, gently lower the jars into the pots. When the water returns to a boil, decrease the heat to an active simmer, and process the jars for 10 minutes. Turn off the heat and leave the jars in the water for 1 to 2 minutes.

Using the jar lifter, transfer the jars from the pots to the baking sheet and let sit for at least 6 hours, until cool enough to handle. Check to be sure the jars have sealed (see page 34). Label and store the sealed jam for 6 months to 2 years. Once open, store in the refrigerator for up to 3 months.

VARIATION

— For Blackberry-Nectarine Jam, add 4 to 5 nectarines, peeled and cut into ½-inch pieces when you add the sugar to the berry puree. The little bites of nectarine in this preserve offer a delicious textural surprise.

BLACKBERRY BRAMBLE JAM

No apples are required for pectin in this jam because the orange and lemons do the job. The bay leaves add a nice woodsy character. You can leave them out, but the jam will be less brambly.

6 cups (8 baskets) blackberries	Juice of 2 lemons, plus more as needed
3 to 4 cups granulated sugar	½ teaspoon ground cloves
½ cup freshly squeezed orange or blood orange juice, plus a bit more as needed	½ teaspoon freshly ground black pepper, plus more as needed
Grated zest of 1 orange or blood orange	2 or 3 bay leaves

Yield: 6 half-pint jars

Place 3 or 4 small plates in the freezer.

In a large preserving pot, combine the blackberries, sugar (adding more or less to taste, depending on the sweetness of the berries), orange juice and zest, and lemon juice. Let sit overnight to macerate.

The next day, place the preserving pot over medium-high heat and bring to a boil. Mash the berries with a potato masher. Cook for 5 minutes.

Process the berries through a food mill to extract the seeds, reserving all fruit pulp and juice.

Place a baking sheet on the counter near your stove. Heat a kettle of water. Set two stock-pots on the stove and fill them with enough water to cover the jars by 1 to 2 inches. Bring the water to a boil over medium-high heat. Sterilize the jars (see page 32) in the water bath.

Transfer the berry pulp and juices to the preserving pot. Add the cloves, black pepper, and bay leaves. Place over medium-high heat and bring to a boil, stirring frequently. Cook until the jam thickens and passes the plate test (see page 30), achieving a soft, slightly runny set. Taste and adjust the lemon juice and pepper. Discard the bay leaves. Remove the pot from the heat.

Bring the water bath back to a boil. If the jars have cooled, warm them in the water bath or in a 200°F oven. Simmer the lids in a saucepan of hot water. Place the jars on the baking sheet.

Ladle the jam into the jars, leaving ¼-inch headspace. Wipe the rims clean and set the lids on the mouths of the jars. Twist on the rings.

Using a jar lifter, gently lower the jars into the pots. When the water returns to a boil, decrease the heat to an active simmer, and process the jars for 10 minutes. Turn off the heat and leave the jars in the water for 1 to 2 minutes.

Using the jar lifter, transfer the jars from the pots to the baking sheet and let sit for at least 6 hours, until cool enough to handle. Check to be sure the jars have sealed (see page 34). Label and store the sealed jam for 6 months to 2 years. Once open, store in the refrigerator for up to 3 months.

BLACKBERRY, BURGUNDY PLUM, MINT, AND BLACK PEPPER JAM

This jam is tart, rich, and delicious. The whole is more than the sum of its parts. The blackberries and plums bring out the best in each other. There is just a hint of mint.

2 pounds plums, preferably red-fleshed

8 cups (10 baskets) blackberries

6 cups granulated sugar

1 cup apple juice

7 large sprigs mint

4 to 5 tablespoons fresh lemon juice

1 teaspoon freshly ground black pepper

Yield: 10 half-pint jars

Place 3 or 4 small plates in the freezer.

Halve, pit, and cut the plums into ½-inch dice. You will have about 8 cups.

In a large preserving pot over medium-high heat, combine the plums, blackberries, sugar, apple juice, 4 of the mint sprigs, and 2 tablespoons of the lemon juice and cook until the fruit softens, about 25 minutes. Discard the mint sprigs.

Process the fruit through a food mill to extract the berry seeds, reserving all fruit pulp and juice. You will have about 8 cups.

Cut the leaves of the remaining 3 sprigs of mint into chiffonade. You should have about 3 tablespoons.

Place two baking sheets on the counter near your stove. Heat a kettle of water. Set two stock-pots on the stove and fill them with enough water to cover the jars by 1 to 2 inches. Bring the water to a boil over medium-high heat. Sterilize the jars (see page 32) in the water bath.

Transfer the fruit pulp and juices to the preserving pot, place over medium-high heat, and bring to a boil. Add the black pepper, decrease the heat to medium-low, and simmer, skimming and stirring occasionally, until thick. Add the mint chiffonade and the remaining 2 to 3 tablespoons of lemon juice, as needed. Cook until the jam thickens and passes the plate test (see page 30), achieving a soft, slightly runny set. Remove the pot from the heat.

Bring the water bath back to a boil. If the jars have cooled, warm them in the water bath or in a 200°F oven. Simmer the lids in a saucepan of hot water. Place the jars on the baking sheets.

Ladle the jam into the jars, leaving ¼-inch headspace. Wipe the rims clean and set the lids on the mouths of the jars. Twist on the rings.

Using a jar lifter, gently lower the jars into the pots. When the water returns to a boil, decrease the heat to an active simmer, and process the jars for 10 minutes. Turn off the heat and leave the jars in the water for 1 to 2 minutes.

Using the jar lifter, transfer the jars from the pots to the baking sheets and let sit for at least 6 hours, until cool enough to handle. Check to be sure the jars have sealed (see page 34). Label and store the sealed jam for 6 months to 2 years. Once open, store in the refrigerator for up to 3 months.

BLACK RASPBERRY JAM

When I was growing up on the East Coast, black raspberries were abundant. Black raspberry jam was one of my favorites, and ice cream made with the berries was highly sought after. Sadly, black raspberries are rarely available in my local markets. I have been able to special-order them a few times, and my family is still dreaming of the black raspberry jam and ice cream I made with them. I had to ration each jar. Since it is a struggle to find these berries, when I do I always buy a couple of flats. The berry puree that you do not use for jam can be frozen and used to make ice cream.

The technique for preparing this jam is a bit different from that used in making raspberry or blackberry jam. Black raspberries are small, dry, and have lots of tiny seeds. They do not respond well to overnight maceration and need heat and a bit of water to give off their juice. I cook them briefly in a bit of water, mash them with a potato masher, and put them through a food mill for a smooth and relatively seedless jam. If you do not want lots of purple drops of berry juice all over the kitchen and you, wear a dark apron when you work and lay out some baking sheets to protect your counters.

Place 3 or 4 small plates in the freezer.

In a large preserving pot over medium-low heat, bring the berries and water to a simmer and cook until soft, about 5 minutes.

Process the berries through a food mill to extract the seeds, reserving the fruit pulp and juice. You will have 6 to 8 cups. It will appear somewhat gelatinous in texture. Measure the puree and note the quantity.

Place two baking sheets on the counter near your stove. Heat a kettle of water. Set two stockpots on the stove and fill them with enough water to cover the jars by 1 to 2 inches. Bring the water to a boil over medium-high heat. Sterilize the jars (see page 32) in the water bath.

Transfer the berry puree to the preserving pot. Add an equal amount of sugar as berry puree, and stir in the lemon juice. Bring to a boil over medium-high heat and cook, stirring frequently. Taste and stir in more lemon juice as needed. Cook until the jam thickens and passes the plate test (see page 30), achieving a soft set that mounds on the plate and is not runny. Remove the pot from the heat.

Bring the water bath back to a boil. If the jars have cooled, warm them in the water bath or in a 200°F oven. Simmer the lids in a saucepan of hot water. Place the jars on the baking sheet.

Ladle the jam into the jars, leaving ¼-inch headspace. Wipe the rims clean and set the lids on the mouths of the jars. Twist on the rings.

Using a jar lifter, gently lower the jars into the pots. When the water returns to a boil, decrease the heat to an active simmer, and process the

---

10 cups (12 baskets) black raspberries

3 cups water

6 to 8 cups granulated sugar

3 to 4 tablespoons fresh lemon juice, plus more as needed

Yield: 12 half-pint jars

jars for 10 minutes. Turn off the heat and leave the jars in the water for 1 to 2 minutes.

Using the jar lifter, transfer the jars from the pots to the baking sheet and let sit for at least 6 hours, until cool enough to handle. Check to be sure the jars have sealed (see page 34). Label and store the sealed jam for 6 months to 2 years. Once open, store in the refrigerator for up to 3 months.

BOYSENBERRY JAM

Boysenberries are a cultivated cross between a raspberry, a loganberry, and a blackberry. (The loganberry is a simpler cross of blackberry and raspberry). Tart and sweet, they are larger than raspberries, softer than blackberries, and have small seeds. Their close relations are the olallieberry and tayberry. All may be prepared in the same way. The season for these berries is short. So if you like them, be ready to jump to it!

6 cups (6 to 8 six-ounce) baskets boysenberries	2 tablespoons fresh lemon juice
4 cups granulated sugar	1 dash to 1 teaspoon vanilla extract

Yield: 5 or 6 half-pint jars

Place 3 or 4 small plates in the freezer.

In a large preserving pot, combine the boysenberries and sugar. Let sit overnight to macerate.

The next day, place the pot over medium-high heat and bring to a boil, cooking until the berries are tender, about 5 minutes.

If you wish to remove the seeds, process the berries through a food mill, reserving all fruit pulp and juice.

Place a baking sheet on the counter near your stove. Heat a kettle of water. Set two stockpots on the stove and fill them with enough water to cover the jars by 1 to 2 inches. Bring the water to a boil over medium-high heat. Sterilize the jars (see page 32) in the water bath.

If you pureed the berries, transfer the berry pulp and juices to the preserving pot. Place over medium-high heat and bring to a boil, stirring frequently. Cook until the jam thickens and passes the plate test (see page 30), achieving a relatively firm set. Add the lemon juice and vanilla to taste. Remove the pot from the heat.

Bring the water bath back to a boil. If the jars have cooled, warm them in the water bath or in a 200°F oven. Simmer the lids in a saucepan of hot water. Place the jars on the baking sheet.

Ladle the jam into the jars, leaving ¼-inch headspace. Wipe the rims clean and set the lids on the mouths of the jars. Twist on the rings.

Using a jar lifter, gently lower the jars into the pots. When the water returns to a boil, decrease the heat to an active simmer, and process the jars for 10 minutes. Turn off the heat and leave the jars in the water for 1 to 2 minutes.

Using the jar lifter, transfer the jars from the pots to the baking sheet and let sit for at least 6 hours, until cool enough to handle. Check to be sure the jars have sealed (see page 34). Label and store the sealed jam for 6 months to 2 years. Once open, store in the refrigerator for up to 3 months.

BLUEBERRY-CITRUS PRESERVES

Blueberries are not high in pectin, so citrus zest and juice are essential for proper gelling. Blueberries may set up fairly firm even if the preserve looks a bit runny during the plate test. Very mysterious! So, when making this recipe, plan to stop cooking and do the plate test a few times. If in doubt, opt for a bit runny rather than a stiff set.

4 cups (2 pint baskets) blueberries, stemmed

½ cup fresh lemon juice

Grated zest of 3 to 4 lemons

2½ to 3 cups granulated sugar, or more as needed

½ teaspoon ground cinnamon

½ teaspoon ground allspice

Yield: 3 or 4 half-pint jars

Place 3 or 4 small plates in the freezer.

In a large preserving pot, combine the blueberries, lemon juice and zest, the sugar (adding more or less, depending on the blueberries' sweetness), cinnamon, and allspice. Place over medium-high heat and bring to a boil, then decrease the heat and simmer for 5 minutes. At this point, the jam can be set aside to rest overnight if you like.

Place a baking sheet on the counter near your stove. Heat a kettle of water. Set a stockpot on the stove and fill it with enough water to cover the jars by 1 to 2 inches. Bring the water to a boil over medium-high heat. Sterilize the jars (see page 32) in the water bath.

Cook the berry mixture until it begins to thicken. Turn off the heat and do the first plate test (see page 30). If the mixture mounds on the plate and does not run much, it is ready. If not, continue to cook and test until it does. Remove the pot from the heat.

Bring the water bath back to a boil. If the jars have cooled, warm them in the water bath or in a 200°F oven. Simmer the lids in a saucepan of hot water. Place the jars on the baking sheet.

Ladle the preserves into the jars, leaving ¼-inch headspace. Wipe the rims clean and set the lids on the mouths of the jars. Twist on the rings.

Using a jar lifter, gently lower the jars into the pot. When the water returns to a boil, decrease the heat to an active simmer, and process the jars for 10 minutes. Turn off the heat and leave the jars in the water for 1 to 2 minutes.

Using the jar lifter, transfer the jars from the pots to the baking sheet and let sit for at least 6 hours, until cool enough to handle. Check to be sure the jars have sealed (see page 34). Label and store the sealed preserves for 6 months to 2 years. Once open, store in the refrigerator for up to 3 months.

VARIATIONS

— For Blueberry–Mixed Citrus Preserves: Substitute 2 tablespoons grated orange zest for the lemon zest, ½ cup orange juice for the lemon juice, and 1 cinnamon stick and 2 star anise pods, tied in a cheesecloth sachet, for the ground cinnamon and allspice. When the jam has thickened, add ¼ cup lemon juice, or a bit more to taste. Remove the sachet before filling the jars.

— For Blueberry-Orange Preserves: Instead of using all lemon, let the orange dominate as a change of pace.

BLUEBERRY-POMEGRANATE JAM

Deep in color and flavor, this jam uses pomegranate to enhance the blueberries' tartness with a sweet-sour accent of its own. The Urfa chile powder adds a raisiny quality and a mild buzz. If you can't find Urfa, use an Aleppo or Maras pepper instead. They are a bit hotter than Urfa peppers, so use a bit less.

8 cups blueberries

4 cups granulated sugar

1½ cups pomegranate juice

2 teaspoons ground Urfa chile

1 teaspoon ground cinnamon

1 teaspoon ground allspice

Grated zest of 2 lemons

3 to 4 tablespoons pomegranate molasses

2 tablespoons fresh lemon juice, plus more as needed

Yield: 8 half-pint jars

Place 3 or 4 small plates in the freezer.

In a large preserving pot, combine the blueberries, sugar, pomegranate juice, Urfa chile, cinnamon, allspice, and lemon zest. Place over medium-high heat and bring to a boil, then decrease the heat and simmer for 5 minutes. At this point, the jam can be set aside to rest overnight if you like.

Place a baking sheet on the counter near your stove. Heat a kettle of water. Set two stockpots on the stove and fill them with enough water to cover the jars by 1 to 2 inches. Bring the water to a boil over medium-high heat. Sterilize the jars (see page 32) in the water bath.

Cook the jam until it has begun to thicken. Stir in 3 tablespoons of the pomegranate molasses and the lemon juice. Taste and add the remaining 1 tablespoon of pomegranate molasses and lemon juice, as needed. Simmer for a few minutes. Turn off the heat and do the first plate test (see page 30). If the jam is slightly runny, it is ready. (Blueberries set up fairly well.) If not, continue to cook over low heat and test until it does. Remove the pot from the heat.

Bring the water bath back to a boil. If the jars have cooled, warm them in the water bath or in a 200°F oven. Simmer the lids in a saucepan of hot water. Place the jars on the baking sheet.

Ladle the jam into the jars, leaving ¼-inch headspace. Wipe the rims clean and set the lids on the mouths of the jars. Twist on the rings.

Using a jar lifter, gently lower the jars into the pots. When the water returns to a boil, decrease the heat to an active simmer, and process the jars for 10 minutes. Turn off the heat and leave the jars in the water for 1 to 2 minutes.

Using the jar lifter, transfer the jars from the pots to the baking sheet and let sit for at least 6 hours, until cool enough to handle. Check to be sure the jars have sealed (see page 34). Label and store the sealed jam for 6 months to 2 years. Once open, store in the refrigerator for up to 3 months.

Plums and Pluots

Some fruits are more interesting when used in condiments rather than prepared as a simple jam. Plums are like that. Plums tend to be tart and rather monochromatic until you add a bit of sugar. Sure, you can add anise or ginger to make them a bit more distinctive, but their powerful tartness will always dominate. However, when it comes to using plums in condiments and chutneys, you hit the jackpot. Because of their tart versatility, they pair well and hold up to other strong flavors. Russian and Georgian plum condiments are eaten with fried chicken or lamb, and Asian-inspired plum sauce is served with duck and pork spareribs. In Italian wine bars, spiced plum condiments are served as accompaniments to cheese plates. And plums make a great mostarda to serve with roast meats and poultry or even to enliven boiled beef or tongue.

For dramatic color, I prefer to use plums that are red on both the outside and inside, but for flavor, plums with yellow flesh will work, too. Japanese plums dominate the start of the season, followed by European varieties.

Japanese plum varieties with red flesh include Burgundy, Elephant Heart, and Satsuma.

Japanese varieties with amber flesh are Friar, Laroda, Mariposa, Santa Rosa, and Casselman.

Japanese green plums are Kelsey and Emerald Beauty.

European plum varieties, such as Italian prune plums, are smaller than Japanese ones, and are oval with purple-blue skin and yellow flesh. French prunes, the gages, and damson plums are also in this category. The Italian prune plums are meatier than the French ones and have a distinct seam so they are easier to cut, pit, and prepare.

We don't see damsons at my San Francisco market very often, so when local grower Blossom Bluff had them for sale, I jumped at the opportunity to preserve them. Their tart flesh is yellow but when cooked turns a remarkable shade of burgundy red, almost maroon. Because they are so small and difficult to pit, they require another cooking technique altogether from the other plums.

As for their name, damsons were supposedly first cultivated around Damascus in antiquity, and the Romans may have brought them to England. However, I have not found any Syrian recipes that use this plum, so this may just be a story to lend them mystique. It is more likely they are related to the tart, round bullace plums, such as the sloe or cherry plums

Let's start with an optimistic but unlikely premise: If the damsons are firm-ripe enough for you to pit them before cooking, do so, because the process will be less messy in the end. But this is a rare occurrence, so most recipes recommend cooking them whole, gently, in water for 45 minutes to 1 hour, until they break down. Then let them cool until you can handle them and pick out the pits with your fingers. It will look as if some terrible carnage has taken place in your kitchen, but you need to get rid of those pits! After you have removed all the pits, you can then put the pulp through a food mill or pulse it in a food processor, much as you do when preparing quince for jam, jelly, or membrillo. Even after cooking and pureeing, a few of those tiny pits always show up.

Damsons make an elegant jam, an excellent plum butter, and a really fine jelly. When cooked long enough, they will also set up into a firm paste that resembles membrillo. Oddly, in England this paste is called damson cheese, which to my mind is an unfortunate name, as it is served with cheese.

The pluot is part of a family of hybrids that includes plumcots, apriplums, and apriums. They are a cross between a plum and an apricot. The first-generation hybrids were the plumcot and apriplum. The pluots and apriums are later generations. The pluot, in my mind, is the most successful of all the crosses. Genetically speaking, pluots are one-quarter apricot and three-quarters plum. They were developed by Floyd Zaiger. The aprium is one-quarter plum and three-quarters apricot.

The most popular and tasty pluots are the Flavor King and Dapple Dandy. They may be used in preserving, but I think plums are a bit richer and tarter in flavor.

Flavor affinities for plums are anise, cinnamon, cloves, ginger, vanilla, orange, lemon, mint, basil, walnuts, black pepper, and pomegranate.

BASIC PLUM JAM

Although you can use water, using prune or pomegranate juice amplifies the flavor of the plums.

4 pounds plums

6 cups granulated sugar

Juice of 2 lemons, plus more as needed

1 cup prune juice, pomegranate juice, or water (optional)

Yield: 7 to 8 half-pint jars

Place 3 or 4 small plates in the freezer.

Halve, pit, and cut the plums into ½-inch dice. You will have about 8 cups.

In a large preserving pot, gently combine the plums, sugar, and lemon juice and toss to mix. Let sit overnight to macerate.

If the plums have not given off at least ½ cup of liquid by the next day, add the prune juice, pomegranate juice, or water.

Bring the plum mixture to a simmer over medium-low heat, stirring frequently and cooking until the fruit is very soft and the jam thickens.

Place a baking sheet on the counter near your stove. Heat a kettle of water. Set two stockpots on the stove and fill them with enough water to cover the jars by 1 to 2 inches. Bring the water to a boil over medium-high heat. Sterilize the jars (see page 32) in the water bath.

For a smooth texture, puree the cooked fruit with an immersion blender or mash with a potato masher. Continue to cook the mixture, stirring frequently, over medium-high heat until it coats the back of a wooden spoon and passes the plate test (see page 30), achieving a soft set that is a bit runny. Watch closely because this jam sets up really thick, even if it tests sort of runny. Opt for a looser set. Remove the pot from the heat.

Bring the water bath back to a boil. If the jars have cooled, warm them in the water bath or in a 200°F oven. Simmer the lids in a saucepan of hot water. Place the jars on the baking sheet.

Ladle the jam into the jars, leaving ¼-inch headspace. Wipe the rims clean and set the lids on the mouths of the jars. Twist on the rings.

Using a jar lifter, gently lower the jars into the pots. When the water returns to a boil, decrease the heat to an active simmer, and process the jars for 10 minutes. Turn off the heat and leave the jars in the water for 1 to 2 minutes.

Using the jar lifter, transfer the jars from the pots to the baking sheet and let sit for at least 6 hours, until cool enough to handle. Check to be sure the jars have sealed (see page 34). Label and store the sealed jam for 6 months to 2 years. Once open, store in the refrigerator for up to 3 months.

BURGUNDY PLUM
AND GINGER JAM

Because plums are so assertively tart, they need a hefty amount of ginger for its presence to be known.

5 pounds Burgundy plums	Juice of 2 lemons, plus more as needed
12 to 16 ounces ginger	1 cup prune juice (optional)
8 cups granulated sugar	

Yield: 8 half-pint jars

Place 3 or 4 small plates in the freezer.

Halve, pit, and cut the plums into ½-inch dice. You will have about 10 cups.

Peel the ginger and slice thin. Grind the ginger in the food processor. You want about 1 cup of ginger puree.

In a large preserving pot, gently combine the plums, sugar, ginger, and lemon juice and toss to mix. Let sit overnight to macerate. (If you do not have time to macerate, then add the prune juice along with the lemon juice.)

The next day, if the plums have not released much liquid, add the prune juice.

Place a baking sheet on the counter near your stove. Heat a kettle of water. Set two stock-pots on the stove and fill them with enough water to cover the jars by 1 to 2 inches. Bring the water to a boil over medium-high heat. Sterilize the jars (see page 32) in the water bath.

Bring the jam to a boil over medium-high heat and cook, stirring frequently, until the jam thickens and coats the back of a wooden spoon. Taste and add a squeeze more lemon juice, as needed. Do the plate test (see page 30). The jam should be a soft but slightly runny set. Watch closely because this jam sets up really thick, even if it tests sort of runny. Opt for a looser set. Remove the pot from the heat.

Bring the water bath back to a boil. If the jars have cooled, warm them in the water bath or in a 200°F oven. Simmer the lids in a saucepan of hot water. Place the jars on the baking sheet.

Ladle the jam into the jars, leaving ¼-inch headspace. Wipe the rims clean and set the lids on the mouths of the jars. Twist on the rings.

Using a jar lifter, gently lower the jars into the pots. When the water returns to a boil, decrease the heat to an active simmer, and process the jars for 10 minutes. Turn off the heat and leave the jars in the water for 1 to 2 minutes.

Using the jar lifter, transfer the jars from the pots to the baking sheet and let sit for at least 6 hours, until cool enough to handle. Check to be sure the jars have sealed (see page 34). Label and store the sealed jam for 6 months to 2 years. Once open, store in the refrigerator for up to 3 months.

BURGUNDY OR RED PLUM JAM WITH STAR ANISE AND BLACK PEPPER

If you like a bit of a kick, double the black pepper in this recipe.

This is a good partner for pork, poultry, and even a cheese assortment.

4 pounds Burgundy or other red plums

6 cups granulated sugar

1 cup prune juice or pomegranate juice

Juice of 2 lemons, plus more to taste

3 teaspoons ground star anise

1 teaspoon freshly ground black pepper, plus more as needed

1 teaspoon Chinese five-spice powder

Yield: 7 or 8 half-pint jars

Place 3 or 4 small plates in the freezer.

Halve, pit, and cut the plums into ½-inch dice. You will have about 8 cups.

In a large preserving pot, gently combine the plums, sugar, prune or pomegranate juice, lemon juice, star anise, black pepper, and five-spice powder and toss to mix.

Place a baking sheet on the counter near your stove. Heat a kettle of water. Set two stockpots on the stove and fill them with enough water to cover the jars by 1 to 2 inches. Bring the water to a boil over medium-high heat. Sterilize the jars (see page 32) in the water bath.

Bring the plum mixture to a boil over medium-high heat and cook, stirring frequently, until the jam thickens. Taste and adjust the seasoning, adding a squeeze more lemon juice or more pepper, if needed.

When the jam coats the back of a wooden spoon, do the plate test (see page 30). You want a soft set that mounds on the plate and is neither runny nor stiff. Watch closely because this jam sets up really thick, even if it tests sort of runny. Remove the pot from the heat.

Bring the water bath back to a boil. If the jars have cooled, warm them in the water bath or in a 200°F oven. Simmer the lids in a saucepan of hot water. Place the jars on the baking sheet.

Ladle the jam into the jars, leaving ¼-inch headspace. Wipe the rims clean and set the lids on the mouths of the jars. Twist on the rings.

Using a jar lifter, gently lower the jars into the pots. When the water returns to a boil, decrease the heat to an active simmer, and process the jars for 10 minutes. Turn off the heat and leave the jars in the water for 1 to 2 minutes.

Using the jar lifter, transfer the jars from the pots to the baking sheet and let sit for at least 6 hours, until cool enough to handle. Check to be sure the jars have sealed (see page 34). Label and store the sealed jam for 6 months to 2 years. Once open, store in the refrigerator for up to 3 months.

BALKAN PLUM AND POMEGRANATE CONSERVE

For this conserve, I prefer firm, red plums that are red all the way through, such as Burgundy or Elephant Heart, but Santa Rosa or even Italian prune plums will work, too. Walnuts and pomegranates are used extensively in preserves in the Balkans and Caucasus. Note that this recipe uses two forms of pomegranate—juice and molasses. The addition of walnuts and raisins turns this condiment into a conserve.

Serve with lamb, poultry, and even salmon. It is good with cheese as well.

4 pounds tart plums, preferably Burgundy, Santa Rosa, or Elephant Heart, but prune plums will also work

2 organic lemons

1 cup pomegranate juice

2 cups granulated sugar, plus more as needed

2 tablespoons ground coriander

1 teaspoon ground cinnamon

½ teaspoon ground allspice

1 tablespoon ground Maras or Aleppo pepper

2 teaspoons salt, plus more as needed

1 cup raisins, plumped in water to just cover

1 teaspoon freshly ground black pepper

¼ cup pomegranate molasses

¼ cup fresh lemon juice, plus more as needed

⅓ cup chopped fresh mint

1 cup chopped walnuts

Yield: About 11 half-pint jars

Place 3 or 4 small plates in the freezer.

Halve, pit, and cut the plums into ½-inch dice. You will have about 8 cups.

Cut the unpeeled lemons into quarters, remove any seeds, and place the quarters in the bowl of a food processor. Pulse until pulverized.

In a large preserving pot, gently combine the plums, lemons, pomegranate juice, sugar, coriander, cinnamon, allspice, Maras or Aleppo pepper, and salt and toss to mix.

Place two baking sheets on the counter near your stove. Heat a kettle of water. Set two stockpots on the stove and fill them with enough water to cover the jars by 1 to 2 inches. Bring the water to a boil over medium-high heat. Sterilize the jars (see page 32) in the water bath.

Bring the conserve to a boil over medium-high heat, decrease the heat, and simmer until the plums are tender, 10 to 20 minutes. Add the raisins, black pepper, pomegranate molasses, lemon juice, and mint. Continue to simmer, stirring frequently (to prevent the raisins from sinking and scorching), until the mixture thickens.

Taste and adjust the tart-sweet ratio, adding more sugar or lemon juice, as needed. Stir in the walnuts. Taste once more to check the salt level and add more if needed. Do a plate test (see page 30). The conserve should mound on the plate and not be runny. Remove the pot from the heat.

Bring the water bath back to a boil. If the jars have cooled, warm them in the water bath or in a 200°F oven. Simmer the lids in a saucepan of hot water. Place the jars on the baking sheets.

Ladle the conserve into the jars, leaving ¼-inch headspace. Wipe the rims clean and set the lids on the mouths of the jars. Twist on the rings.

Using a jar lifter, gently lower the jars into the pots. When the water returns to a boil, decrease the heat to an active simmer, and process the jars for 10 minutes. Turn off the heat and leave the jars in the water for 1 to 2 minutes.

Using the jar lifter, transfer the jars from the pots to the baking sheets and let sit for at least 6 hours, until cool enough to handle. Check to be sure the jars have sealed (see page 34). Label and store the sealed conserve for 6 months to 2 years. Once open, store in the refrigerator for up to 3 months.

PLUM JAM WITH ORANGE AND BLACK PEPPER

I first tasted a version of this condiment served alongside a cheese assortment in an Italian wine bar, and so it seemed logical to use Italian prune plums for the recipe. If you can't find them in your market, any other plum will work.

In the style of the Italians, I like to serve this jam with a cheese course. The slightly peppery prune plum sauce is especially good with robiola cheese and a glass of Amarone. Of course it is delicious with roast pork and chicken, too.

4 pounds Italian prune plums or other plums

2 organic oranges

1 cup water, prune juice, or pomegranate juice

3 cups granulated sugar

3 tablespoons fresh lemon juice, plus more as needed

2 teaspoons freshly ground black pepper

Pinch of salt

Yield: 8 or 9 half-pint jars

Place 3 or 4 small plates in the freezer.

Halve, pit, and quarter the plums. You will have about 8 cups.

Cut the unpeeled oranges into quarters, remove any seeds, and place the quarters in the bowl of a food processor. Pulse until pulverized.

In a large preserving pot, gently combine the plums, orange pulp, and water or juice and toss to mix.

Bring to a boil over medium-high heat, decrease the heat to low, and simmer until the plums are very soft.

Process the fruit mixture through a food mill or puree in a food processor.

Place two baking sheets on the counter near your stove. Heat a kettle of water. Set two stock-pots on the stove and fill them with enough water to cover the jars by 1 to 2 inches. Bring the water to a boil over medium-high heat. Sterilize the jars (see page 32) in the water bath.

Return the puree to the pot. It will be soupy. Add the sugar and lemon juice to taste and simmer over medium heat, stirring frequently, until it coats the back of a spoon and passes the plate test (see page 30), achieving a soft set that is neither runny nor stiff. Stir in the pepper and salt. Remove the pot from the heat.

Bring the water bath back to a boil. If the jars have cooled, warm them in the water bath or in a 200°F oven. Simmer the lids in a saucepan of hot water. Place the jars on the baking sheets.

Ladle the jam into the jars, leaving ¼-inch headspace. Wipe the rims clean and set the lids on the mouths of the jars. Twist on the rings.

Using a jar lifter, gently lower the jars into the pots. When the water returns to a boil, decrease the heat to an active simmer, and process the jars for 10 minutes. Turn off the heat and leave the jars in the water for 1 to 2 minutes.

Using the jar lifter, transfer the jars from the pots to the baking sheets and let sit for at least 6 hours, until cool enough to handle. Check to be sure the jars have sealed (see page 34). Label and store the sealed jam for 6 months to 2 years. Once open, store in the refrigerator for up to 3 months.

PLUM MOSTARDA

The mustard powder–mustard seed combination in this recipe is my attempt to come close to Italian mustard oil. It does not have the same degree of bite and heat, but it is pleasingly hot and sweet, which is the ultimate goal of a mostarda.

Surprise yourself and serve this condiment with poached or baked salmon. It is also good on porchetta, roast pork, chicken, and that bland old turkey. Or add it to ham sandwiches or charcuterie assortments.

3½ to 4 pounds firm red plums, such as Burgundy or Elephant Heart

1 organic orange

8 ounces fresh ginger, peeled and thinly sliced

2 cups apple cider vinegar or red wine vinegar

Grated zest and juice of 2 organic lemons

4 cups granulated sugar

3 tablespoons mustard seeds

6 tablespoons Colman's dry mustard powder

2 teaspoons salt

4 teaspoons freshly ground black pepper

1 teaspoon ground cayenne

Yield: 9 half-pint jars

Place 3 or 4 small plates in the freezer.

Halve and pit the plums, quartering or slicing the halves if large. You will have about 8 cups.

Cut the unpeeled orange into quarters, remove any seeds, and place the quarters in the bowl of a food processor. Add the ginger and ½ cup of the vinegar. Pulse until pulverized.

In a large preserving pot, gently combine the plums, orange-ginger mixture, remaining 1½ cups vinegar, lemon zest and juice, sugar, mustard seeds, mustard powder, salt, black pepper, and cayenne, and toss to mix.

Place two baking sheets on the counter near your stove. Heat a kettle of water. Set two stockpots on the stove and fill them with enough water to cover the jars by 1 to 2 inches. Bring the water to a boil over medium-high heat. Sterilize the jars (see page 32) in the water bath.

Bring the mostarda to a boil over medium-low heat. Decrease the heat to medium and cook, stirring frequently, until the mixture thickens and passes the plate test (see page 30), achieving a soft set that is neither runny nor stiff. Remove the pot from the heat.

Bring the water bath back to a boil. If the jars have cooled, warm them in the water bath or in a 200°F oven. Simmer the lids in a saucepan of hot water. Place the jars on the baking sheets.

Ladle the mostarda into the jars, leaving ¼-inch headspace. Wipe the rims clean and set the lids on the mouths of the jars. Twist on the rings.

Using a jar lifter, gently lower the jars into the pots. When the water returns to a boil, decrease the heat to an active simmer, and process the jars for 10 minutes. Turn off the heat and leave the jars in the water for 1 to 2 minutes.

Using the jar lifter, transfer the jars from the pots to the baking sheets and let sit for at least 6 hours, until cool enough to handle. Check to be sure the jars have sealed (see page 34). Label and store the sealed mostarda for 6 months to 2 years. Once open, store in the refrigerator for up to 3 months.

TKEMALI PLUM SAUCE

This Russo-Georgian plum sauce is traditionally served with *tabaka*, a sour cream and buttermilk-marinated fried chicken, but I have found that *tkemali* is good with all lamb and poultry kebabs, pork chops, roast pork, roast chicken, turkey, and lamb, as well as poached or grilled salmon. The herbs and heat make this sauce distinctive. As a variation, increase the cilantro or use mint or tarragon instead of basil. They love tarragon in the Caucasus.

4 pounds Italian prune plums or Burgundy plums	½ teaspoon ground cayenne
2 large organic lemons	½ teaspoon ground allspice
8 or 9 cloves garlic	1 tablespoon salt, plus more as needed
1 cup prune or pomegranate juice	½ cup chopped fresh basil
1 cup apple cider vinegar	½ cup chopped cilantro
4 cups granulated sugar or white sugar or 5 cups firmly packed light brown sugar	1 tablespoon freshly ground black pepper, plus more as needed
	Fresh lemon juice, as needed

Yield: About 10 half-pint jars

Place 3 or 4 small plates in the freezer.

Halve, pit, and quarter the prune plums. You will have about 8 cups.

Cut the unpeeled lemons into quarters, remove any seeds, and place the quarters in the bowl of a food processor. Pulse until pulverized.

Place two baking sheets on the counter near your stove. Heat a kettle of water. Set two stockpots on the stove and fill them with enough water to cover the jars by 1 to 2 inches. Bring the water to a boil over medium-high heat. Sterilize the jars (see page 32) in the water bath.

In a large preserving pot, gently combine the plums, lemons, garlic, prune or pomegranate juice, vinegar, sugar, cayenne, allspice.

Bring to a boil over medium heat, decrease the heat and simmer, stirring frequently. When the mixture reaches sauce consistency, stir in the basil, cilantro, and black pepper and simmer for 5 minutes.

Taste and add the lemon juice and additional salt, if needed. The sauce should be tart. Continue to simmer, stirring frequently, until the mixture passes the plate test (see page 30), achieving a soft set. Remove the pot from the heat.

Bring the water bath back to a boil. If the jars have cooled, warm them in the water bath or in a 200°F oven. Simmer the lids in a saucepan of hot water. Place the jars on the baking sheets.

Ladle the sauce into the jars, leaving ¼-inch headspace. Wipe the rims clean and set the lids on the mouths of the jars. Twist on the rings.

Using a jar lifter, gently lower the jars into the pots. When the water returns to a boil, decrease the heat to an active simmer, and process the jars for 10 minutes. Turn off the heat and leave the jars in the water for 1 to 2 minutes.

Using the jar lifter, transfer the jars from the pots to the baking sheets and let sit for at least 6 hours, until cool enough to handle. Check to be sure the jars have sealed (see page 34). Label and store the sealed sauce for 6 months to 2 years. Once open, store in the refrigerator for up to 3 months.

FRENCH PLUMS IN PORT SYRUP

Serve with ice cream, yogurt, or as a topping for custardy bread pudding.

2 pounds French plums

2 cups port

2 cups granulated sugar

1 cup water

½ cup orange juice

1 cinnamon stick, broken in half

1 vanilla bean, cut in half

2 long strips orange peel

1 teaspoon freshly ground black pepper

Yield: 2 pint jars

Prick each plum with a toothpick or paring knife (so they don't explode during cooking).

Combine the port, sugar, water, and orange juice in a medium nonaluminum saucepan. Bring to a boil over medium-high heat and boil for 3 minutes, stirring to dissolve the sugar. Add the cinnamon stick, vanilla bean, and orange peel and continue to boil for 5 minutes. Decrease the heat to medium-low.

When the poaching syrup is simmering, add the plums and simmer for 8 minutes. Turn off the heat and let sit overnight in a cool place.

The next day, place a baking sheet on the counter near your stove. Heat a kettle of water. Set a stockpot on the stove and fill it with enough water to cover the jars by 1 to 2 inches. Bring the water to a boil over medium-high heat. Sterilize two wide-mouth pint jars (see page 32) in the water bath.

Bring the plums and syrup to a boil over medium-high heat. Reduce the syrup by one-quarter as it thickens.

Bring the water bath back to a boil. If the jars have cooled, warm them in the water bath or in a 200°F oven. Simmer the lids in a saucepan of hot water. Place the jars on the baking sheet.

Place the jars on the baking sheet.

Using a slotted spoon, distribute the plums evenly between the jars. Ladle the syrup into the jars over the plums, leaving 1-inch headspace. Wipe the rims clean and set the lids on the mouths of the jars. Twist on the rings.

Using a jar lifter, gently lower the jars into the pot. When the water returns to a boil, set the timer for 15 minutes, decrease the heat to an active simmer, and process the jars. Turn off the heat and leave the jars in the water for 1 to 2 minutes.

Using the jar lifter, transfer the jars from the pot to the baking sheet and let sit for at least 6 hours, until cool enough to handle. Check to be sure the jars have sealed (see page 34). Label the sealed plums and let rest for 4 to 6 weeks before eating, then store for up to 1 year. Once open, store in the refrigerator for up to 1 week.

ASIAN-STYLE PLUM SAUCE

This homemade version is not as colorful as the electric-pink sauce served in your neighborhood Chinese restaurant, but it's twice as complex in flavor.

Just as you would enjoy it at the restaurant, serve it with barbecued pork or spareribs. It's also good with sautéed duck breast and even grilled fish.

3 to 4 pounds plums

1 yellow onion, coarsely chopped

4 cloves garlic

5 to 6 ounces ginger, peeled and thinly sliced

1 teaspoon ground cinnamon

1 teaspoon ground allspice

1 teaspoon Chinese five-spice powder

1 teaspoon ground star anise

2 small green apples, peeled, cored, and chopped (optional, for added pectin)

2 cups apple cider vinegar

2½ to 3 cups firmly packed brown sugar

2 teaspoons salt

Yield: 9 or 10 half-pint jars

Place 3 or 4 small plates in the freezer.

Halve and pit the plums, and cut the flesh into ½- to ¾-inch dice. You will have about 8 cups.

In the bowl of a food processor, combine the onion, garlic, ginger, cinnamon, allspice, five-spice powder, star anise, and apples. Pulse until pulverized and then pulse again with 1 cup of the vinegar.

In a large preserving pot, gently combine the plums, the pulverized spice mixture, remaining 1 cup of the vinegar, sugar, and salt, and toss to mix. Bring to a boil over medium-high heat.

Place two baking sheets on the counter near your stove. Heat a kettle of water. Set two stockpots on the stove and fill them with enough water to cover the jars by 1 to 2 inches. Bring the water to a boil over medium-high heat. Sterilize the jars (see page 32) in the water bath.

Cook the sauce, stirring frequently, over medium-high heat until it thickens and passes the plate test (see page 30), mounding on the plate and not runny. Remove the pot from the heat.

Bring the water bath back to a boil. If the jars have cooled, warm them in the water bath or in a 200°F oven. Simmer the lids in a saucepan of hot water. Place the jars on the baking sheets.

Ladle the sauce into the jars, leaving ¼-inch headspace. Wipe the rims clean and set the lids on the mouths of the jars. Twist on the rings.

Using a jar lifter, gently lower the jars into the pots. When the water returns to a boil, decrease the heat to an active simmer, and process the jars for 10 minutes. Turn off the heat and leave the jars in the water for 1 to 2 minutes.

Using the jar lifter, transfer the jars from the pots to the baking sheets and let sit for at least 6 hours, until cool enough to handle. Check to be sure the jars have sealed (see page 34). Label and store the sealed sauce for 6 months to 2 years. Once open, store in the refrigerator for up to 3 months.

PLUM CHUTNEY

Plums work so well in many condiments, making them a natural base for a tangy chutney.

3½ to 4 pounds plums

1½ cups raisins

Water, pomegranate juice, or prune juice, just to cover raisins

2 cups apple cider vinegar

8 ounces apples, peeled, cored and chopped

1 yellow onion, minced

4 cloves garlic, minced

3 serrano chiles, stemmed, seeded, and minced

2 teaspoons ground cinnamon

1 teaspoon ground allspice

1 teaspoon ground cloves

1 tablespoon ground ginger

1 tablespoon salt

3 cups granulated sugar

Yield: 11 half-pint jars

Halve, pit, and coarsely chop the plums. You will have about 8 cups.

In a small bowl, combine the raisins and water or juice and set aside for 5 minutes to plump.

In a large preserving pot, combine the plums, raisins and plumping liquid, vinegar, apples, onion, garlic, chiles, cinnamon, allspice, cloves, ginger, salt, and sugar and toss to mix.

Bring to a boil over medium-high heat, then decrease the heat to medium-low and simmer, stirring frequently, until the chutney thickens, about 30 minutes.

Place two baking sheets on the counter near your stove. Heat a kettle of water. Set two stockpots on the stove and fill them with enough water to cover the jars by 1 to 2 inches. Bring the water to a boil over medium-high heat. Sterilize the jars (see page 32) in the water bath.

Do a plate test (see page 30). The chutney should mound on the plate and be syrupy.

Bring the water bath back to a boil. If the jars have cooled, warm them in the water bath or in a 200°F oven. Simmer the lids in a saucepan of hot water. Place the jars on the baking sheets.

Ladle the chutney into the jars, leaving ¼-inch headspace. Wipe the rims clean and set the lids on the mouths of the jars. Twist on the rings.

Using a jar lifter, gently lower the jars into the pots. When the water returns to a boil, decrease the heat to an active simmer, and process the jars for 10 minutes. Turn off the heat and leave the jars in the water for 1 to 2 minutes.

Using the jar lifter, transfer the jars from the pots to the baking sheets and let sit for at least 6 hours, until cool enough to handle. Check to be sure the jars have sealed (see page 34). Label and store the sealed chutney for 6 months to 2 years. Once open, store in the refrigerator for up to 3 months.

PICKLED PLUMS

Allow these to mellow for about a month in the jar before you serve them as a sweet and tart condiment for charcuterie and other salumi.

Prick each plum with a toothpick or paring knife (so they don't explode during cooking).

6 cups granulated sugar

2 cups red wine vinegar

2 cinnamon sticks

2 tablespoons whole cloves

3 pounds underripe or firm Italian or French plums

Yield: 3 pint jars

Combine the sugar and vinegar in a medium nonaluminum saucepan. Bring to a boil over medium-high heat and boil for 3 minutes, stirring to dissolve the sugar. Add the cinnamon sticks and cloves and continue to boil for 3 more minutes. Decrease the heat to medium-low.

When the poaching syrup is simmering, add the plums and simmer for 3 minutes. Turn off the heat and let sit overnight in a cool place.

Place a baking sheet on the counter near your stove. Heat a kettle of water. Set a stockpot on the stove and fill it with enough water to cover the jars by 1 to 2 inches. Bring the water to a boil over medium-high heat. Sterilize the jars (see page 32) in the water bath; leave in the water to keep warm. Simmer the lids in a saucepan of hot water.

Bring the plums and syrup to a boil over medium-high heat.

Place the jars on the baking sheet.

Using a slotted spoon, transfer the plums to the jars.

Reduce the syrup by one-quarter. Spoon the hot syrup into the jars over the plums, leaving 1-inch headspace. Wipe the rims clean and set the lids over the mouths of the jars. Twist on the rings.

Bring the water bath back to a boil.

Using a jar lifter, gently lower the jars into the pot. When the water returns to a boil, decrease the heat to an active simmer, and process the jars for 15 minutes. Turn off the heat and leave the jars in the water for 1 to 2 minutes.

Using the jar lifter, transfer the jars from the pot to the baking sheet and let sit for at least 6 hours, until cool enough to handle. Check to be sure the jars have sealed (see page 34). Label and store the sealed plums for 6 months to 2 years. Once open, store in the refrigerator for up to 3 months.

PFLAUMENMUS

Italian prune plums are traditionally used for this rich German plum butter, but you could use damsons instead. For the final thickening, you can cook this on stove top or in the oven.

Plum butter is traditionally used as a filling for pastries and dumplings, and spooned on potato pancakes. It pairs well with butter, mascarpone, or clotted cream on toast, biscuits, or crepes. You can also spoon some atop soft polenta with mascarpone or ricotta. Not very German, but very good.

4 pounds Italian prune plums

3 cups granulated sugar

2 tablespoons fresh lemon juice, plus more as needed

1 teaspoon Chinese five-spice powder, or ½ teaspoon ground cloves and ½ teaspoon ground cinnamon, plus more as needed

Dash of vanilla extract (optional), plus more as needed

Yield: 5 half-pint jars

Place 3 or 4 small plates in the freezer.

Halve, pit, and chop the plums into small pieces. You will have about 8 cups.

In a wide, shallow preserving pot, combine the prune plums, 2 cups of the sugar, the lemon juice, five-spice powder or cloves and cinnamon, and the vanilla extract, and toss to mix. Let sit overnight to macerate.

Cook the plum mixture on the stove top over medium heat. When the plums are very soft, remove from the heat and set aside to cool to warm. Puree with a stick blender or food mill or in a food processor. Transfer the puree to the preserving pot.

Bring the puree to a simmer over low heat. Taste, and if you think the mixture needs sweetening, add the remaining 1 cup sugar, stirring with a wooden spoon. Let the mixture cook, stirring frequently until it thickens. Taste and adjust the seasoning, adding a bit more lemon juice, five-spice powder or cloves and cinnamon, and/or a few drops of vanilla extract.

If you prefer, instead of standing at the stove and stirring, you may complete the cooking in a 300°F oven; cook uncovered for about 1 hour, stirring the mixture every 10 to 15 minutes.

While the mixture thickens, place a baking sheet on the counter near your stove. Heat a kettle of water. Set two stockpots on the stove and fill it with enough water to cover the jars by 1 to 2 inches. Bring the water to a boil over medium-high heat. Sterilize the jars (see page 32) in the water bath.

Continue to simmer the mixture (or cook in the oven), stirring frequently, until the mixture thickens and passes the plate test (see page 30), mounding on the plate. Remove the pot from the heat.

Bring the water bath back to a boil. If the jars have cooled, warm them in the water bath or in a 200°F oven. Simmer the lids in a saucepan of hot water. Place the jars on the baking sheets.

Ladle the pflaumenmus into the jars, leaving ¼-inch headspace. Wipe the rims clean and set the lids on the mouths of the jars. Twist on the rings.

Using a jar lifter, gently lower the jars into the pots. When the water returns to a boil, decrease the heat to an active simmer, and process the jars for 15 minutes. Turn off the heat and leave the jars in the water for 1 to 2 minutes.

Using the jar lifter, transfer the jars from the pots to the baking sheets and let sit for at least 6 hours, until cool enough to handle. Check to be sure the jars have sealed (see page 34). Label and store the sealed pflaumenmus for 6 months to 2 years. Once open, store in the refrigerator for up to 3 months.

DAMSON PLUM JAM

This very delicious jam is worth the mess. I like a bit of cardamom as a seasoning. Mild fresh ginger and orange juice and zest might be added as well. These plums are so hard to find—unless you have a tree—that you might want to be a purist and not add any flavorings to them.

Serve the jam on toast. It is especially good paired with cream cheese or other soft cheeses.

3 pounds damson plums

1½ cups water

3 to 4 cups granulated sugar, plus more as needed

Juice of 1 lemon

1 teaspoon ground cardamom (optional)

Yield: 6 half-pint jars

Place 3 or 4 small plates in the freezer.

Stem, halve, pit, and quarter the plums, if possible. If you cannot pit the plums, just stem them.

In a small saucepan over medium-low heat, combine the water and plums. Cook until the plums are very soft. Turn off the heat and let sit to cool.

When the plums are cool enough to handle, remove the pits by hand.

Process the plums through a food mill, or puree in a food processor. Measure the pulp. You should have 3 to 4 cups, but note the exact amount because that determines the amount of sugar you will need to use for this recipe.

Measure out the sugar, using a ratio of 1 cup plum puree to 1 cup sugar.

Transfer the puree to a large preserving pot, and add the sugar. Stir in the lemon juice and cardamom.

Place a baking sheet on the counter near your stove. Heat a kettle of water. Set two stock-pots on the stove and fill them with enough water to cover the jars by 1 to 2 inches. Bring the water to a boil over medium-high heat. Sterilize the jars (see page 32) in the water bath.

Bring the plums to a simmer over medium heat and cook, stirring frequently, until the jam thickens and passes the plate test (see page 30), achieving a soft set that is a bit runny. These plums are pectin bombs, so the jam will set up rather quickly. Remove the pot from the heat.

Bring the water bath back to a boil. If the jars have cooled, warm them in the water bath or in a 200°F oven. Simmer the lids in a saucepan of hot water. Place the jars on the baking sheet.

Ladle the jam into the jars, leaving ¼-inch headspace. Wipe the rims clean and set the lids on the mouths of the jars. Twist on the rings.

Using a jar lifter, gently lower the jars into the pots. When the water returns to a boil, decrease the heat to an active simmer, and process the jars for 10 minutes. Turn off the heat and leave the jars in the water for 1 to 2 minutes.

Using the jar lifter, transfer the jars from the pots to the baking sheet and let sit for at least 6 hours, until cool enough to handle. Check to be sure the jars have sealed (see page 34). Label and store the sealed jam for 6 months to 2 years. Once open, store in the refrigerator for up to 3 months.

VARIATIONS

— For Damson Plum Butter: Double the Damson Plum Jam recipe, cooking 6 pounds of plums and sterilizing 8 or 9 half-pint jars. Combine the fruit puree, sugar, and lemon juice. Heat the puree slowly, stirring frequently, over medium to low heat. After 15 to 20 minutes of cooking, you may want to use a splatter screen if the mixture pops much. Continue cooking, stirring frequently, over low heat, until very thick. You may also complete this butter in the oven, as explained in Pflaumenmus (page 152). Process the jars for 15 minutes in the water bath. From 6 pounds of Damsons, sometimes I get 6 cups of puree; other times I get 8 cups. The variance depends on the size of the plums and the ratio of pit to flesh. As for the amount of sugar needed, ratios vary in recipes, but the average is about equal parts sugar to puree.

— For the membrillo-like Damson Plum Paste: Add 2 to 3 teaspoons grated ginger to the plum jam and cook the mixture until it is so thick that your spoon leaves a trail on the bottom of the pot when dragged through. Line two 8-inch baking pans with parchment paper and coat with cooking spray. (An 8-inch pan holds about 4 cups of plum paste.) Alternatively, lightly oil four half-pint jars (which you will seal and process as you do for the plum butter). Ladle half of the puree into one pan; it should be about 1 inch deep. Ladle the remaining puree into the other pan. Let sit at room temperature until it sets up, about 24 hours. When fully set, wrap the paste completely in parchment, place in a plastic container with a tight-fitting lid, and store in a cool place for 1 to 2 years.

Eggplant

Eggplants originated in southern and eastern Asia and were transported to Spain by the Moors during the Middle Ages. Because they are a fruit, eggplants were served fried and sprinkled with sugar or honey in medieval Spain. So while sweet eggplant preserves may seem a bit strange to those with a Western mindset, treating eggplants as a fruit and preserving them in a rich sugar syrup has a long tradition in the Mediterranean and Sephardic kitchen. The preserved eggplants were served at the end of the meal as an accompaniment to tea, sort of like a Greek spoon sweet.

Most of the recipes for preserving whole eggplants—whether Moroccan, Lebanese, or Arabic in origin—say to soak them in cold water for a day, changing the water three times. A few recipes even say to do this for three days! This step is supposed to cut the bitterness, but the sweet tiny young eggplants that I preserve whole are not very bitter. Nonetheless, I respect tradition, so I soak them, but only overnight.

Another note about eggplant jams and preserves: Most fruit is inherently sweet, so rarely do you use an equal weight of fruit and sugar. Eggplant is an exception; the ratio of sugar to fruit is higher than for a conventional preserve or jam.

MOROCCAN CANDIED EGGPLANT

Known as *confit d'aubergines* in Morocco, these are traditionally served as a sweet with tea after a meal, but you could add them to a lamb tagine instead. If you wish to reduce the amount of refined sugar, use 4 cups sugar and top off each jar with ½ cup of honey.

2½ to 3 pounds small Japanese or round baby eggplants

3 cups water

6 cups granulated sugar

2 cinnamon sticks

12 whole cloves

1 tablespoon ground ginger, or 4 to 5 tablespoons fresh ginger, cut into very thin julienne

½ cup fresh lemon juice

1½ to 2 cups dark honey (optional)

Yield: 3 or 4 pint jars

Prick the eggplants all over with the tines of a fork. Leave the stems attached and trim away the leaves. If you like, peel away the skin in vertical strips so the eggplants have a striped appearance. Soak the eggplants in a bowl of cold water overnight, changing the water a few times. Drain.

Bring a large pan of lightly salted water to a boil over medium-high heat. Add the eggplants and cook for about 10 minutes. Drain again. When the eggplants are cool enough to handle, squeeze them with your hands to rid them of excess water.

In a preserving pot over low heat, combine the 3 cups water, sugar, cinnamon sticks, cloves, and ginger. Simmer the mixture over low heat until it is as thick as honey. Add the lemon juice and eggplants and continue to simmer for 5 to 10 minutes. Turn off the heat and let the eggplants rest for 1 hour. Repeat the process of simmering over low heat and resting three times. The syrup will have reduced and the eggplants will have absorbed most of it, becoming plumped up, tender, and translucent. Remove the pot from the heat.

While the eggplants are cooking, place a baking sheet on the counter near your stove. Heat a kettle of water. Set a stockpot on the stove and fill it with enough water to cover the jars by 1 to 2 inches. Bring the water to a boil over medium-high heat. Sterilize 4 jars (see page 32); leave in the water to keep warm.

Simmer the lids in a saucepan of hot water. Place the jars on the baking sheet.

Remove and discard the whole spices. Using tongs or a slotted spoon, transfer the eggplants to the hot, sterilized jars. If the syrup is thick, spoon it into the jars, leaving 1-inch headspace. If it is not, return the pot to medium-high heat, bring to a gentle boil, and reduce until the syrup thickens, and then spoon it into the jars. (Any excess syrup can be stored in a glass jar with a tight-fitting lid and refrigerated for up to 2 weeks; use for another preserve.)

Spoon honey to taste into the jars, on top of the syrup. Run a chopstick around the inside edge of the jars to distribute the syrup and break up any air bubbles. Wipe the rims clean and set the lids on the mouths of the jars. Twist on the rings.

Bring the water bath back to a boil.

Using a jar lifter, gently lower the jars into the pot. When the water returns to a boil, decrease the heat to an active simmer, and process the jars for 15 minutes. Turn off the heat and leave the jars in the water for 1 to 2 minutes.

Using the jar lifter, transfer the jars from the pot to the baking sheet and let sit for at least 6 hours, until cool enough to handle. Check to be sure the jars have sealed (see page 34). Label and store the sealed candied eggplant for 6 months to 2 years. Once open, store in the refrigerator for up to 3 months.

EGGPLANT CONSERVE

This recipe originates in the Republic of Georgia. A similar preserve is prepared in the Black Sea region of Turkey. And it is akin in flavor to the Moroccan Jewish dish *barania* that is served to break the fast after Yom Kippur. You can cut back on the sugar and add some vinegar to make this sweet and sour (more like a chutney), or add a few tablespoons of honey to make it sweeter.

Serve with clotted cream or mascarpone on bread or toast, or as a condiment for cooked lamb or poultry.

3 pounds small eggplants, peeled and cut into ½-inch dice	¼ teaspoon ground allspice
Grated zest and juice of 3 lemons	½ to ¾ cup raisins
6 cups granulated sugar	¼ cup chopped candied ginger (optional)
2 to 3 tablespoons grated fresh ginger	2 to 4 tablespoons honey (optional)
½ teaspoon ground cinnamon	2¼ to 2½ teaspoons citric acid crystals (optional)

Yield: 9 to 10 half-pint jars

In a stockpot over medium-high heat, bring lightly salted water to a boil. Add the eggplants and blanch until soft, 5 to 8 minutes. Pour into a colander and set aside to drain well.

In a preserving pot over medium-high heat, combine the eggplant, lemon zest and juice, sugar, fresh ginger, cinnamon, and allspice. Bring to a boil, decrease the heat to medium-low, simmer 5 minutes, and then set aside to rest for 1 to 2 hours.

Place two baking sheets on the counter near your stove. Heat a kettle of water. Set two stockpots on the stove and fill them with enough water to cover the jars by 1 to 2 inches. Bring the water to a boil over medium-high heat. Sterilize the jars (see page 32) in the water bath.

Return the pot to medium-high heat and bring back to a boil. Decrease the heat to medium-low and simmer until thick, adding the raisins, candied ginger, and honey during the last 10 to 15 minutes of cooking as the mixture begins to thicken. The raisins may drink up more than their share of pan juices, so you may have to loosen the mixture with enough water to keep it soft and spoonable when you do the plate test (see page 30). Remove the pot from the heat.

Bring the water bath back to a boil. If the jars have cooled, warm them in the water bath or in a 200°F oven. Simmer the lids in a saucepan of hot water. Place the jars on the baking sheets.

As a precaution, spoon ¼ teaspoon citric acid into each jar before filling. Ladle the conserve into the hot, sterilized jars, leaving ¼-inch headspace. Wipe the rims clean and set the lids on the mouths of the jars. Twist on the rings.

Using a jar lifter, gently lower the jars into the pots. When the water returns to a boil, decrease the heat to an active simmer, and process the jars for 15 minutes. Turn off the heat and leave the jars in the water for 1 to 2 minutes.

Using the jar lifter, transfer the jars from the pots to the baking sheets and let sit for at least 6 hours, until cool enough to handle. Check to be sure the jars have sealed (see page 34). Label and store the sealed conserve for 6 months to 2 years. Once open, store in the refrigerator for up to 3 months.

LEBANESE EGGPLANT AND WALNUT CONSERVE

I use the pale lavender Fairy Tale eggplant for this preserve. Some cooks make a slit in each one and tuck in a walnut or almond, but I just add the nuts to the syrup.

 This is an ideal sweetmeat to serve with cheese after a meal.

2½ pounds (16 to 18) 3-inch-long baby eggplants

1 lemon, sliced

4 cups granulated sugar

3 cups water

2 cinnamon sticks

6 whole cloves

3 or 4 thin strips lemon peel (optional)

24 walnut halves, left whole or coarsely chopped

¼ cup fresh lemon juice, or a bit more as needed

1 splash vanilla extract or rose water (optional)

2 teaspoons citric acid crystals

Yield: 3 to 4 pint jars

Prick the eggplants all over with the tines of a fork. Trim away the stems and leaves. Soak the eggplants in a bowl of cold water mixed with a few lemon slices overnight, changing the water once or twice. Drain.

 In a preserving pot over medium-high heat, bring the sugar, 3 cups water, cinnamon sticks, cloves, and lemon peel to a boil. Add the eggplants and walnuts and cook for 5 to 10 minutes. Set aside to rest for 1 hour.

 Place a baking sheet on the counter near your stove. Heat a kettle of water. Set a stockpot on the stove and fill it with enough water to cover the jars by 1 to 2 inches. Bring the water to a boil over medium-high heat. Sterilize the jars (see page 32) in the water bath.

 Add the lemon juice to the eggplant, return the pot to medium-high heat, and boil again for 5 to 10 minutes. Repeat the boiling and resting until the eggplants are translucent. Add the vanilla or rose water. Taste the syrup and adjust the seasoning. Remove the pot from the heat.

 Bring the water bath back to a boil. If the jars have cooled, warm them in the water bath or in a 200°F oven. Simmer the lids in a saucepan of hot water. Place the jars on the baking sheet. As a precaution, spoon ½ teaspoon citric acid into each jar.

 Spoon the eggplant and their syrup into the jars, leaving 1-inch headspace. (Any excess syrup can be stored in a glass jar with a tight-fitting lid and refrigerated for up to 2 weeks; use for another preserve.) Run a knife along the inside of the jars to distribute the syrup and break up any air bubbles. Wipe the rims clean and set the lids on the mouths of the jars. Twist on the rings.

 Using a jar lifter, gently lower the jars into the pot. When the water returns to a boil, decrease the heat to an active simmer, and process the jars for 15 minutes. Turn off the heat and leave the jars in the water for 1 to 2 minutes.

 Using the jar lifter, transfer the jars from the pot to the baking sheet and let sit for at least 6 hours, until cool enough to handle. Check to be sure the jars have sealed (see page 34). Label and store the sealed conserve for 6 months to 2 years. Once open, store in the refrigerator for up to 1 month.

Tomatoes

Like the potato, eggplant, and pepper, the tomato is a member of the nightshade family. It originated in Central and South America and was first used as a food in Mexico. Its name is derived from the Aztec *tomatl* or *jitomatl*. It was discovered during the era of Spanish exploration of the New World, and, along with peppers, vanilla, chocolate, and corn, was transported to Europe on return voyages. The tomato was planted in Spain in the early 1540s but languished as an ornamental plant for years because people did not know if it was safe to eat.

Eventually the tomato was fondly embraced by cooks all over the Mediterranean, but it took a while. Although tomatoes came to Italy in 1548, they were not used in Italian cooking until the late seventeenth century. The earliest Italian recipe for tomatoes was published in 1692, inspired by a Spanish recipe. The tomato was not grown in England until almost 1600. It was introduced in the Middle East circa 1800 by the English ambassador to Aleppo.

The tomato is a fruit but, like eggplant and squashes, has been treated culinarily as a vegetable because if its relatively mild sweetness. In the 1880s, U.S. tariff laws imposed a duty on vegetables (but not fruits). Because tomatoes were not eaten for dessert and instead used as a savory for the main meal, it was officially declared a vegetable by the United States Supreme Court in 1893.

Some of us may have fond memories of eating vine-ripened tomatoes gathered from a home garden. With commercial distribution, the deliciousness of tomatoes has been greatly diminished. Commercial tomatoes are picked green, hard, and unripe for ease of shipping, and later gassed to bring up the bright red color shoppers seek. No wonder we have become disillusioned with supermarket tomatoes! Grow your own if you can or shop at farmers' markets, where the tomatoes are picked ripe and still have aroma. Look for the kinds of tomatoes that offer the most tomato flavor—sweet, earthy, and with some acidity. Beefsteak tomatoes are best for eating in salads and sandwiches, as are the so-called heirloom varieties, as well as the dry-farmed Early Girls. Plum tomatoes and pear-shaped San Marzanos are traditionally used in cooking because they have fewer seeds and the least water content of all the varieties, so they reduce into richer sauces. While some farmers' market plum tomatoes have good flavor, the average supermarket plum tomato can be bland and cottony. Cherry tomatoes, such as Sweet One Hundreds or Sun Golds, are not only good to eat out of hand but cook down into wonderful chunky preserves.

GREEN TOMATO CHUTNEY

For those of you with gardens, this is what you can do with the end-of-season tomatoes that will not have time to ripen. This chutney is good with poultry and fish.

8 ounces ginger, peeled and thinly sliced

2 cups apple cider vinegar, plus more as needed

2 teaspoons ground cinnamon

½ teaspoon ground cloves

4½ pounds green tomatoes, cored and coarsely diced

3 pounds green apples, peeled, cored, and diced

2 to 3 pounds yellow onions

4 or 5 stalks celery (optional)

1 tablespoon salt

4 cups firmly packed brown sugar

Ground cayenne, as needed

2 cups raisins

Water, as needed

Yield: 5 pint jars

In the bowl of a food processor, puree the ginger and ½ cup of the vinegar. Add the cinnamon and cloves and puree again.

In a large preserving pot over medium-high heat, combine the ginger puree, tomatoes, apples, onions, celery, salt, and brown sugar. Add the remaining 1½ cups vinegar and bring to a boil. Decrease the heat and simmer, stirring occasionally, for about 25 minutes.

Place a baking sheet on the counter near your stove. Heat a kettle of water. Set two stockpots on the stove and fill them with enough water to cover the jars by 1 to 2 inches. Bring the water to a boil over medium-high heat. Sterilize the jars (see page 32) in the water bath.

Add the cayenne and raisins to the pot and continue to cook, stirring frequently (to prevent the raisins from sinking and scorching), until the mixture thickens and passes the plate test (see page 30), with pieces of fruit in a syrupy sauce. If the mixture is dry, add water or more vinegar to thin. Remove the pot from the heat.

Bring the water bath back to a boil. If the jars have cooled, warm them in the water bath or in a 200°F oven. Simmer the lids in a saucepan of hot water. Place the jars on the baking sheet.

Ladle the chutney into the jars, leaving ¼-inch headspace. Wipe the rims clean and set the lids on the mouths of the jars. Twist on the rings.

Using a jar lifter, gently lower the jars into the pots. When the water returns to a boil, decrease the heat to an active simmer, and process the jars for 10 minutes. Turn off the heat and leave the jars in the water for 1 to 2 minutes.

Using the jar lifter, transfer the jars from the pots to the baking sheet and let sit for at least 6 hours, until cool enough to handle. Check to be sure the jars have sealed (see page 34). Label and store the sealed chutney for 6 months to 2 years. Once open, store in the refrigerator for up to 3 months.

BASIC SWEET TOMATO JAM

Like the eggplant, the tomato is an example of a fruit that we use as a vegetable. We're more accustomed to seeing ketchup on the shelves, but a sweet tomato jam shouldn't surprise us.

I often serve a salad that combines sliced tomatoes and sliced peaches, as they complement each other so well in sweetness and acidity. As variation, you can use half tomatoes and half peaches for this jam. Vanilla is an optional flavor enhancer.

4 pounds flavorful tomatoes, such as Early Girls or Beefsteaks or red Heirlooms

4 cups granulated sugar, plus more as needed

Juice of 1 lemon, plus more as needed

Grated zest of 1 lemon (optional)

1 vanilla bean, cut up or ground with 1 cup of the sugar (optional)

Salt

Up to 1 cup Homemade Apple Pectin (page 200)

Yield: 4 half-pint jars

Place 3 or 4 small plates in the freezer.

Line a baking sheet with paper towels. Bring a stockpot of water to a boil over medium-high heat. Cut a cross on the bottom of each tomato and cut out the cores. Using a slotted spoon, dip the tomatoes in the boiling water for 1 to 2 minutes, then set on the baking sheet. When cool enough to handle, remove and discard the skins. Cut the tomatoes in half and, holding each over the sink, scoop out the seeds with your fingers and discard. Cut the tomatoes into a large dice. Place the tomatoes in a colander and set aside to drain for 1 to 2 hours.

Transfer the tomatoes to a preserving pot over medium-low heat and add the sugar, lemon juice and zest, vanilla, and salt. Bring to a simmer for a few minutes. Taste and add more sugar, if needed. Turn off the heat and set aside to rest for 1 to 2 hours, or as long as overnight.

Place a baking sheet on the counter near your stove. Heat a kettle of water. Set a stockpot on the stove and fill it with enough water to cover the jars by 1 to 2 inches. Bring the water to a boil over medium-high heat. Sterilize the jars (see page 32) in the water bath.

Bring the tomato mixture to a boil over medium-high heat and cook, stirring often, until it thickens. This could take a while, longer than a half hour, maybe even an hour, depending on the amount of moisture in the tomatoes, so be patient, and vigilant, and stir often. Taste and add more lemon juice if you think it needs it. Do a plate test (see page 30). The jam should not be runny when you tilt the plate. If it is still too runny, continue cooking and stirring. Taste the jam and if you fear you risk ending up with a too-cooked flavor (when the taste of the fresh fruit is literally cooked away), add some of the apple pectin and cook 5 minutes more, and then repeat the plate test. If the jam is still too runny, add more apple pectin, cook, stir, and repeat the plate test until the jam passes. Remove the pot from the heat.

Bring the water bath back to a boil. If the jars have cooled, warm them in the water bath or in a 200°F oven. Simmer the lids in a saucepan of hot water. Place the jars on the baking sheet.

Ladle the jam into the jars, leaving ¼-inch headspace. Wipe the rims clean and set the lids on the mouths of the jars. Twist on the rings.

Using a jar lifter, gently lower the jars into the pot. When the water returns to a boil, decrease the heat to an active simmer, and process the jars for 15 minutes. Turn off the heat and leave the jars in the water for 1 to 2 minutes.

Using the jar lifter, transfer the jars from the pot to the baking sheet and let sit for at least 6 hours, until cool enough to handle. Check to be sure the jars have sealed (see page 34). Label and store the sealed jam for 6 months to 2 years. Once open, store in the refrigerator for up to 3 months.

VARIATIONS

— Use 2 pounds of tomatoes and 2 pounds of peaches, peeled, pitted, and chopped. Add the peaches to the tomatoes when you add the sugar and then macerate overnight. Taste and add more lemon juice as needed.

— Add cinnamon to the mixture instead of the vanilla, or a few tablespoons of chopped fresh mint at the end of cooking.

— Add juice and zest strips of 1 orange, blanching the zest in boiling water for 1 minute, two to three times.

MOROCCAN-SPICED SWEET AND HOT CHERRY TOMATO PRESERVES

I started making cherry tomato preserves in 1968. My original recipe was inspired by one in Catherine Plagemann's *Fine Preserving*. I added the Moroccan seasoning in 1985 so I could serve this with Square One restaurant's Moroccan mixed grills. I have used both red and yellow cherry tomatoes for this preserve. The red ones hold their color longer. The light brown sugar adds a slightly deeper note, but you can use only granulated sugar if you want to see more of the tomatoes' color in the final product.

This condiment is great with lamb burgers or chops, roast chicken or turkey, or even grilled eggplant.

8 ounces fresh ginger, peeled and thinly sliced across the grain

1 teaspoon ground cayenne

1 tablespoon ground cinnamon

1 teaspoon ground cloves

1 tablespoon ground cumin

1 cup apple cider vinegar

8 cups (4 pint baskets) cherry tomatoes, stemmed

2 cups firmly packed light brown sugar

2 cups granulated sugar

2 large, juicy lemons, sliced paper-thin on a mandoline, seeded, and slices cut into eighths

¾ cup water

1 teaspoon salt, plus more as needed

½ teaspoon freshly ground black pepper

Yield: Makes 4 to 5 pint or 8 to 10 half-pint jars

Place 3 or 4 small plates in the freezer.

In the container of a food processor or blender, grind the ginger with the cayenne, cinnamon, cloves, cumin, and vinegar.

In a large preserving pot over high heat, combine the spice mixture, tomatoes, brown and granulated sugars, lemon slices, water, salt, and pepper, stirring to combine. Bring to a boil over high heat and cook for about 15 minutes.

Place one or two baking sheets on the counter near your stove. Heat a kettle of water. Set two stockpots on the stove and fill them with enough water to cover the jars by 1 to 2 inches. Bring the water to a boil over medium-high heat. Sterilize the jars (see page 32) in the water bath.

Decrease the heat under the tomatoes to medium and cook the mixture, stirring frequently, until it is thick and passes the plate test (see page 30). It should not be very runny. Season to taste with salt. Remove the pot from the heat.

Bring the water bath back to a boil. If the jars have cooled, warm them in the water bath or in a 200°F oven. Simmer the lids in a saucepan of hot water. Place the jars on the baking sheet(s).

Ladle the preserves into the jars, leaving ¼-inch headspace. Wipe the rims clean and set the lids on the mouths of the jars. Twist on the rings.

Using a jar lifter, gently lower the jars into the pots. When the water returns to a boil, decrease the heat to an active simmer, and process the jars for 10 minutes. Turn off the heat and leave the jars in the water for 1 to 2 minutes.

Using the jar lifter, transfer the jars from the pots to the baking sheet(s) and let sit for at least 6 hours, until cool enough to handle. Check to be sure the jars have sealed (see page 34). Label and store the sealed preserves for 6 months to 2 years. Once open, store in the refrigerator for up to 3 months.

SPICY TOMATO KETCHUP

Traditionally, ketchup was a savory condiment, and this recipe follows that flavor path.

This is, of course, good with burgers, lamb chops, and fried potatoes.

6 pounds flavorful red tomatoes

2 yellow onions

2 tablespoons minced garlic

1 tablespoon salt

1 tablespoon sweet paprika or sweet and smoky Pimentón de la Vera

1 teaspoon ground cinnamon

½ teaspoon ground cloves

1 to 2 tablespoons ancho chile powder

1 teaspoon freshly ground black pepper

½ to 1 teaspoon ground cayenne

1 cup apple cider vinegar

4 to 6 tablespoons light brown sugar

¾ teaspoon citric acid crystals

Yield: 3 pint jars

Place 3 or 4 small plates in the freezer.

Line a baking sheet with paper towels. Bring a stockpot of water to a boil over medium-high heat. Cut a cross on the bottom of each tomato and cut out the cores. Using a slotted spoon, dip the tomatoes in the boiling water for 1 to 2 minutes, then set on the baking sheet. When cool enough to handle, remove the skins and discard. Cut the tomatoes in half and, holding each over the sink, scoop out the seeds with your fingers. Place the tomato halves in the bowl of a food processor and pulse until smooth. You will have 10 to 12 cups. Transfer the tomato pulp to a large preserving pot.

Puree the onions in the food processor. Add the onions to the preserving pot.

Place a baking sheet on the counter near your stove. Heat a kettle of water. Set a stockpot on the stove and fill it with enough water to cover the jars by 1 to 2 inches. Bring the water to a boil over medium-high heat. Sterilize the jars (see page 32) in the water bath.

Place the tomato mixture over medium heat and add the garlic, salt, paprika, cinnamon, cloves, chile powder, black pepper, ½ teaspoon of the cayenne, the vinegar, and 4 tablespoons of the brown sugar. Cook, stirring frequently, until the mixture thickens. Taste and add the remaining ½ teaspoon cayenne and 2 tablespoons of brown sugar, as needed. Continue to cook until the ketchup reduces by half and passes the plate test (see page 30), achieving a soft set that mounds on the plate and is not runny. Remove the pot from the heat.

Bring the water bath back to a boil. If the jars have cooled, warm them in the water bath or in a 200°F oven. Simmer the lids in a saucepan of hot water. Place the jars on the baking sheet.

Spoon ¼ teaspoon of citric acid into each sterilized jar.

Ladle the ketchup into the jars, leaving ¼-inch headspace. Wipe the rims clean and set the lids on the mouths of the jars. Twist on the rings.

Using a jar lifter, gently lower the jars into the pot. When the water returns to a boil, decrease the heat to an active simmer, and process the jars for 20 minutes. Turn off the heat and leave the jars in the water for 1 to 2 minutes.

Using the jar lifter, transfer the jars from the pot to the baking sheet and let sit for at least 6 hours, until cool enough to handle. Check to be sure the jars have sealed (see page 34). Label and store the sealed ketchup for 6 months to 2 years. Once open, store in the refrigerator for up to 3 months.

TURKISH TOMATO AND POBLANO RELISH

This is a wonderful tart, spicy relish that I first tasted many years ago at a small restaurant on the Asian side of Istanbul. The restaurant, now long gone, specialized in the regional food of Gazantiep (near the Syrian border) and this relish, called *ezme,* (which I now know is synonymous with "sauce") was served as an accompaniment to lamb sausage and puffed flatbread. Pomegranate molasses adds that ineffable sweet-sour finish that cannot be replicated with sugar and lemon. If you can't find poblano peppers, use jalapeños, but increase the amount. You can order the Turkish red pepper known as *kirmizi biber* from Kalustyans in New York City.

Be sure that that the tart-sweet elements dominate and the heat is just a mild buzz on the tongue. Test this by dipping a piece of bread into the relish to see if it is well seasoned.

Serve the relish with pita bread or as a condiment for lamb, chicken, and fish. And, of course, on lamb burgers.

2 fresh poblano chiles

2 pounds ripe red tomatoes

1 yellow onion

2 tablespoons minced garlic

½ teaspoon ground Aleppo or Maras pepper or cayenne, or more or less (depending on heat of peppers)

1 teaspoon sweet paprika or Turkish paprika (kirmizi biber; see headnote)

¼ cup pomegranate molasses, plus more as needed

⅓ cup apple cider vinegar

2 tablespoons brown sugar

1½ teaspoons salt

1 teaspoon citric acid crystals

Roast the poblanos on a griddle or over a direct flame until the skin is black and charred. Place the peppers in a paper bag or small plastic container with the lid on and let steam for 15 minutes. Peel, seed, and finely chop the chiles. You will have about ½ cup.

Line a baking sheet with paper towels. Bring a stockpot of water to a boil over medium-high heat. Cut a cross on the bottom of each tomato and cut out the cores. Using a slotted spoon, dip the tomatoes in the boiling water for 1 to 2 minutes, then set on the baking sheet. When cool enough to handle, remove the skins and discard. Cut the tomatoes in half and, holding each over the sink, scoop out the seeds with your fingers. Coarsely chop the tomato halves. You will have about 4 cups.

In the bowl of a food processor, puree the onion.

Place a baking sheet on the counter near your stove. Heat a kettle of water. Set a stockpot on the stove and fill it with enough water to cover the jars by 1 to 2 inches. Bring the water to a boil over medium-high heat. Sterilize the jars (see page 32) in the water bath.

In a large preserving pot over medium heat, combine the tomatoes, onion, garlic, Aleppo or Maras pepper, and paprika and cook until the mixture thickens. Add the roasted chiles, pomegranate molasses, vinegar, brown sugar, and salt. Simmer, stirring frequently, until thick. Taste and add more pomegranate molasses and ground pepper as needed. Remove the pot from the heat.

Yield: 3 or 4 half-pint jars

Bring the water bath back to a boil. If the jars have cooled, warm them in the water bath or in a 200°F oven. Simmer the lids in a saucepan of hot water. Place the jars on the baking sheet.

Spoon ¼ teaspoon of citric acid into each sterilized jar.

Ladle the relish into the jars, leaving ¼-inch headspace. Run a knife along the inside of the jars to break up any air bubbles. Wipe the rims clean and set the lids on the mouths of the jars. Twist on the rings.

Using a jar lifter, gently lower the jars into the pot. When the water returns to a boil, decrease the heat to an active simmer, and process the jars for 20 minutes. Turn off the heat and leave the jars in the water for 1 to 2 minutes.

Using the jar lifter, transfer the jars from the pot to the baking sheet and let sit for at least 6 hours, until cool enough to handle. Check to be sure the jars have sealed (see page 34). Label and store the sealed relish for 6 months to 2 years. Once open, store in the refrigerator for up to 3 months.

TOMATO SAUCE

A few years ago, in a mad moment of seasonal enthusiasm or temporary insanity, my daughter-in-law, Barbara, and I peeled, seeded, and chopped 35 pounds of tomatoes and cooked them down into sauce. The sauce was delicious, but the process was so messy and time-consuming that I vowed never to do it again.

Our family goes through lots of tomato sauce, so naturally I eventually bought two tomato strainers—the Victorio and the KitchenAid mixer attachment—to expedite the processing. Through experimenting, I found that processing uncooked tomatoes produces sauce with the freshest flavor and the deepest color, and for that you need a tomato strainer. Soon after, Barbara and I processed more than 90 pounds of tomatoes. I guess you could say we are obsessed.

The yield from the food mill and the coarse strainer in the Victorio is similar. There will be some seeds but no peel. You will have to reduce the puree produced this way less than if you use the fine strainer.

If you use the fine strainer on the Victorio or KitchenAid, the yield will be a bit more but the puree will be much thinner and you will need to reduce the sauce longer, cutting your final yield.

If you do not have a Victorio tomato strainer or KitchenAid attachment, do not get too ambitious and try to make such a large batch.

If you want to put up a large batch of tomato sauce, first you need to make a decision about tomato variety. You want to use the most flavorful, sweet tomatoes with ample acidity, so taste as many varieties as you can. Most supermarket tomatoes are dismal and overly refrigerated. The average Roma tomato is highly touted for sauce because it has fewer seeds and less waste. I often find Romas bland and cottony, without much tomato flavor or acidity, so taste before automatically choosing them. If you shop at farmers' markets you will have better luck.

At my farmers' markets, I can get assorted heirloom tomatoes, San Marzanos (sort of an Italian Roma), and dry-farmed Early Girls. Heirloom tomatoes are often great for flavor but can be watery, so if you use them expect to significantly reduce the puree to produce a sauce that is thick enough the jar. Heirloom varieties are more expensive than Early Girls and San Marzanos, as well; look for the heaviest, most dense varietals. You can also opt to use a blend of varieties.

For my sauce, I use a blend of San Marzanos and dry-farmed Early Girls. Sauce made from only San Marzanos is earthy, deep, and very tomato-y. It tastes like Italy. The sauce made from Early Girls is sweet, tastes like truly great tomatoes, and delivers the largest yield.

What follows is a recipe for an all-purpose sauce—not marinara—that you can customize by adding onions, garlic, and herbs. It is endlessly adaptable to any recipe and keeps in the jar for more than a year. The final yield depends on how watery the tomatoes are and how long you reduce the sauce to achieve the texture you prefer.

CONTINUED

20 pounds San Marzano
or Early Girl tomatoes

2 to 3 tablespoons salt

2½ teaspoons citric
acid crystals or
10 tablespoons
bottled lemon juice

12 to 16 basil leaves
(optional)

Yield: 6 to 8 quart or 12 to 16 pint jars

You have two options for making sauce without a tomato strainer. One method: Bring a stockpot of water to a boil over medium-high heat. Cut a cross on the bottom of each tomato and cut out the cores. Using a slotted spoon, dip the tomatoes in the boiling water for 1 to 2 minutes and then set on the baking sheet. When cool enough to handle, remove the peels and discard. Cut the tomatoes in half and, holding each over the sink, scoop out the seeds with your fingers and discard. Transfer the tomatoes to a cutting board set over a baking sheet, to capture any juices, and chop them. Transfer the tomatoes and juice to a large stainless steel or enamel-covered, cast-iron preserving pot. (Aluminum interacts badly with tomatoes, and the acid in tomatoes can interact badly with copper.) Cook over medium heat until the tomatoes reach the desired saucelike consistency.

The second method is to use a food mill: Core the tomatoes. Peel them if you prefer (see previous step). Coarsely chop the tomatoes and transfer them and their juice to a large stainless steel or enamel-covered, cast-iron preserving pot. Cook over medium heat for 10 to 15 minutes, until they soften and give off more juice.

Then set the mill over a bowl and process the warm tomatoes. Return the puree to the pot over medium heat and reduce to desired saucelike consistency.

If you have a Victorio strainer or KitchenAid attachment, which enables you to process raw tomatoes, cut up the tomatoes so they fit in the feeding chute. Process the tomatoes into a bowl. Collect the peels and seeds in another container as they emerge from the machine and discard them. With luck, you will have about 16 cups of puree, depending upon the tomatoes that you use.

Transfer the tomato puree to the preserving pot and bring to a simmer over medium-low heat. Cook down until the puree thickens into a saucelike consistency. Add the salt to taste at the end of cooking.

Place two baking sheets on the counter near your stove. Heat a kettle of water. Set two stockpots on the stove and fill them with enough water to cover the jars by 1 to 2 inches. Bring the water to a boil over medium-high heat. Sterilize the jars and lids (see page 32) in the water bath.

Place the jars on the baking sheets.

If using quart jars, add ½ teaspoon citric acid or 2 tablespoons bottled lemon juice to each sterilized jar before adding the tomatoes. If using pint jars, add ¼ teaspoon citric acid or 1 tablespoon bottled lemon juice. Add 1 or 2 basil leaves to each jar.

Ladle the sauce into the jars, leaving ¼-inch headspace. Run a knife along the inside of the jars to break up any air bubbles. Wipe the rims clean and set the lids on the mouths of the jars. Twist on the rings.

Using a jar lifter, gently lower the jars into the pots. When the water returns to a boil, decrease the heat to an active simmer, and process the jars for 45 minutes for quarts and 35 minutes for pints. Turn off the heat and leave the jars in the water for 1 to 2 minutes.

Using the jar lifter, transfer the jars from the pots to the baking sheets and let sit for at least 6 hours, until cool enough to handle. Check to be sure the jars have sealed (see page 34). Label and store the sealed sauce for 6 months to 2 years. Once open, store in the refrigerator for up to 3 months.

VARIATIONS

— In case you want to do a small batch or enough for a year's supply, here are my ratios for scaling:

- 2½ pounds San Marzanos produces ¾ quart of puree and reduces to 2 cups of sauce.

- 2½ pounds Early Girls produces 1 quart of puree and reduces to 2½ cups of sauce.

- 10 pounds Early Girls produces 4½ to 5 quarts of puree and reduces to 3½ to 4 quarts of sauce.

- 10 pounds San Marzanos produces 3½ to 4 quarts of puree and reduces to 3 quarts of sauce.

- 20 pounds San Marzanos produces 8 quarts of puree and reduces to 6 quarts of sauce.

- 20 pounds Early Girls produces 9 to 10 quarts of puree and reduces to 7½ to 8 quarts of sauce.

- 40 pounds tomatoes reduces to 14 to 16 quarts of sauce.

Figs

Because I grew up in New York, I did not experience the joy of eating fresh figs. We could buy dried figs from Greece, and they were good but dangerously chewy for a girl with braces. When I moved to Italy, I finally understood the seductive deliciousness of this most-prized fruit. To me, the fig is the quintessential fruit of the Mediterranean.

The fig tree is not native to the Mediterranean but was brought there in Roman times from Asia Minor. It was known to the Sumerians and the Assyrians. The best figs were thought to be from Smyrna. The Phoenicians and the Greeks were responsible for spreading fig cultivation in the ancient world. In the 1880s, the first cuttings of Calimyrna figs were planted in California at the Spanish missions, soon followed by what we now call Black Mission figs.

The fig varieties available include Black Mission, Turkey, Adriatic, and Panache (green with white stripes and very red flesh). Figs have two crops. The first is in late June, but the larger crop with more flavorful fruit comes in the fall, usually in September. Perfumed, voluptuous, fragile, and, dare I say, sexy, the fig is best when eaten out of hand, warm and perfectly ripe. For eating, you want the ones that are cracked and oozing a bit of juice. When you buy figs, eat the softest and ripest ones first. The ones that are slightly firm will soften a bit when stored at room temperature, but you must arrange them on a tray or plate so they are not touching. (That way, they will resist molding.) Figs have a brief shelf life at room temperature, usually 1 to 2 days. Refrigeration will keep them from spoiling for a few more days but will cause them to lose their perfume and some of their voluptuousness. Buy a little more than 3 pounds of figs—some to eat within a day or two and the rest to preserve. You won't be sorry.

Natural flavor affinities for figs are orange and lemon, cinnamon, cloves, fennel, bay, ginger, Chinese five-spice powder, anise, star anise, vanilla, raspberry, walnuts, and almonds.

As an added safety precaution, if there is not much lemon juice in your preserves, you may add a bit of citric acid (¼ teaspoon per half pint) or 1 tablespoon of bottled lemon juice to the jars before you fill them.

Serve fig preserves on toast, with cheese assortments, on grilled cheese sandwiches, on ham and cheese, or atop ricotta toast. Or with soft polenta and mascarpone. Or warmed and spooned on cheesecake or almond cake. They are also good paired with grilled or roast pork, poultry, ham, and duck.

SPICED FIG JAM

You can make a simple fig jam without the spices or the ground-up citrus or ginger. But as the fig season is short and the fruit so fragile, I do not want to make the simplest, just the best. When you dip a spoon into this jam, it will remind you of late summer all winter long.

This jam is great on toast with cream cheese or mascarpone, paired with blue cheese and walnut bread, or spread on a grilled cheese sandwich. It also may be used as a cookie filling or with soft polenta and mascarpone for breakfast.

3 pounds ripe Black Mission figs

4 cups granulated sugar

1 small organic lemon, unpeeled, cut into chunks, seeds removed

1 small organic orange, unpeeled, cut into chunks, seeds removed

4 ounces fresh ginger, peeled and thinly sliced across the grain (optional)

⅓ cup orange juice

¼ cup fresh lemon juice, plus more as needed

2 teaspoons ground cinnamon or Chinese five-spice powder

Yield: About 10 half-pint jars

Place 3 or 4 small plates in the freezer.

Stem the figs and cut them into 1- to 1½-inch chunks. (There's no need to peel them because the peel gives this jam a gorgeous maroon color.)

In a large preserving pot, combine the cut figs and sugar. Set aside to macerate for a few hours or preferably overnight if you have time.

In the bowl of a food processor, grind the lemon, orange, and ginger to a fine puree. Add to the figs, which should have given off quite a bit of liquid. Add the orange juice, lemon juice, and cinnamon or five-spice powder, stir well, and bring to a boil over medium-high heat, stirring occasionally. Decrease the heat to low and simmer for 10 minutes, stirring often. Let rest for 2 hours.

Place two baking sheets on the counter near your stove. Heat a kettle of water. Set two stockpots on the stove and fill them with enough water to cover the jars by 1 to 2 inches. Bring the water to a boil over medium-high heat. Sterilize the jars (see page 32) in the water bath.

Taste the figs and add more lemon juice if the mixture seems dry or needs acidity. Return the mixture to medium-low heat and simmer until thickened, stirring frequently to prevent scorching. Do a plate test (see page 30). The mixture should mound on the plate. Remove the pot from the heat.

Bring the water bath back to a boil. If the jars have cooled, warm them in the water bath or in a 200°F oven. Simmer the lids in a saucepan of hot water. Place the jars on the baking sheets.

Ladle the jam into the jars, leaving ¼-inch headspace. Wipe the rims clean and set the lids on the mouths of the jars. Twist on the rings.

Using a jar lifter, gently lower the jars into the pots. When the water returns to a boil, decrease the heat to an active simmer, and process the jars for 10 minutes. Turn off the heat and leave the jars in the water for 1 to 2 minutes.

Using the jar lifter, transfer the jars from the pots to the baking sheets and let sit for at least 6 hours, until cool enough to handle. Check to be sure the jars have sealed (see page 34). Label and store the sealed jam for 6 months to 2 years. Once open, store in the refrigerator for up to 3 months.

FIG PRESERVES WITH PORCHETTA FLAVORS

I like to pair fresh or dried figs with roast pork, especially with pork that is seasoned in the manner of Italian porchetta, with sage, rosemary, garlic, fennel, and black pepper. A word of advice: Stay by the stove to stir the preserves during the last 30 minutes of cooking, so that the figs do not scorch.

In addition to roast pork, serve this preserve with roast chicken, turkey, or lamb; at brunch or after dinner with cheese; or spread on toast with mascarpone.

2 pounds ripe Black Mission or green Adriatic figs

2 cups granulated sugar

Grated zest of 2 lemons

1 cup water or apple juice, as needed

2 fresh bay leaves

1 sprig rosemary in a sachet or tea ball

1½ to 2 teaspoons ground fennel seeds

1 teaspoon ground cloves

1 teaspoon freshly ground black pepper

Pinch of salt

½ cup fresh lemon juice, or a bit more as needed

Yield: 6 to 8 half-pint jars

Place 3 or 4 small plates in the freezer.

Stem and halve the figs, cutting them into quarters if they are large. In a large preserving pot, combine the cut figs and sugar. Set aside to macerate overnight.

The next day, add the lemon zest and just enough water or juice to barely cover the fruit. Add the bay leaves, rosemary, fennel, cloves, pepper, and salt and stir well. Bring to a boil over medium heat, stirring occasionally to prevent scorching and sticking. Decrease the heat and simmer for 15 minutes. Turn off the heat and set aside and let rest for 1 hour, to allow the figs to plump up a bit.

Place a baking sheet on the counter near your stove. Heat a kettle of water. Set two stockpots on the stove and fill them with enough water to cover the jars by 1 to 2 inches. Bring the water to a boil over medium-high heat. Sterilize the jars (see page 32) in the water bath.

Bring the fig mixture to a boil again and cook over medium heat, stirring frequently, until the preserves are thick and large bubbles appear on the surface. Add the lemon juice to taste during the last 10 minutes of cooking. Cook until the preserves pass the plate test (see page 30), achieving a soft set that mounds on the plate. (These preserves set up quickly.) Discard the bay leaves and rosemary sachet. Remove the pot from the heat.

Bring the water bath back to a boil. If the jars have cooled, warm them in the water bath or in a 200°F oven. Simmer the lids in a saucepan of hot water. Place the jars on the baking sheet.

Ladle the preserves into the jars, leaving ¼-inch headspace. Wipe the rims clean and set the lids on the mouths of the jars. Twist on the rings.

Using a jar lifter, gently lower the jars into the pots. When the water returns to a boil, decrease the heat to an active simmer, and process the jars for 10 minutes. Turn off the heat and leave the jars in the water for 1 to 2 minutes.

Using the jar lifter, transfer the jars from the pots to the baking sheet and let sit for at least 6 hours, until cool enough to handle. Check to be sure the jars have sealed (see page 34). Label and store the sealed preserves for 6 months to 2 years. Once open, store in the refrigerator for up to 3 months.

SICILIAN FIG MARMALADE

This recipe, known as *marmellata di fichi* in Italy, is inspired by one from Anna Tasca Lanza, a fine cook who ran a cooking school at Regaleali Winery for many years and wrote three lovely books about the food of Sicily. Keep an eye on the figs as they cook, so the mixture doesn't get too thick too quickly. The subtle hint of heat adds an intriguing note to this sweet marmalade.

Serve the marmalade with cheesecake, with polenta pound cake, or on toast.

2 cups dry white wine

2 cups granulated sugar

4 pounds ripe Black Mission or other figs, quartered

2 teaspoons ground cinnamon

Juice of 1 lemon

¼ teaspoon ground cayenne or other ground chile

Yield: 8 half-pint jars

Place 3 or 4 small plates in the freezer.

Place a baking sheet on the counter near your stove. Heat a kettle of water. Set two stockpots on the stove and fill them with enough water to cover the jars by 1 to 2 inches. Bring the water to a boil over medium-high heat. Sterilize the jars (see page 32) in the water bath.

In a preserving pot over medium-low heat, combine the wine and sugar and bring to a simmer, stirring to dissolve the sugar. Add the figs and cook over medium heat for about 20 minutes, stirring so the mixture does not stick. Add the cinnamon, lemon juice, and cayenne and cook until the jam thickens and passes the plate test (see page 30), achieving a soft set that mounds on the plate. Remove the pot from the heat.

Bring the water bath back to a boil. If the jars have cooled, warm them in the water bath or in a 200°F oven. Simmer the lids in a saucepan of hot water. Place the jars on the baking sheet.

Ladle the marmalade into the jars, leaving ¼-inch headspace. Wipe the rims clean and set the lids on the mouths of the jars. Twist on the rings.

Using a jar lifter, gently lower the jars into the pots. When the water returns to a boil, decrease the heat to an active simmer, and process the jars for 10 minutes. Turn off the heat and leave the jars in the water for 1 to 2 minutes.

Using the jar lifter, transfer the jars from the pots to the baking sheet and let sit for at least 6 hours, until cool enough to handle. Check to be sure the jars have sealed (see page 34). Label and store the sealed marmalade for 6 months to 2 years. Once open, store in the refrigerator for up to 3 months.

FIG CHUTNEY

The heat of the ground chile add excitement, and the Lapsang Souchong tea adds a hint of smoke.

Serve the chutney with poultry, lamb, or cheese.

1 large red onion, cut into chunks

2 organic lemons, unpeeled, cut into eighths, seeds removed

8 ounces fresh ginger, peeled and sliced

3 cups apple cider vinegar, plus more as needed

3 pounds just-ripe Black Mission figs

4 cups firmly packed brown sugar

1 tablespoon salt, plus more as needed

1 teaspoon ground cinnamon

1 teaspoon ground cloves

2 teaspoons ground Maras or Aleppo chile

1 tablespoon Lapsang Souchong tea, ground to a powder

½ teaspoon freshly ground black pepper, or ¼ teaspoon ground cayenne (optional)

1 cup raisins (optional)

Water, as needed

Yield: 7 pint jars

Combine the onion, lemons, and ginger in the bowl of a food processor and pulse until finely chopped. Add a splash of the vinegar and pulse once or twice.

Stem and halve the figs, cutting them into quarters if they are large.

In a large preserving pot over medium-low heat, combine the onion-ginger mixture, figs, the remainder of the vinegar, and the brown sugar, salt, cinnamon, cloves, ground chile, and tea and then simmer for 20 minutes. Set aside to allow the figs to plump.

Place a baking sheet on the counter near your stove. Heat a kettle of water. Set two stockpots on the stove and fill them with enough water to cover the jars by 1 to 2 inches. Bring the water to a boil over medium-high heat. Sterilize the jars (see page 32) in the water bath.

Return the figs to medium-high heat and continue to cook, adding the tea and black pepper. After 20 minutes, add the raisins, keeping an eye on the amount of liquid in the chutney, as raisins tend to drink up the juices, and you do not want this to be too dry. Add water or more vinegar to loosen the chutney, if necessary. Cook until the mixture passes the plate test (see page 30), with pieces of fruit in a syrupy sauce.

Bring the water bath back to a boil. If the jars have cooled, warm them in the water bath or in a 200°F oven. Simmer the lids in a saucepan of hot water. Place the jars on the baking sheet.

Ladle the chutney into the jars, leaving ¼-inch headspace. Wipe the rims clean and set the lids on the mouths of the jars. Twist on the rings.

Using a jar lifter, gently lower the jars into the pots. When the water returns to a boil, decrease the heat to an active simmer, and process the jars for 10 minutes. Turn off the heat and leave the jars in the water for 1 to 2 minutes.

Using the jar lifter, transfer the jars from the pots to the baking sheet and let sit for at least 6 hours, until cool enough to handle. Check to be sure the jars have sealed (see page 34). Label and store the sealed chutney for 6 months to 2 years. Once open, store in the refrigerator for up to 3 months.

FIG AND PEAR PRESERVES

Their paths cross in mid-fall, the figs on their way out and the pears on their way in, so I always have to jump to it to capture this happy confluence of flavors and textures. I use Black Mission figs, but Adriatic or green figs work well, too, and offer a lighter color profile. Substituting other figs does not change the taste, just the aesthetic. Aomboon Deasy at K & J, one of my local farms in the San Francisco Bay Area, grows Panache figs, which are green with white stripes on the outside and raspberry flesh. Deasy also cultivates Italian Morettini pears, which are pale green, some with a blush of red on the outside. They are fragrant and hold their shape without breaking down. If you can't get Morettinis, use Comice or not-too-soft Bartletts, so the pear slices are still identifiable after cooking. If you like, you could increase the amount of pears by 8 ounces, in which case you'd probably get six half-pint jars instead of five.

Serve with cheese, lamb, poultry, and pork. This would also be good with soft polenta or on polenta croutons with a bit of soft robiola cheese.

1½ pounds ripe figs, stemmed and chopped

1 pound small pears, peeled, cored, and sliced

3 cups granulated sugar

Grated zest and juice of 1 orange

Grated zest and juice of 1 lemon, or a bit more as needed

1 teaspoon cardamom seeds, crushed or coarsely ground

1¼ teaspoons citric acid crystals

Yield: 5 half-pint jars

Place 3 or 4 small plates in the freezer.

In a large preserving pot, combine the figs, pears, sugar, orange zest and juice, lemon zest and juice, and cardamom. Let sit overnight to macerate. Alternatively, bring the pot to a boil over medium-high heat and cook for 2 minutes, then set aside, uncovered, for 1 hour.

Place a baking sheet on the counter near your stove. Heat a kettle of water. Set two stockpots on the stove and fill them with enough water to cover the jars by 1 to 2 inches. Bring the water to a boil over medium-high heat. Sterilize the jars (see page 32) in the water bath.

Return the pot to medium-high heat and bring to a boil. Cook until the mixture thickens and passes the plate test (see page 30), mounding on the plate. Remove the pot from the heat.

Bring the water bath back to a boil. If the jars have cooled, warm them in the water bath or in a 200°F oven. Simmer the lids in a saucepan of hot water. Place the jars on the baking sheet. Add ½ teaspoon citric acid to each jar.

Ladle the preserves into the jars, leaving ¼-inch headspace. Wipe the rims clean and set the lids on the mouths of the jars. Twist on the rings.

Using a jar lifter, gently lower the jars into the pots. When the water returns to a boil, set the timer for 15 minutes, decrease the heat to an active simmer, and process the jars. Turn off the heat and leave the jars in the water for 1 to 2 minutes.

Using the jar lifter, transfer the jars from the pots to the baking sheet and let sit for at least 6 hours, until cool enough to handle. Check to be sure the jars have sealed (see page 34). Label and store the sealed preserves for 6 months to 2 years. Once open, store in the refrigerator for up to 3 months.

WHOLE SPICED FIGS
IN TEA SYRUP

Cooking figs in tea is an old culinary tradition. Black Mission figs make the most beautiful red syrup, but you could do this with green figs as well.

These are delicious served over ice cream, panna cotta, or simple pound cake or with soft cheese.

1½ pounds ripe figs, with short stems	3 (1½- to 2-inch-long) strips lemon zest
2½ cups granulated sugar	2 tablespoons julienned fresh, young ginger
2½ cups water	½ teaspoon citric acid crystals, or 2 tablespoons bottled lemon juice
2 Earl Grey tea bags, or another fragrant tea	
2 star anise pods	Fresh lemon juice, as needed
1 cinnamon stick	

Yield: 3 pint jars

Prick the figs once with a skewer or knife point.

In a saucepan, combine the sugar, water, tea bags, star anise, cinnamon stick, lemon zest, and ginger and bring to a boil over medium-high heat. Decrease the heat to low and simmer for 5 minutes. Add the figs and simmer over low heat until they feel soft and tender, about 30 minutes.

Place a baking sheet on the counter near your stove. Heat a kettle of water. Set a stockpot on the stove and fill it with enough water to cover the jars by 1 to 2 inches. Bring the water to a boil over medium-high heat. Sterilize the jars (see page 32) in the water bath. Simmer the lids in a saucepan of hot water.

Place the jars on the baking sheet.

Spoon ¼ teaspoon citric acid or 1 tablespoon bottled lemon juice into each sterilized jar. Remove the figs from the syrup with a slotted spoon and transfer them to the jars.

Discard the tea bags, star anise, and cinnamon stick from the syrup. Taste the syrup and add a bit of fresh lemon juice if you think it is needed. If the syrup seems thin, reduce over medium-low heat until it thickens, about 10 minutes. Remove the pot from the heat.

Ladle the syrup into the jars, leaving 1-inch headspace. Wipe the rims clean and set the lids on the mouths of the jars. Twist on the rings.

Using a jar lifter, gently lower the jars into the pot. When the water returns to a boil, decrease the heat to an active simmer, and process the jars for 15 minutes. Turn off the heat and leave the jars in the water for 1 to 2 minutes.

Using the jar lifter, transfer the jars from the pot to the baking sheet and let sit for at least 6 hours, until cool enough to handle. Check to be sure the jars have sealed (see page 34). Label and store the sealed syrup for 6 months to 2 years. Once open, store in the refrigerator for up to 3 months.

VARIATIONS

— Instead of the star anise, cinnamon, and ginger, flavor the syrup with 2 bay leaves, fennel seed, and 1 vanilla bean, cut into 3 pieces.

— Substitute 1 cup red or white wine and 1½ cups water for the 2½ cups water.

Mid-September Through
Mid-November

Fall

Pears

I am of the opinion that pears are better eaten fresh than turned into jam. I guess others share this view, and that is probably why you don't see lots of pear preserves on the shelves. The exception might be pear butter, which is not quite as popular as apple butter. I prefer to preserve pear halves or slices in syrup, or pickle them. Unlike apples, pears are low in pectin and need to be acidified for safe preserving. Pears are good for chutney, which is vinegar-based. When I put them up, I use lots of fresh lemon juice or add bottled lemon juice or citric acid crystals.

There are two kinds of pears: European and Asian. In most instances, you want to use European pears for preserving. They are sweet, fine-grained in texture, and can be creamy on the tongue when ripe. They have a good balance of sweetness and mild acidity. Look for pears that are firm-ripe but not soft. Pears will ripen at room temperature at home. Very firm green ones may take longer than a week. Pears bruise easily, so handle them with care, or you will be cutting out brown spots.

The best pears for preserving are Comice, Anjou, and Bartlett (which are the same as the European Williams pear). One of my local farm stands has Morettini pears, which resemble Comice in texture and flavor but are smaller in size and thus ideal for preserving in syrup.

A word about Asian pears, (which are sometimes called apple pears): They are crisp and sweet but do not have much acidity. Unlike regular pears, they ripen on the tree. The ripe fruit is yellow-brown or yellow-green. They can be stored for about one week at room temperature and up to two months in the refrigerator. In other words, they are hardy! But they do not have the voluptuous texture of a ripe European pear nor the European pear's balanced contrast of sweetness and acidity. Because of their excellent crunch, you may want to use them in chutneys, but not in jams or butters as they are not creamy enough.

Complementary flavor pairings for pears are vanilla, citrus, cinnamon, anise, ginger, and cloves.

PEAR BUTTER

This one is delicately perfumed with lemon and vanilla and not too sweet. It is ideal for topping toast and pancakes.

3 pounds Comice or Bartlett pears, peeled, cored, and chopped

Grated zest and juice of 2 lemons, plus more juice as needed

¾ cup water

2 cups granulated sugar

2 teaspoons vanilla extract, plus more as needed

1½ teaspoons citric acid crystals

Yield: 6 half-pint jars

Place 3 or 4 small plates in the freezer.

In a large preserving pot over medium heat, combine the pears, lemon zest and juice, and water. Cook until the pears are soft, 20 to 30 minutes. When the pears are translucent and tender, puree them through a food mill or in the bowl of a food processor. Return the puree to the pot.

Place a baking sheet on the counter near your stove. Heat a kettle of water. Set two stock-pots on the stove and fill them with enough water to cover the jars by 1 to 2 inches. Bring the water to a boil over medium-high heat. Sterilize the jars (see page 32) in the water bath.

Return the fruit puree to low heat and add the sugar and vanilla. Increase the heat to medium and cook, stirring frequently, until the mixture thickens. It may spit and pop a bit, so if you have a splatter screen, you may want to use it. Wear long pot-holder gloves, too. Alternatively, after 15 minutes of stove-top cooking you may transfer the mixture to a shallow baking pan and finish the butter in a 300°F oven, stirring every 10 to 15 minutes until the mixture is very thick. This can take 60 minutes or longer. Add a bit more lemon or vanilla to taste. Do the plate test (see page 30); the pear butter should mound and hold its shape. Remove the pot from the heat.

Bring the water bath back to a boil. If the jars have cooled, warm them in the water bath or in a 200°F oven. Simmer the lids in a saucepan of hot water. Place the jars on the baking sheet.

Spoon ¼ teaspoon citric acid into each jar.

Ladle the pear butter into the jars, leaving ¼-inch headspace. Wipe the rims clean and set the lids on the mouths of the jars. Twist on the rings.

Using a jar lifter, gently lower the jars into the pots. When the water returns to a boil, decrease the heat to an active simmer, and process the jars for 15 minutes. Turn off the heat and leave the jars in the water for 1 to 2 minutes.

Using the jar lifter, transfer the jars from the pots to the baking sheet and let sit for at least 6 hours, until cool enough to handle. Check to be sure the jars have sealed (see page 34). Label and store the sealed pear butter for 6 months to 2 years. Once open, store in the refrigerator for up to 3 months.

VARIATIONS

— Use 1 cup of vanilla sugar (see page 22) in place of 1 cup of the granulated sugar and omit the vanilla extract.

— You can also spice pear butter with ½ teaspoon or more of ground cinnamon, ginger, or cloves (choose two of the three) instead of vanilla. Using freshly grated ginger is also an option. Add it to the pears during the initial cooking.

PEAR CHUTNEY

I often use Anjou or Comice pears for this chutney, but I also like Asian pears for their nice crunch and shape retention. No citric acid is needed, because ample vinegar and citrus are included.

Serve the chutney with curries, roast chicken, or pork. It also pairs well with cheese and is great on a grilled cheese sandwich.

5 ounces ginger, peeled and sliced	2½ cups firmly packed light brown sugar
1 large yellow onion, diced	1 teaspoon ground cloves
2 organic oranges, unpeeled, cut into chunks	1 teaspoon ground cinnamon
1½ to 2 cups apple cider vinegar	1 teaspoon salt
5 pounds firm-ripe Anjou or Comice pears or Asian pears, peeled, cored, and cut into large dice	½ teaspoon ground cayenne
	1½ cups golden raisins
	Water or apple juice, as needed

Yield: 4 to 5 pint jars

Place 3 or 4 small plates in the freezer.

Combine the ginger, onion, oranges, and a splash of the vinegar in the bowl of a food a processor and pulse until pureed.

In a large preserving pot over medium heat, combine the pears and orange mixture, 1½ cups vinegar, brown sugar, cloves, cinnamon, salt, and cayenne. Cook over medium heat, stirring occasionally, until the mixture thickens.

Place a baking sheet on the counter near your stove. Heat a kettle of water. Set two stockpots on the stove and fill them with enough water to cover the jars by 1 to 2 inches. Bring the water to a boil over medium-high heat. Sterilize the jars (see page 32) in the water bath.

When the chutney is thick, add the raisins, stirring frequently (to prevent the raisins from sinking and scorching), and cook for 15 to 20 minutes longer. If the raisins start to drink all of the liquid, add a bit more water, apple juice, or apple cider vinegar to keep the mixture syrupy. Do a plate test (see page 30). The chutney should mound on the plate but still be syrupy. If the chutney is not ready, cook a few more minutes and repeat the plate test until it passes. Remove the pot from the heat.

Bring the water bath back to a boil. If the jars have cooled, warm them in the water bath or in a 200°F oven. Simmer the lids in a saucepan of hot water. Place the jars on the baking sheet.

Ladle the chutney into the jars, leaving ¼-inch headspace. Wipe the rims clean and set the lids on the mouths of the jars. Twist on the rings.

Using a jar lifter, gently lower the jars into the pots. When the water returns to a boil, decrease the heat to an active simmer, and process the jars for 10 minutes. Turn off the heat and leave the jars in the water for 1 to 2 minutes.

Using the jar lifter, transfer the jars from the pots to the baking sheet and let sit for at least 6 hours, until cool enough to handle. Check to be sure the jars have sealed (see page 34). Label and store the sealed chutney for 6 months to 2 years. Once open, store in the refrigerator for up to 3 months.

ROSEMARY PICKLED AND SPICED PEARS

You can use Comice, Anjou, Seckel, or Bartlett pears for this recipe, but I prefer Morettini, which are an Italian pear variety bred in 1956 in New Zealand. They are a cross between an Italian Coscia pear and a French butter pear. Small and easy to fit in jars, they're greenish yellow with a red blush. Their flesh is creamy white, sweet, and spicy and somewhat reminiscent of Comice pears. In the San Francisco Bay Area, I get them from Aomboon at K & J Farm.

These are great as an accompaniment to roast chicken or lamb.

2 cups apple cider vinegar

1 cup water

2 cups granulated sugar

2 to 3 teaspoons dried hot red pepper flakes

4 large sprigs rosemary

2 pounds small Comice, Anjou, Seckel, or Bartlett pears, or 8 Morettini pears, peeled, halved, and cored

Yield: 2 pint jars

Place a baking sheet on the counter near your stove. Heat a kettle of water. Set a stockpot on the stove and fill it with enough water to cover the jars by 1 to 2 inches. Bring the water to a boil over medium-high heat. Sterilize the jars (see page 32) in the water bath.

In a medium saucepan over medium heat, combine the vinegar, 1 cup water, and sugar and bring to a boil. Add the red pepper flakes and rosemary. Boil the syrup for 5 minutes, until it is slightly thickened. Add the pear halves and simmer for 10 to 15 minutes, or until a skewer inserted into the largest pear penetrates easily.

Bring the water bath back to a boil. If the jars have cooled, warm them in the water bath or in a 200°F oven. Simmer the lids in a saucepan of hot water. Place the jars on the baking sheet.

Transfer the pears to the sterilized jars.

Discard the rosemary sprigs from the syrup. Return the syrup to a boil and reduce until it thickens, 8 to 10 minutes.

Ladle the syrup into the hot, sterilized jars, leaving ¼-inch headspace. Wipe the rims clean and set the lids on the mouths of the jars. Twist on the rings.

Using the jar lifter, gently lower the jars into the pot. When the water returns to a boil, decrease the heat to an active simmer, and process the jars for 20 minutes. Turn off the heat and leave the jars in the water for 1 to 2 minutes.

Using the jar lifter, transfer the jars from the pot to the baking sheet and let sit for at least 6 hours, until cool enough to handle. Check to be sure the jars have sealed (see page 34). Label and store the sealed pears for 6 months to 2 years. Once open, store in the refrigerator for up to 3 months.

Apples

Apples are used in jams and jellies because of their high pectin content, but on their own, they produce rather bland preserves. Apple butter is comforting but hardly a groundbreaking topping for toast. Apple jelly is mild and needs a flavor accent, such as mint or rosemary, to make it interesting. In my opinion, the best use for apples in preserving is to make pectin-rich apple jelly to help set all of your other preserves.

I prefer to use tart green apples such as Newton Pippin or Granny Smith for pectin and jelly and a mixture of apples for butter. Avoid pretty but bland mass-market apples, such as Red Delicious, as they will disappoint. You want apples with some acidity and spice. Try Gravenstein, Pink Pearl, Sierra Beauty, Macintosh, Arkansas Black, Winesap, or Fuji apples for a more complex flavor profile.

APPLE BUTTER

Once friends discover your passion for preserving, they will make requests. That is how I came to make apple butter. Fruit butters are quintessentially American. They are symbolic of the loving-hands-at-home culinary tradition and a reminder of America's agrarian past. Those who love fruit butters really love them, especially as a comforting spread for toast and pancakes and even pork chops.

Using a food mill will get rid of peels and any tough pieces, so save time and skip the peeling. If you prefer to puree in the food processor, peel the fruit.

4 pounds tart cooking apples, or 3 pounds apples and 1 pound quince

4 cups apple cider, plus more as needed

Grated zest and juice of 2 lemons

4 to 6 cups granulated sugar

2 teaspoons ground cinnamon or a mixture of other apple pie spices, such as ground ginger, cloves, allspice, and nutmeg

Yield: 6 half-pint jars

Place 3 or 4 small plates in the freezer.

Peel, core, and dice or slice the apples. If using the quince, peel, core, and dice.

In a large preserving pot over medium-high heat, combine the apples or the apples and quince, apple cider, and lemon zest and juice and cover. If the cider does not cover the fruit, add more cider (or water) to cover. Check on the pot occasionally to note the liquid level, as the apples can scorch. When the apples are soft, set the pot aside to cool. When cool enough to handle, pass the fruit through food mill or puree in the bowl of a food processor.

Measure the puree. For every 2 cups of puree, measure out 1 cup of sugar. Because the fruit butter does not have to reach gel point and must simply mound on a spoon, it does not require much sugar and can be tart rather than very sweet. Return the fruit puree to the pot.

Place a baking sheet on the counter near your stove. Heat a kettle of water. Set two stock-pots on the stove and fill them with enough water to cover the jars by 1 to 2 inches. Bring the water to a boil over medium-high heat. Sterilize the jars (see page 32) in the water bath.

Return the fruit puree to medium heat and add the, sugar and cinnamon. Gently cook, stirring frequently, until it thickens, approximately 1 hour. It may spit and pop a bit, so if you have a splatter screen, you may want to use it. Wear long pot-holder gloves, too. Alternatively, after 15 minutes of stove-top cooking, you may transfer the mixture to a shallow baking pan and finish the butter in a 300°F oven, stirring every 10 to 15 minutes, until the mixture is thick. If you use quince, the mixture will be red.

Bring the water bath back to a boil. If the jars have cooled, warm them in the water bath or in a 200°F oven. Simmer the lids in a saucepan of hot water. Place the jars on the baking sheet.

Do the plate test (see page 30); the apple butter should mound and hold its shape. If it isn't ready, continue to cook and stir until it passes the plate test. Remove the pot from the heat.

Ladle the apple butter into the jars, leaving ¼-inch headspace. Wipe the rims clean and set the lids on the mouths of the jars. Twist on the rings.

Using a jar lifter, gently lower the jars into the pots. When the water returns to a boil, decrease the heat to an active simmer, and process the jars for 15 minutes. Turn off the heat and leave the jars in the water for 1 to 2 minutes.

Using the jar lifter, transfer the jars from the pots to the baking sheet and let sit for at least 6 hours, until cool enough to handle. Check to be sure the jars have sealed (see page 34). Label and store the sealed apple butter for 6 months to 2 years. Once open, store in the refrigerator for up to 3 months.

VARIATIONS

— For apple-ginger butter, peel and slice 5 to 6 ounces fresh ginger and cook it in the cider with the apples. Puree with the apples.

— For apple butter with a kick, stir in a few tablespoons of Calvados with the cinnamon.

HOMEMADE APPLE PECTIN

The classic use of apple pectin is to enrich and thicken fruit preserves when the fruit needs a boost to set. To do so, use 1 cup per 1 quart batch of jam. You can freeze apple juices or "pectin stock" to add to low-pectin fruit jams and preserves, but you have to either refrigerate it for a day or two or freeze it, which is impractical because, if you need it while you are in the middle of cooking a fruit jam, you have to stop and thaw it in the microwave.

For long-term storage and immediate access, you need to cook the apple juices (pectin stock) with sugar and lemon until it gels, and preserve it in jars. Simply put, Homemade Apple Pectin is really an unflavored apple jelly—there's no need to flavor it if you are just going to use it to thicken other preserves.

This recipe may be increased by half to make 6 half-pint jars at a time. For the larger batch (6 cups) of Apple Pectin Stock, use 5½ to 6 pounds tart apples and 8 to 9 cups water, or more as needed, and stir in 5 cups sugar and 3 tablespoons lemon juice.

Note that you can make quince pectin stock and quince pectin jelly in the same way.

3½ to 4 pounds tart green apples

7 to 8 cups water, or to cover

Juice of 1 large lemon

4 cups granulated sugar

Yield: 4 half-pint jars

Place 3 or 4 small plates in the freezer.

Stem and coarsely chop the apples but do not peel or core them. You will have about 16 cups.

The first step is to make the apple juices or pectin stock.

In a large preserving pot over medium-high heat, combine the apples and water to cover and bring to a boil. Decrease the heat and simmer until the apples are totally soft. Check on them occasionally to note the liquid level in the pot, as apples can scorch. Add more water if needed. Mash the apples a bit with a potato masher.

When the apples are very soft, turn them into a dampened cheesecloth–lined colander set over a bowl or chinois set over a container and press gently on the fruit. Do not press too hard or the jelly will be cloudy. (Either discard the smooshed cooked fruit or puree it in a food mill and turn it into a rustic applesauce that you can sweeten to taste.) Now pour the apple juice remaining in the pot through the dampened cheesecloth–lined colander or chinois, and set aside to drip into the same bowl for a few hours, or longer if you have the patience, though most of the yield will be collected in the first few hours. For 4 pounds of apples, you will get about 4 cups reduced juice or apple pectin stock.

You are now ready for step two, making the jellied apple pectin.

Place a baking sheet on the counter near your stove. Heat a kettle of water. Set a stockpot on the stove and fill it with enough water to cover the jars by 1 to 2 inches. Bring the water to a boil over medium-high heat. Sterilize the jars (see page 32) in the water bath.

CONTINUED

Pour the strained juices (aka apple pectin stock) into the preserving pot, stir in the lemon juice and sugar, and bring to a boil over high heat. Boil until the mixture thickens and passes the plate test (see page 30), firmly gelling, or it registers 220°F on a candy thermometer. This happens quickly, so start checking the set point 5 to 7 minutes after the mixture boils. Remove the pot from the heat.

Bring the water bath back to a boil. If the jars have cooled, warm them in the water bath or in a 200°F oven. Simmer the lids in a saucepan of hot water. Place the jars on the baking sheet.

Ladle the apple pectin into the jars, leaving ¼-inch headspace. Wipe the rims clean and set the lids on the mouths of the jars. Twist on the rings.

Using a jar lifter, gently lower the jars into the pot. When the water returns to a boil, decrease the heat to an active simmer, and process the jars for 5 minutes. Turn off the heat and leave the jars in the water for 1 to 2 minutes.

Using the jar lifter, transfer the jars from the pot to the baking sheet and let sit for at least 6 hours, until cool enough to handle. Check to be sure the jars have sealed (see page 34). Label and store the sealed apple pectin for 6 months to 2 years. Once open, store in the refrigerator for up to 3 months.

VARIATIONS

— For Apple Jelly: Flavorings are added to apple jelly to make it more interesting. Make the jelly as if making apple pectin. For every 4 cups of Apple Pectin Stock, use 3 cups of sugar. To make 4 half-pint jars, sterilize the jars as directed. Measure 4 cups of the stock into the preserving pot, leaving any sediment. Stir in the sugar and lemon juice. Add the flavorings (see options, below). Bring to a boil over medium-high heat, skim frequently, and boil until the mixture thickens and registers 220°F on a candy thermometer. The mixture is ready when it passes the plate test (see page 30) and firmly gels on the plate. Rewarm the jars, fill, and process as directed for the Homemade Apple Pectin.

- For spiced apple jelly: Add 1 cinnamon stick or a few star anise pods.

- For minted apple jelly: Add 1 cup chopped mint leaves and strain them out before ladling into jars or add 3 mint tea bags. (No green food coloring, please!) Or you can put a few mint leaves in each empty jar and pour the apple jelly over them. Regardless of which mint-flavoring option you choose, also add lemon juice to taste.

- For rosemary-scented apple jelly: Add 2 to 3 tablespoons chopped rosemary in a tea ball or sachet. Also increase the lemon juice, to taste.

- For spicy apple jelly: Add a few chile flakes or ground fresh red chiles. Increase the lemon juice for this option, too.

- For ginger-apple jelly: Add a few tablespoons of ginger juice. (If you don't have a juicer, finely grate ginger and squeeze it through a strainer.) Adjust the lemon juice to taste, if needed, to highlight the ginger.

APPLE CHUTNEY

This is a workhorse winter chutney. It's good with baked ham, pork chops, or roast chicken. And it adds a little zip to the Thanksgiving turkey. Omit the red peppers if you like and increase the onions by 1 cup, or substitute cranberries for the peppers and cut back a bit on the raisins.

2 large yellow onions, chopped

4 cloves garlic, minced

5 ounces fresh ginger, peeled and sliced

3 to 4 cups apple cider vinegar

3 pounds Pippin or Granny Smith apples, peeled and chopped

2 red bell peppers, seeded and chopped

4 cups firmly packed brown sugar

3 tablespoons mustard seeds

1½ teaspoons ground allspice

1 teaspoon ground cayenne

2 teaspoons salt

2 cups raisins

Water or apple juice, as needed

Yield: 5 pint jars

Place 3 or 4 small plates in the freezer.

Combine the onions, garlic, ginger, and a splash of the vinegar in the bowl of a food processor and pulse to puree.

Place a baking sheet on the counter near your stove. Heat a kettle of water. Set two stockpots on the stove and fill them with enough water to cover the jars by 1 to 2 inches. Bring the water to a boil over medium-high heat. Sterilize the jars (see page 32) in the water bath.

In a large preserving pot, combine 3 cups vinegar, the apples, bell peppers, brown sugar, mustard seeds, allspice, cayenne, and salt. Bring to a boil over medium-high heat, decrease the heat to medium, and cook until it thickens, then add the raisins, stirring frequently (to prevent the raisins from sinking and scorching), during the last 15 minutes of cooking. If the raisins have absorbed too much of the juices add water or apple juice so that the mixture is syrupy. Do the plate test (see page 30). Remove the pot from the heat.

Bring the water bath back to a boil. If the jars have cooled, warm them in the water bath or in a 200°F oven. Simmer the lids in a saucepan of hot water. Place the jars on the baking sheet.

Ladle the chutney into the jars, leaving ¼-inch headspace. Wipe the rims clean and set the lids on the mouths of the jars. Twist on the rings.

Using a jar lifter, gently lower the jars into the pots. When the water returns to a boil, decrease the heat to an active simmer, and process the jars for 15 minutes. Turn off the heat and leave the jars in the water for 1 to 2 minutes.

Using the jar lifter, transfer the jars from the pots to the baking sheet and let sit for at least 6 hours, until cool enough to handle. Check to be sure the jars have sealed (see page 34). Label and store the sealed chutney for 6 months to 2 years. Once open, store in the refrigerator for up to 3 months.

Quince

The quince is a member of the Rosaceae family, which also includes apples and pears. It is native to Southwest Asia and Iran. Quince made their way to Greece, where quince conserve or jam became known as *kythoni glyko*, and to Turkey, where it is called *ayva receli*. In Portugal, the fruit is known as *marmelo* and the paste made from it is called *marmelada* (the origin of the word *marmalade*). Today, quince paste, or *membrillo*, is still eaten as a sweetmeat, often with a soft fresh white cheese, and in Spain it is classically paired with Manchego. In Italy, quince is called *cotogna* and the paste *cotognata*.

The quince resembles a lumpy apple and, when ripe, turns from green to gold and becomes highly aromatic. A few quince varieties do not require cooking, but the ones we cultivate in the United States are inedible when raw. They must be cooked to be enjoyed. The Romans used to submerge them in honey, leaves and all, and simmer them until they were totally tender. When cooked long enough, quince turn a magnificent shade of terra-cotta red. This takes time, and a day resting between periods of simmering helps the color develop. One year, I was given a batch of quince that were picked too green, and after hours and hours of simmering, they still had not turned color. I called culinary science expert Harold McGee to find out why, and he told me that if the quince were not ripe when picked they would not turn red, no matter how long I cooked them. Quince turn red when the phenolic compounds in the fruit interact with oxygen and create anthrocyanins, which are responsible for the red, purple, and blue colors in plants. (I sent him some membrillo in exchange for his troubleshooting.)

I am always excited when I see the first quince at the market. For me, they officially announce the arrival of autumn in California. I keep a bowl of them on my dining table for as long as the season lasts. They perfume the entire house. I am so enamored of quince that for a while my family called me the "quince queen." I make quince jam flavored with Meyer lemon or with cardamom and rose sugar. Next comes quince butter seasoned with citrus and ginger and cooked down to an unctuous puree.

I enjoy making my own membrillo, the quince paste traditionally served with cheese, a perfect dessert. And I put up jars of sliced spiced quince to add to North African tagines.

Prepping quince for cooking is a chore. Most traditional recipes casually advise you to peel and core the fruits before cooking—as if it were a breeze, like peeling apples. What they don't tell you is that the fruit is as hard as a rock and getting the core out requires more than a knife or a melon baller (or even a special quince-coring knife). The task requires strength and caution so you don't cut yourself. Other recipes will tell you to put the cut quince in lemon water to keep it white, but why bother when you want the quince to take on color?

For many years, I have been making membrillo for friends and for Bi-Rite Market in San Francisco, and if I had to peel, core, and slice each quince I'd have given up long ago. I knew there had to be a better way to process the fruit, and I found it in Maria Grammatico and Mary Taylor Simeti's book *Bitter Almonds*. Maria ran a pastry shop in the tiny Sicilian town of Erice. In her recipe for *marmellata di cotogna,* she calls for putting the whole washed and defuzzed quince and some lemons in a deep pot, covering them with water, weighing them down if necessary, and cooking them, covered, until they are totally soft. It takes 45 to 60 minutes, depending on the size of the fruit. I use this technique if I am making quince jam or jelly or membrillo. It saves time and fingers. But for quince mostarda and sliced preserved quince I still have to resort to the knife and peeler to produce distinct pieces.

Be sure to reserve every drop of the quince cooking liquid. This is what I call quince tea, and it is loaded with pectin. It can be saved and diluted and reused many times. It can be refrigerated for a week or two and also frozen. At the end of quince season, I put some in the freezer so I can start my first batch of quince with some of the quince tea from the season before. If you do not boil the quince, here's another way to make quince tea: Put all the quince peels, cores, and seeds in a large pot. Cover with cold water and bring to a boil over medium-high heat. Decrease the heat to medium and simmer for 30 minutes to extract the flavor. Strain, discarding the solids.

BASIC QUINCE PRESERVES

You can make the puree one day and finish with sugar the next. Or add the sugar and let the preserve sit overnight. It takes time for the quince to become that gorgeous red, so turning the heat off and letting it rest a few times will allow it to bring up the color.

To make larger batches, scale the ingredients as such: 5 pounds quince makes 7 to 8 cups puree. For 8 cups of puree, add 7 cups sugar, 2 teaspoons ground cardamom or cinnamon, 4 tablespoons lemon juice, and 2 to 3 cups quince tea. This will make 14 to 15 half-pint jars.

For 6 pounds quince, you will get about 10 cups puree. For 10 cups of puree, add 9 cups sugar, 5 to 6 tablespoons lemon juice, 1 tablespoon cardamom or cinnamon, and 3 to 4 cups quince tea. This will make 16 to 18 half-pint jars.

Serve as you would serve applesauce or apple butter, on toast or pancakes. It's a great topping for latkes, too. And it's also good with poultry and cheese.

2 pounds quince

1 or 2 Meyer or Eureka lemons, thinly sliced

Water, to cover, or replace 3 to 4 cups of the water with quince tea from cooking the quince (see page 207)

Scant 3½ cups granulated sugar

2 to 3 tablespoons fresh lemon juice

1 teaspoon ground cardamom or cinnamon (optional)

Yield: 6 half-pint jars

Place 3 to 4 small plates in the freezer.

Wash and defuzz the quince. I use a plastic scrubby to remove the fuzz.

Combine the quince and lemon slices in a large stockpot for a snug fit. Add the water and bring to a boil over high heat. Decrease the heat to medium-low, cover, and simmer until the quince are soft and easily pierced with a skewer; 45 minutes for small quince and 1 hour for larger ones. When they are done, a skewer will slide in easily and the skin on some of the quince will have split. When tender, using a slotted spoon, transfer the quince and lemon slices from the cooking water to a baking sheet and set aside just until they are cool enough to handle. (Quince can be pureed most easily when they are still warm.) Save all of the cooking water, or quince tea; you will need 3 cups of this tea for the preserves. Refrigerate any remaining quince tea for up to 2 weeks, or freeze.

There is no need to peel the quince, as the skin will have practically disintegrated after the long cooking and provides additional pectin. It vanishes after pureeing. Set the cooked quince upright and cut down on all four sides to remove the flesh, leaving just the central core. Scoop out and discard any pieces of core and seeds that remain in the slices, and transfer the quince pieces and lemon slices in batches to the bowl of a food processor. Pulse first to break down the flesh, and then puree.

Measure the quince puree. You should have 3½ to 4 cups.

CONTINUED

In a preserving pot over medium-high heat, combine the quince puree, 2 cups of the quince tea, sugar, lemon juice, and cardamom or cinnamon and bring to a boil, stirring frequently. Remove the pot from the heat and set aside to rest for 1 hour. Then, return to a boil, stirring frequently. Remove from the heat and let rest overnight to give the cooked preserves time to turn red.

The next day, place a baking sheet on the counter near your stove. Heat a kettle of water. Set two stockpots on the stove and fill them with enough water to cover the jars by 1 to 2 inches. Bring the water to a boil over medium-high heat. Sterilize the jars (see page 32) in the water bath.

Place the quince mixture over medium-high heat and bring to a boil. Decrease the heat to medium and simmer, stirring frequently, until the preserves thicken and pass the plate test (see page 30), mounding on the plate. Remove the pot from the heat.

Bring the water bath back to a boil. If the jars have cooled, warm them in the water bath or in a 200°F oven. Simmer the lids in a saucepan of hot water. Place the jars on the baking sheet.

Ladle the preserves into the hot, sterilized jars, leaving ¼-inch headspace. Wipe the rims clean and set the lids on the mouths of the jars. Twist on the rings.

Using a jar lifter, gently lower the jars into the pots. When the water returns to a boil, decrease the heat to an active simmer, and process the jars for 15 minutes. Turn off the heat and leave the jars in the water for 1 to 2 minutes.

Using the jar lifter, transfer the jars from the pots to the baking sheet and let sit for at least 6 hours, until cool enough to handle. Check to be sure the jars have sealed (see page 34). Label and store the sealed preserves for 6 months to 2 years. Once open, store in the refrigerator for up to 3 months.

VARIATIONS

— Use 1 teaspoon ground ginger in place of the cardamom or cinnamon. Taste and increase if you like. You may also stir in honey to taste at the end of cooking.

— You can substitute up to 1 cup sliced Buddha's Hand citron per 4 to 5 pounds quince for the sliced lemons.

QUINCE AND HONEY BUTTER

This fruit butter is voluptuous and perfumed. I prefer to use a rich, dark honey for this recipe.

4 cups quince puree, made from 2½ pounds quince (see page 209)

1½ cups apple cider or apple juice

2½ cups granulated sugar

1½ teaspoons ground cinnamon

½ teaspoon ground cloves

½ teaspoon ground ginger

½ teaspoon ground nutmeg

Grated zest and juice of 1 small orange

Pinch of salt

Grated zest and juice of 1 lemon, plus more juice as needed

½ cup dark honey

Yield: 8 half-pint jars

Place 3 or 4 small plates in the freezer.

In a large preserving pot over medium-high heat, combine the quince puree, apple cider or apple juice, sugar, cinnamon, cloves, ginger, nutmeg, orange juice and zest, and salt and stir until the sugar is dissolved and the mixture is starting to bubble. Remove the pot from the heat and set aside to rest for 1 hour.

Return to the pot to medium heat and bring to a gentle boil for a few minutes, stirring frequently, and then set aside to rest for 1 hour. Repeat this process until the mixture has turned red. Once the mixture has reddened, you can proceed or let it rest overnight.

Place a baking sheet on the counter near your stove. Heat a kettle of water. Set two stock-pots on the stove and fill them with enough water to cover the jars by 1 to 2 inches. Bring the water to a boil over medium-high heat. Sterilize the jars (see page 32) in the water bath.

Bring the quince mixture to a boil over medium-high heat. Decrease the heat to low and cook, stirring frequently. It may spit and pop a bit, so if you have a splatter screen, you may want to use it. Wear long pot-holder gloves, too. Alternatively, after 15 minutes of stove-top cooking, you may transfer the mixture to a shallow baking pan and finish the quince butter in a 300°F oven, stirring every 10 to 15 minutes, until the mixture is very thick. This can take 1 hour or longer.

Add the lemon zest and juice and honey to the quince butter, tasting and adding more lemon juice as needed. Do the plate test (see page 30); the quince butter should mound and hold its shape on the plate. Remove the pot from the heat.

Bring the water bath back to a boil. If the jars have cooled, warm them in the water bath or in a 200°F oven. Simmer the lids in a saucepan of hot water. Place the jars on the baking sheet.

Ladle the quince butter into the jars, leaving ¼-inch headspace. Wipe the rims clean and set the lids on the mouths of the jars. Twist on the rings.

Using a jar lifter, gently lower the jars into the pots. When the water returns to a boil, decrease the heat to an active simmer, and process the jars for 15 minutes. Turn off the heat and leave the jars in the water for 1 to 2 minutes.

Using the jar lifter, transfer the jars from the pots to the baking sheet and let sit for at least 6 hours, until cool enough to handle. Check to be sure the jars have sealed (see page 34). Label and store the sealed quince butter for 6 months to 2 years. Once open, store in the refrigerator for up to 3 months.

VARIATION

— Add up to ¼ cup freshly grated ginger, stirring it in with the ground spices.

QUINCE JAM WITH ROSE AND CARDAMOM

When I was traveling in Iran, I was astounded by the size of the quince I saw on the trees and the abundance of fruit on each tree. Persians love quince. They stuff the fruit with ground meat and braise it and add slices of quince to their meat stews, called *khoreshe*. This jam uses rose and cardamom—classic flavors in Persian cooking.

7 cups granulated sugar

2 cups dried organic rose petals

7 to 8 cups quince puree, made with about 5 pounds quince (see page 209)

4 cups quince tea from cooking the quince (see page 207)

2 teaspoons ground cardamom

¼ cup fresh lemon juice

Rose water (optional)

Yield: 14 to 15 half-pint jars

Place 3 or 4 small plates in the freezer.

In the bowl of a food processor, blend 4 cups of the sugar and the rose petals until the petals are broken down and well distributed.

In a large preserving pot over medium-high heat, combine the quince puree, quince tea, rose sugar, remaining 3 cups granulated sugar, cardamom, and lemon juice. Bring to a boil, stirring frequently. Remove the pot from the heat and set aside to rest for 1 hour. Then, return to a boil, stirring frequently. Remove from the heat and let rest overnight to give the jam time to turn red.

The next day, place two baking sheets on the counter near your stove. Heat a kettle of water. Set two stockpots on the stove and fill them with enough water to cover the jars by 1 to 2 inches. Bring the water to a boil over medium-high heat. Sterilize the jars (see page 32) in the water bath.

Place the quince mixture over medium-high heat and bring to a boil. Decrease the heat to low and simmer, stirring frequently, until the jam thickens and passes the plate test (see page 30), mounding on the plate. Taste and add a splash of rose water if you want an even stronger floral note. Remove the pot from the heat.

Bring the water bath back to a boil. If the jars have cooled, warm them in the water bath or in a 200°F oven. Simmer the lids in a saucepan of hot water. Place the jars on the baking sheets.

Ladle the jam into the jars, leaving ¼-inch headspace. Wipe the rims clean and set the lids on the mouths of the jars. Twist on the rings.

Using a jar lifter, gently lower the jars into the pots. When the water returns to a boil, decrease the heat to an active simmer, and process the jars for 15 minutes. Turn off the heat and leave the jars in the water for 1 to 2 minutes.

Using the jar lifter, transfer the jars from the pots to the baking sheets and let sit for at least 6 hours, until cool enough to handle. Check to be sure the jars have sealed (see page 34). Label and store the sealed jam for 6 months to 2 years. Once open, store in the refrigerator for up to 3 months.

MEMBRILLO

The traditional cheese pairing for membrillo is Manchego, but I also love serving it with soft fresh goat cheese. Walnut bread is a nice accompaniment.

To make an 8 by 8-inch pan, use 5 cups quince puree plus 5 cups sugar and 3 table-spoons of lemon juice.

To make a 12 by 18-inch half-sheet pan, use 12 cups quince puree plus 12 cups sugar, 4 to 5 tablespoons lemon juice (or a bit more, to taste), and 1 to 2 teaspoons ground cardamom.

7 to 8 cups quince puree, made with about 5 pounds quince (see page 209)

Juice of 2 lemons

7 to 8 cups granulated sugar

1 cup quince tea from cooking the quince (see page 207)

2 teaspoons ground cardamom, or 1 teaspoon ground cinnamon (optional)

Yield: 11 by 15-inch jelly-roll pan

Line an 11 by 15-inch jelly-roll pan or sheet pan with parchment paper and coat it lightly with nonstick cooking spray.

In a large preserving pot over medium-high heat, combine the quince puree, lemon juice, as much sugar as quince puree, quince tea, and cardamom or cinnamon. Cook, stirring almost constantly, wearing long pot-holder gloves and scraping the sides and bottom with a long-handled wooden spoon or silicone spatula, until very thick, 30 to 40 minutes. The mixture will bubble up like molten lava, so if you have a splatter screen, you may want to use it; you might even consider goggles if you have them!

When the mixture is very thick, carefully ladle it onto the prepared pan and spread it evenly. It should be ¾ to 1 inch thick. Set the paste aside in a clean, warm, dust-free place, such as in an oven with a pilot light. After 3 days, if the top feels firm, line a second pan with parchment paper, flip the quince sheet paste over onto the second pan, and place the pan in the same spot to dry for 2 to 3 days longer.

Cut the membrillo into squares or rectangles, wrap in parchment, and transfer to airtight plastic containers. Store in a cool place (like a cellar) for up to 9 months. No need to refrigerate; refrigeration may make the membrillo too stiff.

SLICED PRESERVED QUINCE WITH MOROCCAN FLAVORS

If you want to put up sliced preserved quince for lamb or chicken tagines, or as a condiment to serve with the Thanksgiving turkey, there is no way to escape the torture of peeling, coring, and slicing the quince. Gather a sharp peeler and paring knife and a melon baller, take a deep breath, and prepare to slow down. This recipe can be doubled.

4 pounds quince

8 cups water or quince tea (see page 207)

4 cups granulated sugar

1 tablespoon fresh lemon juice

1 lemon, thinly sliced on a mandoline and then the slices quartered or halved

¼ cup peeled, thinly sliced, and julienned fresh ginger

1 teaspoon cardamom pods

1 teaspoon ras el hanout, mixed Moroccan spices, or garam masala

½ teaspoon ground cinnamon, or 1 cinnamon stick

1 star anise pod

½ teaspoon whole cloves

Yield: 6 pint jars

Wash and defuzz the quince. I use a plastic scrubby to remove the fuzz. Peel, halve, and core the quince, then cut them into ½-inch-thick slices. You should have about 3 pounds after trimming. Set aside.

In a heavy, nonreactive pot, combine the water or quince tea, sugar, lemon juice and slices, ginger, cardamom, ras el hanout or mixed Moroccan spices or garam masala, cinnamon, star anise, and cloves and bring to a boil over high heat, stirring to dissolve the sugar. Decrease the heat to medium-low and cook for 15 to 20 minutes to thicken the syrup. Add the quince slices, decrease the heat to low, and cook for 10 minutes. Turn off the heat and let rest for 2 to 3 hours to allow the quince slices to begin to redden.

Place a baking sheet on the counter near your stove. Heat a kettle of water. Set two stockpots on the stove and fill them with enough water to cover the jars by 1 to 2 inches. Bring the water to a boil over medium-high heat. Sterilize the jars (see page 32) in the water bath.

Return the quince to high heat, bring back to a boil, and then decrease the heat to low and simmer until the quince slices turn red, 20 to 30 minutes longer. Repeat this process of boiling and resting, if necessary to bring up the color.

Bring the water bath back to a boil. If the jars have cooled, warm them in the water bath or in a 200°F oven. Simmer the lids in a saucepan of hot water. Place the jars on the baking sheet.

Transfer the quince slices to the sterilized jars.

Return the syrup to a boil and reduce until it thickens, 8 to 10 minutes.

Ladle the syrup, with the lemon peel, ginger, cardamom, cinnamon, star anise, and cloves into the jars over the quince, leaving ¼-inch headspace. Wipe the rims clean and set the lids on the mouths of the jars. Twist on the rings.

Using a jar lifter, gently lower the jars into the pots. When the water returns to a boil, decrease the heat to an active simmer, and process the jars for 15 minutes. Turn off the heat and leave the jars in the water for 1 to 2 minutes.

Using the jar lifter, transfer the jars from the pots to the baking sheet and let sit for at least 6 hours, until cool enough to handle. Check to be sure the jars have sealed (see page 34). Label and store the sealed quince for 6 months to 2 years. Once open, store in the refrigerator for up to 3 months.

QUINCE, PEAR, AND NUT CONSERVE

This conserve, known as *cogna* in Italian, is a specialty of the Piemontese town of Monferrato and is usually served with cheese. As quince and pears come into season at the same time, they are a natural pairing for this rich sweet. Late September or early October is an ideal time to make this preserve. Some versions of the recipe call for figs, which may or may not still be available at the market, but if they are, by all means add them. Hazelnuts, also a regional specialty, are added for texture. Some recipes even add pumpkin squash to the fruit mixture.

The fruits can be chopped and cooked down in grape must (reduced grape juice) into a paste with bits of nuts, or they can be preserved in large pieces in the manner of *mostarda di frutta*. As we do not have easy access to grape must, I use grape juice or a combination of grape juice and dry white or red wine.

1 pound quince	2 cups granulated sugar
1 pound pears	Grated zest of 2 lemons or 1 orange
12 cloves	
2 cinnamon sticks	1 pound figs, stemmed and halved (optional)
4 to 5 cups grape juice, or a combination of grape juice and dry white or red wine	½ cup hazelnuts
	Fresh lemon juice, as needed

Yield: 2 to 3 pint jars

Wash and defuzz the quince. I use a plastic scrubby to remove the fuzz. Peel, halve, core, and cut the quince into thick slices.

Peel, core, and cut the pears into thick slices.

Gather the cloves and cinnamon in a square of cheesecloth to make a sachet.

In a large preserving pot over medium-high heat, combine the grape juice, sugar, citrus zest, and spice sachet. Bring to a boil and cook for 5 minutes. Add the quince, pears, and figs and cook for 5 minutes. Set aside and let rest overnight.

The next day, preheat the oven to 300°F. Place the hazelnuts on a baking sheet and toast for 8 to 10 minutes, until golden brown and aromatic. Transfer to a clean kitchen towel, wrap them up, and set aside for 10 minutes. Then, rub vigorously with the towel to remove the hazelnut skins. Chop coarsely and set aside.

Place a baking sheet on the counter near your stove. Heat a kettle of water. Set a stockpot on the stove and fill it with enough water to cover the jars by 1 to 2 inches. Bring the water to a boil over medium-high heat. Sterilize the jars (see page 32) in the water bath.

Return the fruit preserves to a boil over medium-high heat. Add lemon juice to taste. Decrease the heat to medium and continue to cook until the fruit is tender and the syrup is condensed. If the fruit is getting too soft during this step, use a slotted spoon to transfer the pieces to a colander, continue to reduce the syrup to thicken, and then return the fruit to the pot. When the fruit is translucent and the syrup is thick, add the nuts.

Bring the water bath back to a boil. If the jars have cooled, warm them in the water bath or in a 200°F oven. Simmer the lids in a saucepan of hot water. Place the jars on the baking sheet.

Ladle the conserve into the jars, leaving ¼-inch headspace. Run a knife along the inside of the jars to break up any air bubbles. Wipe the rims clean and set the lids on the mouths of the jars. Twist on the rings.

Using a jar lifter, gently lower the jars into the pot. When the water returns to a boil, decrease the heat to an active simmer, and process the jars for 20 minutes. Turn off the heat and leave the jars in the water for 1 to 2 minutes.

Using the jar lifter, transfer the jars from the pot to the baking sheet and let sit for at least 6 hours, until cool enough to handle. Check to be sure the jars have sealed (see page 34). Label and store the sealed conserve for 6 months to 2 years. Once open, store in the refrigerator for up to 3 months.

Late November Through March

Winter

Citrus

As you may have noticed, lemons are used in almost all of the recipes in this book, because they bring out flavor and intensify the pectin in other fruits. Home preservers, and most home cooks, would be at a loss without them. Lemons came from Southeast Asia to southern Italy during the time of ancient Rome and were widely disseminated in the Arab world and the Mediterranean between 1000 and 1150. When initially introduced, they were treated as garden ornamentals.

The first substantial cultivation of lemons began in the fifteenth century. Christopher Columbus brought lemons on his voyage to the New World. They were planted in Florida in the sixteenth century. In the eighteenth century Spanish missionaries planted them in California. The most common lemons are the Eureka and the Lisbon. A few lucky souls have Sorrento lemon trees, which have almost seedless fruit that is prized for its medium-thick and juicy peel and is ideal for making Moroccan-style preserved lemons and candied lemon peel. Californians proudly extol the state's culinary citrus superstar, the Meyer lemon. Imported from China by Frank Meyer in 1908, it is a cross between a lemon and a mandarin. Meyers are sweet, mild, thin skinned, and perfumed. They need to be picked when ripe and golden. They are lower in acid than other lemons, so their juice should not be used in place of regular lemon juice when making preserves.

Oranges came to the Mediterranean from China, where they had been cultivated since 2500 BC. They were introduced to the Iberian Peninsula by the Moors. The Portuguese were active in the orange trade, and as a reminder of their role in the dissemination of the sweet orange, the Greek word for "orange" is *portokal*. After the Columbian Exchange, oranges arrived in the New World and were planted in the Spanish missions. Oranges are still grown in great quantity in California, although most juice oranges are cultivated in Florida. Valencias, Cara Caras, eating oranges (such as navels), and the beautiful red-streaked blood oranges make their way into preserves. I remember my shock the first time I ordered *spremuta d'arancia* (orange juice) in Italy. I was handed a glass of what looked like blood. It was musky, sweet, and perfumed. I've been hooked ever since. The US used to import blood oranges from Sicily, but now they are cultivated in California and have found their way to supermarkets nationwide. The two most popular are the Moro and the Tarocco. Seville or bitter oranges are native to Southeast Asia and arrived in the Mediterranean before the Portuguese started transporting the sweet oranges. They are used to make orange-flower water and perfume and to flavor liqueurs, and they are the proper orange for classic authentic marmalade. They are hard to find at the market. Either you know someone with a tree, or you will have to special-order them. Even more difficult to track down is the bergamot orange, whose intensely perfumed peel is used to flavor Earl Grey tea. Bergamot is usually used in combination with other citrus; by itself it is rather overpowering.

Mandarins, tangerines, and clementines are close relatives of oranges. Mandarins originated in China. Tangerines were discovered in Morocco, and clementines in Algeria. All three have a thin, bright orange peel that is somewhat loose from the fruit. The fruit segments are easy to separate for eating out of hand. Japanese satsumas are seedless, so they are a preserver's dream. Select ones with peels that are not too puffy or loose. They will keep for a week or so at room temperature.

At my market, I get the best limes from Brokaw Ranch, where they also specialize in the cultivation of superb avocados, a perfect marriage of flavors. They cultivate Bearss limes, also known as Persian or Tahitian limes, which are fragrant and a bit spicy as well as tart. They make great marmalade, and their juice adds tang to Green Mango Chutney (page 98) as well.

MOROCCAN PRESERVED LEMONS

A signature condiment in the North African kitchen, preserved lemons are unique in flavor and texture. Once you have prepared them, they must cure for 4 to 6 weeks before they can be used, so try to put up a new jar as soon as you see that you are running low.

Most of us will use only 1 or 2 lemons at a time, so pint jars, rather than quart jars, are more practical, as they take up less room in the refrigerator once opened.

Keep in mind that with preserved lemons you primarily are using the peel, diced or in strips. Eureka and Lisbon lemons have thick peels, so they are the best choice for preserving. Using Meyer lemons may seem tempting, but they are not the ideal choice for preserving because their skins are so thin and soft that the lemons turn to mush if not used quickly. The shelf life of preserved Meyer lemon is less than half that of regular lemons.

While preserved lemons are traditionally used in tagines, you will also probably find ways to use them in dishes that are not North African. Their tart brininess will enliven vinaigrettes, fish stews, and vegetable and legume dishes.

Scrub the lemons well with a brush under running cold water. Place the lemons in a bowl, add water to cover, and let soak for 1 day, changing the water a few times. (If you are short on time, soak for at least 2 hours.)

Set a stockpot on the stove and fill it with enough water to cover the jars by 1 to 2 inches. Bring the water to a boil over medium-high heat. Sterilize the jars (see page 32) in the water bath.

Drain the lemons and dry well. Using a sharp knife, cut each lemon lengthwise into quarters, cutting just short of all the way through and leaving the bottom peel intact. The cut lemon should resemble a tulip. Push a heaping tablespoon of salt into the center of each lemon. Also spoon a heaping tablespoon of salt into the bottom of each jar and pack the salted lemons tightly in the jars. You will be able to fit 3 or 4 per jar.

Pour lemon juice into each jar to completely cover the lemons, leaving 1-inch headspace. Wipe the rims clean and set the lids on the mouths of the jars. Twist on the rings to seal the jars.

There is no need to process the jars in a boiling water bath, as they do not need to vacuum seal; the salt and acid fully preserve the lemons.

2 pounds Eureka or Lisbon lemons

About 1¼ cups kosher salt, plus more as needed

Juice of 4 lemons, plus more as needed

Yield: 2 to 3 pint jars

CONTINUED

For the first few days, turn the jars upside down and then right-side up to distribute the salt. Store the jars in a cool, dry place for at least 4 weeks before using. Unopened jars will keep for 1 year. The color of the lemons will fade over time. Once a jar has been opened and the contents have come into contact with oxygen, store it in the refrigerator, where it will keep for at least 4 months. If a white film forms on the lemons, just rinse it off; the lemons are still good.

To use the lemons, rinse briefly under cool running water and pat dry. Cut away and discard the pulp. Cut the peel as directed by the recipe.

VARIATIONS

— Add cinnamon sticks and/or cloves to the jars. (I don't do this, as the flavors do not really penetrate the fruit. It's more for looks.)

— For Quick-Brine Lemons, dissolve ⅓ cup kosher salt in 1 cup boiling water and let cool. Scrub and cut 4 lemons as directed, put the lemons in the sterilized jars, pour the brine over the lemons to cover, and close the jars. Store the jars in a cool cupboard for 2 weeks before using the lemons, turning them occasionally. This is the brining technique used at the Culinary Institute of America in Napa, California, where they put up preserved lemons in great quantities.

BASIC CITRUS MARMALADE

When we hear the word *marmalade*, we automatically think of a spreadable preserve made with the peel and pulp of citrus fruits. The first marmalade, however, was not made with citrus fruits. It was a Portuguese preserve made with quince, much like membrillo. *Marmelo* is the Portuguese word for "quince," and *marmelada* is the condiment derived from the fruit. The earliest citrus marmalades as we know them began to appear in England and Scotland in the eighteenth century, when cooks started adding more water to the fruit paste, making it more spreadable. Marmalade for mass consumption did not catch on until later in the nineteenth century when the price of sugar dropped.

Technically, marmalade has a jelly base with small pieces of fruit peel suspended in the jelly. Some, like lime or lemon, are light and clear in appearance. Others, such as most of the orange marmalades, are darker and less translucent.

Making a classic English-style citrus marmalade is a time-consuming process that requires patience and good knife skills. There are many methods of production, and each has its aficionados.

In one method, you simmer the whole fruit in water to cover, either on the stove top or in a 350°F oven for 2½ to 3 hours. When they are cool enough to handle, you lift the fruits from the liquid, halve them, scoop out the inside pulp, and set it aside. Then you save all of the cooking liquids and put the pith and seeds in a cheesecloth sachet. Since the fruit is soft, it is easy to slice the peel into thin strips. Next you combine the peels, reserved pulp, and juices and add sugar. Stir until the sugar is dissolved and then cook until the set point is achieved.

For another method, you remove the colored part of the rind with a very sharp peeler, scrape away the excess pith and save it, and then cut the peel into fine julienne strips. Cut the fruit in half and squeeze the juice. Save the pith and seeds and wrap them in a cheesecloth sachet. Put all in a pan with water to cover and let it sit overnight. The next day, bring to a boil and simmer for about 1 hour, until the peel is soft and cooked through. Add sugar and cook until the set point is reached.

Yet another method has you remove the rind with a sharp peeler and cut it into fine julienne strips. Then cook the peel and thinly sliced or chopped pulp in water until tender, add sugar, and cook to the set point. Some recipes encourage overnight soaking. Others do not.

If the appearance of the peel is important to you, you can either remove the peel and slice it by hand or, better yet, thinly slice the citrus fruit on a sharp mandoline and then cut those slices into quarters. Cook them in ample water, let the mixture sit overnight, add sugar, cook again briefly, let sit overnight again, and finally cook until the set point in reached.

The easiest method is what I call the Grammatico-Davidson chop. This technique is used by Sicilian pastry shop owner Maria Grammatico as described in her and Mary Taylor Simeti's book *Bitter Almonds*, and by the late Alan Davidson, renowned English food historian, author, and former chairman of the Oxford Symposium on Food. He used to make 75 pounds of marmalade each year, using this practical technique for production: Chop the fruit in small batches in the food processor, transfer to a preserving pot, cover with ample water, and boil until the fruit is completely softened and the water is reduced, about 40 minutes. Add the sugar and cook over low heat while stirring, until the sugar dissolves. It's not essential, but I like to let the mixture sit overnight after the sugar is added and before the final boiling. Bring to a boil and cook until the set point is reached. This method is efficient. No fancy knife skills are needed. Just a food processor with a sharp blade.

So how do you decide which method to use? It all comes down to aesthetics and practicality. Having tested and tasted the results of these various techniques, I can report that they all make delicious marmalades. The question is, do you want to see elegant little strips of peel when you open your jar of marmalade? Or do you just want a tasty marmalade with smaller pieces of peel whose shape and size are not important? If looks are important, use the mandoline technique or cut the peel into strips by hand. If the appearance of the peel is not crucial and flavor takes precedence, use the Grammatico-Davidson chop technique.

Appearance counts the most with lime marmalade, because limes have the toughest peel and the clearest gel. I use the mandoline. It is also good for lemons. The appearance of the peel matters less for orange marmalades because they are darker and less translucent. And your jar yield is greater when you use the Grammatico-Davidson chop technique than with the other techniques.

For marmalade, buy unsprayed, organic citrus fruit. Some supermarket citrus fruit is sold waxed, so you will have to scrub the fruit in hot water to remove the wax before proceeding. Seville oranges are often hard to come by at the market, but there are many other citrus options. Cara Cara oranges,

Valencias, navels, and blood oranges are all available, as are tangerines, lemons and Meyer lemons, and limes.

Don't worry about the precise amount of water. If you have used too much, it will all be absorbed in the final cooking once the balance of water and sugar is achieved at gel point. Cook the fruit in large amounts of water. It has to be enough for the initial cooking.

Peels that are not cooked all the way through before you add the sugar will become tough, so give them enough time to soften. It takes 45 to 60 minutes or longer for the peels to become totally tender and translucent. Cut into a piece and look at it or give it a bite. When it's ready, add the sugar. To determine the amount of sugar to add, measure the fruit pulp and add approximately 2 cups of sugar for every 3 cups of fruit. Stir until the sugar is warm and totally dissolved before you bring the mixture to a boil.

Most recipes advise you to let the mixture rest overnight before proceeding with the final cooking. Some have you add sugar and cook to completion. I prefer to wait overnight, so I can see how much gel set there is before the final boil.

When making marmalade, use a large, deep pot. At no point should it ever be more than half full. It may froth and bubble up and need skimming. Cooking times will vary from fruit to fruit. Cook the fruit and sugar at a boil, not a simmer.

The keys to successful marmalade are acidity and texture. They are supposed to be tart as well as sweet, and texture is crucial. Citrus is loaded with pectin, and thus

CONTINUED

marmalade may reach the gel point faster than you expect and, with an overnight rest with the sugar (this is a two-day project), it will have almost set up by itself without additional simmering. If necessary, add a bit more lemon juice or water to thin it before bringing it back to a boil for packing and sealing. Plan to do the plate test a few times as the mixture starts to thicken. You want it to set up, but to be a bit loose and syrupy when you put it in jars, especially for lime and lemon marmalades (which are especially high in pectin), as you do not want to open the jars later and discover a tough, rubbery preserve. As the mixture thickens and gets close to the set point, stir often so the peel is well distributed in the gel. Stop short of 220°F, please, or you will have rubber.

The shelf life of a good marmalade is long—up to 3 years—so you might want to make more than a few jars. And if you have made too much, keep in mind that while these marmalades are great on toast, they can easily be transformed into marinades for fish, poultry, and pork. Just combine them with grated ginger, garlic, and soy sauce, and thin with citrus juices. For another marinade or a zippy salad dressing, thin marmalade with citrus juice and olive oil and add some salt and spices or chopped herbs, such as mint or basil. A few tablespoons also can be stirred into pan juices to make a tangy sauce for chicken, veal, or fish piccata.

2½ pounds Meyer lemons, limes, blood oranges, Cara Cara, Valencia or navel oranges, tangerines, or a mixture

3 quarts water

5 to 6 cups granulated sugar

Juice of 1 to 2 Eureka or Lisbon lemons, plus more as needed

1 vanilla bean, cut into 3 pieces (optional)

Yield: 9 to 10 half-pint jars

Place 3 or 4 small plates in the freezer.

Wash the citrus and cut out the small stem-end pieces. Cut up the fruit, pick out as many seeds as possible, and then chop the fruit in small batches in the bowl of a food processor, pulsing 12 to 14 times, until evenly processed but not very fine. You will have 6 to 8 cups.

In a large preserving pot, combine the chopped citrus and water to cover (about three times as much water as cut-up fruit). Bring to a boil over medium-high heat and cook, uncovered, until the liquid is reduced by one-third. Bite a piece of peel; if it is tender, proceed to measure the fruit. If not, cook a little longer.

Measure the chopped fruit and then return it to the pot. For every 3 cups of fruit, gradually add 2 cups of sugar, stirring until dissolved. Continue to pick out seeds. Add the lemon juice for flavor balance. Add the vanilla bean. Set aside to rest overnight.

Place two baking sheets on the counter near your stove. Heat a kettle of water. Set two stockpots on the stove and fill them with enough water to cover the jars by 1 to 2 inches. Bring the water to a boil over medium-high heat. Sterilize the jars (see page 32) in the water bath.

Inspect the mixture in the pot. It may appear gelled and ready to jar (it probably is). If it is too set, stir in water to loosen. Bring the mixture to a boil over high heat, stirring often. Do the plate test (see page 30). The marmalade is ready when it sets up on a chilled plate but is still syrupy. Stop before the mixture measures 220°F on an instant-read thermometer. Remove the pot from the heat and set aside to rest for 10 minutes. Stir well to distribute the peel.

Bring the water bath back to a boil. If the jars have cooled, warm them in the water bath or in a 200°F oven. Simmer the lids in a saucepan of hot water. Place the jars on the baking sheets.

Ladle the marmalade into the jars, leaving ¼-inch headspace. Wipe the rims clean and set the lids on the mouths of the jars. Twist on the rings.

Using a jar lifter, gently lower the jars into the pots. When the water returns to a boil, decrease the heat to an active simmer, and process the jars for 10 minutes. Turn off the heat and leave the jars in the water for 1 to 2 minutes.

Using the jar lifter, transfer the jars from the pots to the baking sheets and let sit for at least 6 hours, until cool enough to handle. Check to be sure the jars have sealed (see page 34). Label and store the sealed marmalade for 6 months to 2 years. Once open, store in the refrigerator for up to 3 months.

VARIATIONS

— Add 2 tablespoons Fiori di Sicilia or 2 teaspoons vanilla extract at the end of cooking.

— Add up to ½ cup chopped mint leaves at the end of cooking.

— Thin the Meyer lemon marmalade with blood orange juice for an amazingly colorful preserve.

MEYER LEMON–RASPBERRY MARMALADE

Combining raspberries and Meyer lemons makes them both more intriguing—tartness two ways. Plus, the marmalade is the most gorgeous color.

This is great on toast or English muffins.

2 pounds Meyer lemons

8 to 10 cups water

5 cups granulated sugar, plus more as needed after adding raspberries

½ cup fresh lemon juice, plus more as needed

2 cups (3 six-ounce baskets) raspberries

Yield: 10 to 12 half-pint jars

Place 3 or 4 small plates in the freezer.

Wash the lemons and cut out the small stem-end pieces. Cut up the lemons, pick out as many seeds as possible, and then chop the lemons in small batches in the bowl of a food processor, pulsing 12 to 14 times, until evenly processed but not very fine. You will have 3 to 4 cups.

In a large preserving pot over medium-high heat, combine the lemons and water to cover. Bring to a boil. Cook, uncovered, for about 30 minutes, until the peel is tender to the bite. Meyer lemon peel tends to be much softer than regular lemon peel, so it will soften quickly. When the peel is tender, add the sugar and lemon juice. Set it aside and let rest overnight.

The next morning, place two baking sheets on the counter near your stove. Heat a kettle of water. Set two stockpots on the stove and fill them with enough water to cover the jars by 1 to 2 inches. Bring the water to a boil over medium-high heat. Sterilize the jars (see page 32) in the water bath.

Inspect the fruit. It may appear gelled and ready to jar (it probably is). If it is too set, stir in water to loosen. Add the raspberries and cook, stirring frequently, over medium-high heat for 10 minutes. Add more sugar and lemon juice to taste. Do the plate test (see page 30). The marmalade is ready when it sets up on a chilled plate but is still syrupy. Stop before the mixture measures 220°F on an instant-read thermometer. Remove the pot from the heat and set aside to rest for 10 minutes. Stir well to distribute the peel.

Bring the water bath back to a boil. If the jars have cooled, warm them in the water bath or in a 200°F oven. Simmer the lids in a saucepan of hot water. Place the jars on the baking sheets.

Ladle the marmalade into the jars, leaving ¼-inch headspace. Wipe the rims clean and set the lids on the mouths of the jars. Twist on the rings.

Using a jar lifter, gently lower the jars into the pots. When the water returns to a boil decrease the heat to an active simmer, and process the jars for 10 minutes. Turn off the heat and leave the jars in the water for 1 to 2 minutes.

Using the jar lifter, transfer the jars from the pots to the baking sheet and let sit for at least 6 hours, until cool enough to handle. Check to be sure the jars have sealed (see page 34). Label and store the sealed marmalade for 6 months to 2 years. Once open, store in the refrigerator for up to 3 months.

MEYER LEMON CHUTNEY

This is sort of a cross between an Indian lemon pickle and a marmalade. I prefer to use white sugar rather than brown because I want the color of the chutney to be bright and clear, not muddy. I like this quite tart, but you may prefer it to be a bit sweeter.

If you want to make this with standard lemons, keep in mind that they are not as tender or mild as Meyers and will need to cook longer.

This chutney is especially good with fish and seafood, as well as shrimp or crab curry, curried lentils, or eggplant. It is also delicious with roast chicken or turkey.

2 pounds Meyer lemons	1 tablespoon salt
5 to 6 ounces fresh ginger	1 teaspoon ground coriander
4 cups granulated sugar	1 to 2 teaspoons mustard seeds
1 cup apple cider vinegar	1 teaspoon freshly ground black pepper
1½ cups fresh lemon juice, plus more as needed	½ teaspoon ground cloves
3 or 4 fresh red chiles, minced (leave in the seeds if you want it spicy)	Water, as needed
	1 cup raisins
1 tablespoon minced garlic	¼ teaspoon ground cayenne, plus more as needed (optional)

Yield: 8 half-pint jars

Wash the lemons and cut out the small stem end pieces. Cut the lemons in half lengthwise and slice thinly. Cut those slices in half so you have strips that are not longer than 1 inch. In other words, you have quarters. You may use a mandoline or do it by hand as they are very tender. After slicing, you will have about 5 cups of sliced lemons.

Peel the ginger and slice thinly on a mandoline. Then cut those slices into very thin strips, 1 to 1½ inches in length.

In a large preserving pot over medium-high heat, combine the lemons, ginger, sugar, vinegar, lemon juice, chiles, garlic, salt, coriander, mustard seeds, black pepper, ground cloves, and water to cover. Bring to a boil over medium-high heat and simmer until the peel is tender, about 20 minutes. (Standard lemons will take twice as long to get tender.) Set aside to rest overnight.

The next day, place a baking sheet on the counter near your stove. Heat a kettle of water. Set two stockpots on the stove and fill them with enough water to cover the jars by 1 to 2 inches. Bring the water to a boil over medium-high heat. Sterilize the jars (see page 32) in the water bath.

Return the lemon mixture to a boil over medium-high heat, adding water or more lemon juice if the mixture is dry. Add the raisins. Taste and, if the fresh red chiles are not hot enough and you'd like it zippier, add the cayenne. Decrease the heat to low and simmer, stirring frequently (to prevent the raisins from sinking and scorching) for about 10 minutes. The raisins will have absorbed some of the liquid; add more lemon

CONTINUED

juice or water if you think the mixture is too thick. It should be quite syrupy. Adjust the sweetness. Stir well to distribute the ingredients and syrup. Remove the pot from the heat.

Bring the water bath back to a boil. If the jars have cooled, warm them in the water bath or in a 200°F oven. Simmer the lids in a saucepan of hot water. Place the jars on the baking sheet.

Ladle the chutney into the jars, leaving ¼-inch headspace. Wipe the rims clean and set the lids on the mouths of the jars. Twist on the rings.

Using a jar lifter, gently lower the jars into the pots. When the water returns to a boil, decrease the heat to an active simmer, and process the jars for 10 minutes. Turn off the heat and leave the jars in the water for 1 to 2 minutes.

Using the jar lifter, transfer the jars from the pots to the baking sheet and let sit for at least 6 hours, until cool enough to handle. Check to be sure the jars have sealed (see page 34). Label and store the sealed chutney for 6 months to 2 years. Once open, store in the refrigerator for up to 3 months.

CRANBERRY-TANGERINE PRESERVES

You've got to have a fail-safe recipe for cranberry preserves, as Thanksgiving dinner requires it and family will be disappointed if it does not appear at the table. Actually, I also enjoy this throughout the year with roast chicken.

Grated zest of
4 tangerines

4 cups tangerine juice

4 cups granulated sugar

4 ounces fresh ginger,
peeled and grated

1 teaspoon freshly
ground black pepper

1 teaspoon Chinese
five-spice powder, or
a combination of five-
spice, ground cinnamon,
and ground cloves

12 cups (4 twelve-ounce
bags) cranberries

Yield: 5 pint jars

Place 3 or 4 small plates in the freezer.

Place a baking sheet on the counter near your stove. Heat a kettle of water. Set two stockpots on the stove and fill them with enough water to cover the jars by 1 to 2 inches. Bring the water to a boil over medium-high heat. Sterilize the jars (see page 32) in the water bath.

In a large preserving pot over medium-high heat, bring the tangerine zest and juice, sugar, ginger, black pepper, and five-spice powder or combination of five-spice, cinnamon, and cloves to a boil. Add the cranberries and cook, stirring frequently, until they pop and bubble up and the juices thicken, about 5 minutes. The preserves are done when it passes the plate test (see page 30) and is spoonable but not stiff. Remove the pot from the heat.

Bring the water bath back to a boil. If the jars have cooled, warm them in the water bath or in a 200°F oven. Simmer the lids in a saucepan of hot water. Place the jars on the baking sheet.

Ladle the preserves into the jars, leaving ¼-inch headspace. Wipe the rims clean and set the lids on the mouths of the jars. Twist on the rings.

Using a jar lifter, gently lower the jars into the pots. When the water returns to a boil, decrease the heat to an active simmer, and process the jars for 10 minutes. Turn off the heat and leave the jars in the water for 1 to 2 minutes.

Using the jar lifter, transfer the jars from the pots to the baking sheet and let sit for at least 6 hours, until cool enough to handle. Check to be sure the jars have sealed (see page 34). Label and store the sealed preserves for 6 months to 2 years. Once open, store in the refrigerator for up to 3 months.

SATSUMA MANDARIN MARMALADE

Satsumas are tender, so they are very easy to slice by hand. And there are no seeds to pick out! Select ones with skin that is taut and close to the fruit, not puffy and loose. The color of this marmalade is beautiful, and the flavor is delicate.

While this is good on English muffins and toast, you can also use it in a marinade. Thinned with a bit of juice and soy, it makes a tangy glaze on roast duck, pork, or chicken.

2½ pounds Satsuma mandarins

2 quarts water, plus more as needed

4 cups granulated sugar

¼ cup fresh lemon juice, plus more as needed

½ teaspoon ground cinnamon or Chinese five-spice powder

¼ cup orange-flower water, or 2 tablespoons vanilla extract or Fiori di Sicilia (optional)

Yield: 7 or 8 half-pint jars

Place 3 or 4 small plates in the freezer.

Cut the mandarins in half across their equators, then cut each half in half vertically. Slice very thinly by hand (they are often too squooshy to slice on a mandoline). You will have about 8 scant cups of sliced fruit.

In a large preserving pot over medium-high heat, combine the mandarins and water to cover. Bring to a boil, and cook for 20 to 30 minutes. Remove from the heat. Add the sugar and lemon juice. Let sit overnight.

The next day, place a baking sheet on the counter near your stove. Heat a kettle of water. Set two stockpots on the stove and fill them with enough water to cover the jars by 1 to 2 inches.

Bring the water to a boil over medium-high heat. Sterilize the jars (see page 32) in the water bath.

Bring the mandarin mixture to a boil over medium-high heat and stir in the cinnamon or five-spice powder. Cook, stirring frequently, until the mixture registers 215°F on a candy thermometer and passes the plate test (see page 30) but is still syrupy. Add the orange-flower water, vanilla, or Fiori di Sicilia to taste at the end of cooking. Their perfume will fade with time, but the marmalade will still be delicious. Taste to make sure the marmalade has enough acidity, as the mandarins themselves are sweet and mild. Add lemon juice if you think it needs more acidity. Remove the pot from the heat.

Bring the water bath back to a boil. If the jars have cooled, warm them in the water bath or in a 200°F oven. Simmer the lids in a saucepan of hot water. Place the jars on the baking sheet.

Ladle the marmalade into the jars, leaving ¼-inch headspace. Wipe the rims clean and set the lids on the mouths of the jars. Twist on the rings.

Using a jar lifter, gently lower the jars into the pots. When the water returns to a boil, decrease the heat to an active simmer, and process the jars for 10 minutes. Turn off the heat and leave the jars in the water for 1 to 2 minutes.

Using the jar lifter, transfer the jars from the pots to the baking sheet and let sit for at least 6 hours, until cool enough to handle. Check to be sure the jars have sealed (see page 34). Label and store the sealed marmalade for 6 months to 2 years. Once open, store in the refrigerator for up to 3 months.

LIME MARMALADE

This marmalade is so intensely limey that it needs a squeeze of lemon juice for balance. Lime peel is a bit tougher than lemon or orange, so be sure it is truly tender before you add the sugar.

It is great on breakfast toast but also may be thinned with broth and used to deglaze a pan after sautéing a fillet of sole or chicken piccata.

2 pounds limes

7 to 8 cups water

6 to 7 cups granulated sugar

Fresh lemon juice, as needed

Yield: 12 half-pint jars

Place 3 or 4 small plates in the freezer.

Wash the limes and cut out the small stem-end pieces. Cut up the limes, pick out as many seeds as possible, and then chop the limes in small batches in the bowl of a food processor, pulsing 12 to 14 times, until evenly processed but not very fine. You will have 7 to 8 cups.

In a large preserving pot, combine the limes and water to cover. Let sit overnight.

The next day, bring the pot to a boil over medium-high heat and cook, uncovered, for about 40 minutes, or until the lime peels are soft. Gradually add 6 cups of the sugar, stirring until it dissolves. Continue to pick out seeds. Taste and add the remaining 1 cup of sugar as needed, gradually stirring until it dissolves. At this point, you can let the mixture sit overnight.

The next day, place two baking sheets on the counter near your stove. Heat a kettle of water. Set two stockpots on the stove and fill them with enough water to cover the jars by 1 to 2 inches. Bring the water to a boil over medium-high heat. Sterilize the jars (see page 32) in the water bath.

The lime mixture may appear gelled and ready to jar (it probably is). If it is too set, stir in water to loosen. Bring the mixture to a boil over high heat, stirring often. Do the plate test (see page 30). The marmalade is ready when it sets up on a chilled plate but is still syrupy. Stop when the mixture measures 215°F on a candy thermometer; this marmalade has a tendency to set up quite firm. Add the lemon juice to taste. Remove the pot from the heat and set aside to rest for 10 minutes. Stir well to distribute the peel.

Bring the water bath back to a boil. If the jars have cooled, warm them in the water bath or in a 200°F oven. Simmer the lids in a saucepan of hot water. Place the jars on the baking sheets.

Ladle the marmalade into the jars, leaving ¼-inch headspace. Wipe the rims clean and set the lids on the mouths of the jars. Twist on the rings.

Using a jar lifter, gently lower the jars into the pots. When the water returns to a boil, decrease the heat to an active simmer, and process the jars for 10 minutes. Turn off the heat and leave the jars in the water for 1 to 2 minutes.

Using the jar lifter, transfer the jars from the pots to the baking sheets and let sit for at least 6 hours, until cool enough to handle. Check to be sure the jars have sealed (see page 34). Label and store the sealed marmalade for 6 months to 2 years. Once open, store in the refrigerator for up to 3 months.

VARIATION

— Use the mandoline method, which yields about 6 cups thinly sliced limes and 9 half-pint jars of marmalade. Slice the limes thinly on the mandoline and cut the slices into quarters. Place in the preserving pot with water to cover and let soak for a few hours or overnight. The next day, bring to a boil and then simmer until the peels are soft, about 40 minutes. Measure the sliced fruit and add an equal amount of sugar. Let sit overnight once more. The next day, over low heat, stir the mixture until the sugar has dissolved and then boil until it reaches 215°F on a candy thermometer and passes the plate test (see page 30) but is still a bit syrupy as this marmalade sets up surprisingly firm. Add lemon juice to taste. Let rest for 10 minutes, stir, and then ladle into the sterilized jars and process as directed.

BLOOD ORANGE–ROSE MARMALADE

This is a pretty marmalade in the jar. The hint of rose gives it a mysterious undertone.
   Toast or muffins will be special with the addition of this preserve.

2½ pounds blood oranges, Moro or Tarocco varieties

About 3 quarts water

2 cups rose sugar (see page 22)

Up to 1 cup granulated sugar

Juice of 1 to 2 Eureka or Lisbon lemons, plus more as needed

Yield: About 8 half-pint jars

Place 3 or 4 small plates in the freezer.

Wash the oranges and cut out the small stem-end pieces. Cut up the unpeeled oranges, pick out as many seeds as possible, and then chop the oranges in small batches in the bowl of a food processor, pulsing 12 to 14 times, until evenly processed but not very fine. You will have 8 to 10 cups.

In a preserving pot over medium-high heat, combine the oranges and water to cover. Bring to a boil and cook, uncovered, until the mixture reduces by one-third and the peels are tender, about 40 minutes.

Gradually add the rose sugar, stirring constantly until it dissolves. Continue to pick out the seeds. Taste and add the granulated sugar, as needed. Add lemon juice to taste. Boil for 5 more minutes and then set aside to rest overnight.

The next day, place a baking sheet on the counter near your stove. Heat a kettle of water.

Set two stockpots on the stove and fill them with enough water to cover the jars by 1 to 2 inches. Bring the water to a boil over medium-high heat. Sterilize the jars (see page 32) in the water bath.

The blood orange mixture may appear gelled and ready to jar (it probably is). If it is too set, stir in water to loosen. Bring the mixture to a boil over high heat, stirring often. Do the plate test (see page 30). The marmalade is ready when it sets up on a chilled plate but is still syrupy. Stop when the mixture measures 215°F on a candy thermometer. Remove the pot from the heat and set aside to rest for 10 minutes. Stir well to distribute the peel.

Bring the water bath back to a boil. If the jars have cooled, warm them in the water bath or in a 200°F oven. Simmer the lids in a saucepan of hot water. Place the jars on the baking sheet.

Ladle the marmalade into the jars, leaving ¼-inch headspace. Wipe the rims clean and set the lids on the mouths of the jars. Twist on the rings.

Using a jar lifter, gently lower the jars into the pots. When the water returns to a boil, decrease the heat to an active simmer, and process the jars for 10 minutes. Turn off the heat and leave the jars in the water for 1 to 2 minutes.

Using the jar lifter, transfer the jars from the pots to the baking sheet and let sit for at least 6 hours, until cool enough to handle. Check to be sure the jars have sealed (see page 34). Label and store the sealed marmalade for 6 months to 2 years. Once open, store in the refrigerator for up to 3 months.

Pumpkin and Winter Squash

The pumpkin, or winter squash, is native to the Americas and was introduced in Europe by the Spanish explorers during the Columbian Exchange. In most countries of the Old and New Worlds, pumpkin or winter squash is enjoyed both as a savory and as a sweet. We Americans love pumpkin pie and enjoy a rich pumpkin butter to spread on toast. The word *pumpkin* seems to be more appealing than *winter squash* to the dining public, despite the fact that most canned "pumpkin" is butternut squash. I suspect our preference must be due to all those stories about the pilgrims and Native Americans at Thanksgiving.

For the sake of simplicity, I refer to these hardy winter squashes as pumpkin or pumpkin squash. As most true pumpkins are watery and often stringy when cooked, I opt for butternut squash when making pumpkin preserves or pumpkin butter. Kabocha would also work well. Pumpkin squash may be cooked in water or roasted in the oven. For smooth jams and butters, I prefer roasting.

In Spain, Portugal, and Sicily, cooks have established a successful preserving technique. First the pumpkin squash is cooked in water until tender and drained, and then it is cooked in sugar syrup until it becomes a spoonable preserve. The pumpkin may be diced or cut into strips, but it can also be grated for a finer texture

if it is to be used exclusively as a preserve or cake filling. Cooks like to perfume preserved pumpkin squash with a little cinnamon or clove and orange-flower water. From Spain and Portugal, pumpkin sweets made their way to Turkey and the Balkans, where they prefer their pumpkin preserves chunky, like a spoon sweet. Walnuts or pine nuts may be added to provide even more texture.

For hundreds of years, families have prepared pumpkin squash preserves without a concern about food safety, but recently the U.S. National Center of Home Food Preservation has issued a warning about canning pumpkin. It raised these safety concerns because pumpkins lack proper acidity for long-term preserving with the boiling water-bath method. To quote, "Gelled preserves rely on the natural acidity in most fruits for safe food preservation. Most fruits have natural acids, so the resulting jams can be safely canned in a boiling water bath. Pumpkin, however, is a low-acid fruit and cannot be safely canned in a boiling water bath. A jam or sweetened preserve would have to have enough sugar and/or added acid to be treated safely without concerns for botulism. A certain acidity level is also required to cause the pectin molecule to form a gel structure. The USDA and Georgia Cooperative Extension currently do not have any tested recipes to recommend for safely canning pumpkin preserves and storing them at room temperature." They also say that pureed pumpkin is too dense for the heat to penetrate in the boiling water bath. I am bewildered by this, because I do not find pureed pumpkin squash any denser than quince or carrot puree, for which they offer no density warning.

I do not, however, put up plain canned pumpkin. My pumpkin preserves have lots of sugar and ample, some might even say excessive, acidity from citrus fruits. And I add citric acid crystals as insurance. These preserves have sufficient body, so they do not need to gel. I process them in a boiling water bath for 20 to 25 minutes—plenty of time for them to heat through. My recipes follow the traditions and techniques of the Turks, Armenians, Greeks, Germans, French, Spaniards, and Portuguese, as well as of many American families.

So caveat emptor. You may make these pumpkin preserves and freeze or refrigerate them. Or you may follow the recipes and add lots of citrus and sugar, along with citric acid to each jar, as insurance, and process in a boiling water bath. Once opened, pumpkin jams and butters do not hold for a long time and so should be refrigerated and eaten within 2 weeks.

ROASTED PUMPKIN BUTTER

Fruit butters are classic Americana, and for many years, my culinary interests have been tilted toward the Mediterranean, so fruit butters had not been in my preserving repertoire until just a few years ago, when I was asked to produce a pumpkin butter for Bi-Rite Market. It sold very well, and then my daughter gave jars as holiday gifts to my grandson's teachers, and they requested more—independent confirmation that this recipe is a hit.

You may like this sweeter than I do. I start with 3 cups of sugar and add more to taste.

This butter is great on toast, pancakes, and waffles. Or turn it into a tart or pie filling, using it in place of the same amount of canned pumpkin the recipe calls for. It can also be folded into cheesecake filling to flavor it.

8 pounds butternut squash

2 organic lemons

1 organic orange

6 to 8 ounces fresh ginger, peeled (optional)

2 cups apple cider

½ cup fresh lemon juice, plus more as needed

3 to 4 cups granulated sugar, plus more as needed

2 teaspoons salt

1 teaspoon ground ginger

1 teaspoon ground cinnamon

2 teaspoons vanilla extract, or 1 tablespoon Fiori di Sicilia

½ teaspoon ground Maras pepper, if the fresh ginger is too mild (optional)

1½ to 1¾ teaspoons citric acid crystals

Yield: 6 to 7 half-pint jars

Place 3 or 4 small plates in the freezer.

Preheat the oven to 400°F. Line one baking sheet with parchment paper.

Place the whole squash on the baking sheet or halve the squash and place it cut-side up. Roast until tender, 2 to 3 hours if whole, 1 to 1½ hours if halved. Remove from the oven.

When the squash is cool enough to handle, peel it and discard the seeds. Transfer the squash to the bowl of a food processor and pulse until pureed. Place the puree in a fine-mesh strainer set over a bowl and drain off the excess water, which takes about 60 minutes. You will need 6 cups of drained puree for this recipe. Save any extra to use for soup.

Wash and dry the food processor bowl and then add the lemons and pulse until finely pureed. You will have ½ to ⅔ cup.

Place the orange in the food processor bowl and pulse until finely pureed. You will have about ½ cup.

Place the fresh ginger in the food processor bowl and pulse until finely pureed. You will have about 1 cup.

Place a baking sheet on the counter near your stove. Heat a kettle of water. Set two stockpots on the stove and fill them with enough water to cover the jars by 1 to 2 inches. Bring the water to a boil over medium-high heat. Sterilize the jars (see page 32) in the water bath.

In a large preserving pot over medium-low heat, combine the 6 cups of squash puree, lemons, orange, pureed ginger, apple cider, lemon juice, 3 cups of the sugar, salt, ground ginger, and cinnamon and simmer, stirring frequently with a long-handled silicone spatula or wooden spoon, until the mixture is very thick, scraping the bottom and the sides of the pot to prevent sticking and scorching. This can take 60 minutes or longer. Add up to the remaining 1 cup sugar and/or lemon juice to taste. The mixture may spit and pop a bit, so if you have a splatter screen, you may want to use it. Wear long pot-holder gloves, too. Alternatively, after 15 minutes of stove-top cooking, you may transfer the mixture to a shallow baking pan and finish the butter in a 300°F oven, stirring every 10 to 15 minutes until the mixture is very thick. Taste again and add the vanilla or Fiori di Sicilia and the Maras pepper. The butter is ready when it is very thick and passes the plate test (see page 30), mounding on the plate. Remove the pot from the heat.

Bring the water bath back to a boil. If the jars have cooled, warm them in the water bath or in a 200°F oven. Simmer the lids in a saucepan of hot water. Place the jars on the baking sheet.

Spoon ¼ teaspoon citric acid into each sterilized jar.

Ladle the pumpkin butter into the jars, leaving ¼-inch headspace. Wipe the rims clean and set the lids on the mouths of the jars. Twist on the rings.

Using a jar lifter, gently lower the jars into the pots. When the water returns to a boil, decrease the heat to an active simmer, and process the jars for 20 minutes. Turn off the heat and leave the jars in the water for 1 to 2 minutes.

Using the jar lifter, transfer the jars from the pots to the baking sheet and let sit for at least 6 hours, until cool enough to handle. Check to be sure the jars have sealed (see page 34). Label and store the sealed pumpkin butter for 6 months to 2 years. Once open, store in the refrigerator for up to 2 weeks.

MEDITERRANEAN-STYLE PUMPKIN PRESERVES

In Turkey and Greece, the pumpkin squash for this preserve is cut into large dice or strips. It is eaten as a spoon sweet with a glass of ice water, but there is nothing stopping you from spooning it over rice pudding or ice cream.

3 cups granulated sugar

1 cup water

Juice of 3 to 4 lemons, plus more as needed

5 strips lemon peel

2 pounds pumpkin or butternut squash, peeled and cut into 1-inch dice or strips that are ½ inch by 2 inches

3 whole cloves, or 1 cinnamon stick or 3 star anise pods or 1 vanilla bean (optional), plus more as needed

1 cup chopped toasted walnuts

Orange-flower water (optional)

1¼ to 1½ teaspoons citric acid crystals

Yield: 5 to 6 half-pint jars

Place 3 or 4 small plates in the freezer.

In a large preserving pot over medium-high heat, combine the sugar, water, lemon juice, and lemon peel and boil until the syrup begins to thicken. Set aside.

Place the pumpkin in a saucepan with water to cover. Cook over medium heat until the pumpkin is just barely tender but still holding its shape, about 15 minutes. Remove from the heat and transfer the pumpkin to a colander to drain.

Add the pumpkin to the syrup along with the cloves or cinnamon or star anise or vanilla bean. Set aside and let the pumpkin sit in the syrup overnight.

The next day, place a baking sheet on the counter near your stove. Heat a kettle of water. Set two stockpots on the stove and fill them with enough water to cover the jars by 1 to 2 inches. Bring the water to a boil over medium-high heat. Sterilize the jars (see page 32) in the water bath.

Bring the pumpkin mixture to a boil over medium-high heat. Taste and add more lemon juice or spice. Continue to cook, stirring frequently with a long-handled silicon spatula or wooden spoon, scraping the bottom and the sides of the pot to prevent sticking and scorching. The preserves are ready when it is very thick and passes the plate test (see page 30), mounding on the plate. Stir in the walnuts and orange-flower water at the end of cooking. Remove the pot from the heat.

Bring the water bath back to a boil. If the jars have cooled, warm them in the water bath or in a 200°F oven. Simmer the lids in a saucepan of hot water. Place the jars on the baking sheet.

Spoon ¼ teaspoon citric acid into each sterilized jar.

Ladle the preserves into the jars, leaving ¼-inch headspace. Run a knife along the inside of the jars to break up any air bubbles. Wipe the rims clean and set the lids on the mouths of the jars. Twist on the rings.

Using a jar lifter, gently lower the jars into the pots. When the water returns to a boil, decrease the heat to an active simmer, and process the jars for 20 minutes. Turn off the heat and leave the jars in the water for 1 to 2 minutes.

Using the jar lifter, transfer the jars from the pots to the baking sheet and let sit for at least 6 hours, until cool enough to handle. Check to be sure the jars have sealed (see page 34). Label and store the sealed preserves for 6 months to 2 years. Once open, store in the refrigerator for up to 2 weeks.

VARIATIONS

— Omit the strips of lemon peel from the syrup.

— Slice 2 Meyer lemons or Eureka lemons thinly on a mandoline, cut the slices in halves or quarters, and blanch for 30 seconds in boiling water, repeating the blanching two times for Meyer lemons and three times for Eureka or Lisbon lemons. Add the cooked lemon slices to the syrup when you add the pumpkin and cook until all are tender.

GRATED WINTER
SQUASH JAM

This is a Spanish preserve called *cabello de angel,* which translates to "angel hair." It is used as a pie and tart filling and would be good layered in a filo pie.

You may also want to try this jam using only orange peel and orange juice, not a mix of lemon and orange. This recipe has so much citrus in it that I do not add citric acid, but you can if you prefer the insurance.

2 pounds butternut squash, peeled and trimmed	**4 to 5 cups granulated sugar**
2 cups water, plus more as needed	**1 walnut-size knob fresh ginger, peeled and grated (optional)**
1 cup lemon juice, plus grated zest and juice of 2 lemons, and more juice as needed	**1 to 2 teaspoons ground cinnamon**
Grated zest and juice of 2 oranges	**Orange-flower water or vanilla extract (optional)**
	1¾ teaspoons citric acid crystals (optional)

Yield: 6 to 7 half-pint jars

Place 3 or 4 small plates in the freezer.

Grate the squash, using a food processor fitted with the grater blade. You will have 6 to 7 cups.

Place a baking sheet on the counter near your stove. Heat a kettle of water. Set two stockpots on the stove and fill them with enough water to cover the jars by 1 to 2 inches. Bring the water to a boil over medium-high heat. Sterilize the jars (see page 32) in the water bath.

In a large preserving pot over medium-high heat, combine the squash, 2 cups water, and 1 cup lemon juice and bring to a boil. Decrease the heat and simmer for 10 minutes. Set aside to rest for 10 to 15 minutes.

Add the lemon zest and juice and orange zest and juice to the squash, along with the sugar, ginger, and cinnamon, and cook over medium heat until it thickens. Simmer a few minutes longer and then do the plate test (see page 30). The jam should be thick and the juices condensed, but not stiff or dry. If the juices have mostly been absorbed, add more water or lemon juice to thin the preserves. Add a dash of orange-flower water or vanilla if you like. Increase the heat to high and bring the jam to a boil briefly, stirring constantly. Remove the pot from the heat.

Bring the water bath back to a boil. If the jars have cooled, warm them in the water bath or in a 200°F oven. Simmer the lids in a saucepan of hot water. Place the jars on the baking sheet.

Spoon ¼ teaspoon citric acid into each jar.

Ladle the jam into the jars, leaving ¼-inch headspace. Run a knife along the inside of the jars to break up any air bubbles. Wipe the rims clean and set the lids on the mouths of the jars. Twist on the rings.

Using a jar lifter, gently lower the jars into the pots. When the water returns to a boil, decrease the heat to an active simmer, and process the jars for 20 minutes. Turn off the heat and leave the jars in the water for 1 to 2 minutes.

Using the jar lifter, transfer the jars from the pots to the baking sheet and let sit for at least 6 hours, until cool enough to handle. Check to be sure the jars have sealed (see page 34). Label and store the sealed jam for 6 months to 2 years. Once open, store in the refrigerator for up to 3 weeks.

ACKNOWLEDGMENTS

Thank you to

My daughter-in-law Barbara Pino, for being my preserving partner.

My grandchildren, Elena, Adam, and Antonio, for loving Grandma's preserves.

Bill LeBlond, for connecting me with Lorena Jones and enjoying many preserves.

Dave McElroy, for serving my preserves at his many dinners and fundraisers.

Mark Furstenberg, for carrying my membrillo at Bread Furst Bakery in Washington, DC.

Jo Lynne Lockley, for her prolific Sorrento lemon tree.

Sam Mogannam and Simon Richard and Jason Rose at Bi-Rite market, for carrying my preserves and membrillo.

My wonderful quince network: Adrian Card, Suki Weir, Mattole Meadows, David Cooper at Oak Hill Farm, and Tim Bates at the Apple Farm in Philo.

Cliff Jones at Greenleaf Produce, for getting currants and black raspberries.

CUESA, for running our Ferry Plaza Farmers Market and for my greatly appreciated chef parking pass.

Publisher and editor Lorena Jones, for wanting a preserving book just as I was wanting to do one.

Photographer Ed Anderson, whose work is earthy and beautiful and who I always love running into at the market.

Food stylist Christine Wolheim, for her artistry on set.

Creative Director Emma Campion, for visual guidance.

Senior Art Director and designer Kara Plikaitis, for elegant layout.

Senior Production Designer Mari Gill, for all the finishing touches.

Production manager Jane Chinn, for beautiful printing.

Publicist Erin Welke and marketer Allison Renzulli, for their creativity in getting the word out.

**And thanks also to the following farms
and farmers at the Ferry Building:**

Al Courchesne at Frog Hollow Farm

Aomboon (Boonie) Deasy at K & J

Bill Crepps at Everything Under the Sun

Bella Viva Orchards

Brokaw Ranch Company

Joe Schirmer at Dirty Girl Farm

Kenny Baker at Lonely Mountain Farm

Knoll Farms

Lagier Ranches, Inc.

The Loewen family at Blossom Bluff Orchards

Lucero Organic Farms

The Peach Farm

Poli Yerena at Yerena Farms

Rojas Family Farms

Swanton Berry Farm

Tim Bates at The Apple Farm

Tory Farms

Twin Girls Farm

INDEX

Library of Congress Cataloging-in-Publication Data is on
file with the publisher.

Hardcover ISBN: 978-0-399-57961-5
Ebook ISBN: 978-0-399-57962-2

Printed in China

Design by Kara Plikaitis
Recipe photo styling by Christine Wolheim

10 9 8 7 6 5 4 3 2 1

First Edition